International Environmental Law-making and Diplomacy

Bringing together contributions from diplomats, UN agency officials, lawyers and academics, this book provides unique insight into the evolution of international environmental law, diplomacy and negotiating techniques.

Based on first-hand experiences and extensive research, the chapters offer a blend of practice and theory, history and analysis, presenting a range of historical episodes and nuances and drawing lessons for future improvements to the processes of law-making and diplomacy.

The book represents a synthesis of the most important messages to emerge from the annual course on Multilateral Environmental Agreements, delivered to diplomats and negotiators from around the world for the last decade by the University of Eastern Finland and the United Nations Environment Programme. The book will be of interest as both a supplementary textbook and a reference volume for a wide range of students of law and environmental issues.

Tuomas Kuokkanen is a Ministerial Adviser with the Ministry of the Environment, Helsinki, Finland, and a part-time Professor of International Environmental Law at the University of Eastern Finland.

Ed Couzens is an Associate Professor at Sydney Law School, University of Sydney, Australia.

Tuula Honkonen is a Post-Doctoral Researcher at the University of Eastern Finland.

Melissa Lewis is a Doctoral Researcher in the Department of European and International Public Law at Tilburg University, the Netherlands, and an Honorary Research Fellow in the School of Law, University of KwaZulu-Natal, South Africa.

Routledge Research in International Environmental Law

Available titles in this series:

International Environmental Law and the Conservation of Coral Reefs
Edward J. Goodwin

Common Pools of Genetic Resources
Equity and Innovation in International Biodiversity Law
Evanson Chege Kamau and Gerd Winter

The Precautionary Principle in Marine Environmental Law
With Special Reference to High Risk Vessels
Benedicte Sage-Fuller

International Environmental Law and Distributive Justice
The Equitable Distribution of CDM Projects under the Kyoto Protocol
Tomilola Akanle Eni-Ibukun

International Climate Change Law and Policy
Cultural Legitimacy in Adaption and Mitigation
Thoko Kaime

International Liability Regime for Biodiversity Damage
The Nagoya-Kuala Lumpur Supplementary Protocol
Akiho Shibata

Climate Change, Forests and REDD
Lessons for Institutional Design
Joyeeta Gupta, Nicolien van der Grijp and Onno Kuik

Environmental Governance in Europe and Asia
A Comparative Study of Institutional and Legislative Frameworks
Jona Razzaque

Climate Change and Forest Governance
Lessons from Indonesia
Simon Butt, Rosemary Lyster & Tim Stephens

Research and Development on Genetic Resources
Public domain approaches to implementing the Nagoya Protocol
Edited by Evanson Chege Kamau, Gerd Winter and Peter-Tobias Stoll

Forthcoming titles in this series:

Sustainable Development Principles in the Decisions of International Courts and Tribunals
1992–2012
Marie-Claire Cordonier Segger and Yolanda Saito

Law and Practice on Public Participation in Environmental Matters
The Nigerian Example in Transnational Comparative Perspective
Uzuazo Etemire

Culture and International Economic Law
Valentia Vadi and Bruno de Witte

Climate Change and Human Rights
An International and Comparative Law Perspective
Ottavio Quirico and Mouloud Boumghar

Human Rights Approaches to Climate Change
Challenges and Opportunities
Sumudu Atapattu

Ecological Restoration in International Environmental Law
Afshin Akhtarkhavari, An Cliquet and Anastasia Telesetsky

International Environmental Law-making and Diplomacy
Insights and Overviews
Edited by Tuomas Kuokkanen, Ed Couzens, Tuula Honkonen and Melissa Lewis

Natural Resources Law, Investment and Sustainability
Shawkat Alam, Jahid Hossain Bhuiyan, Carmen Gonzalez and Jona Razzaque

International Environmental Law-making and Diplomacy

Insights and overviews

Edited by Tuomas Kuokkanen, Ed Couzens, Tuula Honkonen and Melissa Lewis

Routledge
Taylor & Francis Group
LONDON AND NEW YORK

earthscan
from Routledge

First published 2016
by Routledge

2 Park Square, Milton Park, Abingdon, Oxfordshire OX14 4RN
711 Third Avenue, New York, NY 10017

Routledge is an imprint of the Taylor & Francis Group, an informa business

First issued in paperback 2017

British Library Cataloguing-in-Publication Data
A catalogue record for this book is available from the British Library

Library of Congress Cataloging in Publication Data
International environmental law-making and diplomacy : insights and overviews / Edited by Tuomas Kuokkanen, Ed Couzens, Tuula Honkonen and Melissa Lewis.
pages cm
Includes bibliographical references and index.
1. Environmental law, International. 2. Environmental law. 3. International relations. I. Kuokkanen, Tuomas, editor. II. Couzens, Ed, editor. III. Honkonen, Tuula, editor.
K3585.I5795 2015
344.04'6—dc23
2015023814

ISBN: 978-1-138-85124-5 (hbk)
ISBN: 978-0-8153-9542-3 (pbk)

Typeset in Goudy
by Fish Books Ltd., Enfield, Middlesex.

Contents

Contributors

Sylvia Bankobeza Legal Officer, National Environmental Law Unit, UNEP Division of Environmental Law and Conventions (DELC), Nairobi, Kenya. *LLB (Dar-es-Salaam), LLM International Law (Hull), PGDip (DSM).*
Sylvia Bankobeza has been a lawyer at the United Nations Environment Programme since 1999. She handles environmental law issues relating to national and international legal instruments. Her responsibilities include directing environmental law activities by developing environmental law related programmes and coordinating their implementation; providing legal support to international processes and instruments; providing advisory services and technical assistance in developing and strengthening national laws and institutional frameworks; building capacity of government officials and related legal stakeholders in environmental law through facilitating forums for sharing information and expertise; imparting knowledge and skills sets in environmental law and policy and developing environmental information tools on both national and international environmental law issues. Prior to joining UNEP, she worked with various institutions at national and international levels, including the Ministry of Foreign Affairs, Kenya, where she handled international institutional issues and treaties.

Ed Couzens Associate Professor, Sydney Law School, University of Sydney, Australia. *BA Hons LLB (Wits), LLM (Natal & Nottingham), PhD (KZN).*
Ed Couzens is the author of *Whales and Elephants in International Law and Politics: A comparative study* (Earthscan/Routledge, 2014); and co-author, with Melissa Lewis, of *Environmental Law: South Africa* (2013). He has taught on the UEF/UNEP Course on MEAs since 2004; and was the IUCN Academy of Environmental Law Visiting Professor, Faculty of Law, University of Ottawa, in January 2015. He has been recognized as an 'Established Researcher' by South Africa's National Research Foundation, 2013–2018. He has been an editor on the *South African Journal of Environmental Law and Policy* since 2001; and a co-editor on the University of Eastern Finland – UNEP *Review of International Environmental Law-making and Diplomacy* since 2006. From 2015 he will be an editor on the *Asia Pacific Journal of Environmental Law*; and a member of the Advisory Boards of *Transnational Environmental Law* and the *Journal of Interna-*

tional Wildlife Law and Policy. He has attended four Meetings of the International Whaling Commission (2007, 2011, 2012 and 2014) as a member of the South African delegation; and attended the 17th CoP of the UN Framework Convention on Climate Change (2011). He is an attorney of the High Court of South Africa; and has also been a qualified Field Guide in South Africa since 1997.

Tewolde Berhan Gebre Egziabher Advisor to the Ministry of Environment and Forest, Ethiopia. *BSc (Addis Ababa), PhD (Wales)*.
Before becoming involved in the development of Ethiopian and international environmental policies, Tewolde Egziabher had an academic career at the Addis Ababa and Asmara Universities. From 1995 until 2013 he was the Director of the Ethiopian Environmental Protection Authority. During this period he participated in numerous international environmental law-making processes, including the Rio process and the negotiations toward the Convention on Biological Diversity and the Desertification Convention. From 1996 to 2000, he led Africa in the negotiations toward the Cartagena Protocol on Biosafety, and also led the Like-minded Group for a shorter time in these negotiations. In addition, he led the African Group in negotiating the International Treaty on Plant Genetic Resources for Food and Agriculture; and in 2002 he led the Ethiopian delegation at the World Summit on Sustainable Development. In 2000, he received the Right Livelihood Award for his work in biosafety and community rights; in 2006, UNEP awarded him the Champion of the Earth award for being 'a champion against the patenting of life forms and for community rights in Africa'; and in 2013 he was awarded the insignia of the Legion of Honour with the rank of Officer from the President of France.

Tuula Honkonen Post-Doctoral Researcher, University of Eastern Finland. *LLM (LSE), DSc (Joensuu)*.
In her studies and subsequent academic research work, Tuula Honkonen has specialized in international environmental law and policy. She has published on a wide range of topics, including the regulation of transboundary freshwater resources and water security, natural resources governance (especially related to mining and genetic resources), common but differentiated responsibilities, and compliance under international environmental regimes. She is the author of *The Common but Differentiated Responsibility Principle in Multilateral Environmental Agreements: Regulatory and Policy Aspects* (2009). Her special interests lie in the dynamics of multilateral environmental agreements, natural resources governance and the climate change regime. She has worked as a part-time lecturer at the University of Eastern Finland and as a consultant for the Finnish Ministry of the Environment. She has been part of the organizing team of the UEF/UNEP Course on Multilateral Environmental Agreements since 2004; and a co-editor of the University of Eastern Finland – UNEP *Review of International Environmental Law-making and Diplomacy* since 2006.

Tadanori Inomata Inspector of the Joint Inspection Unit of the United Nations system, 2005–2014. *LLB, LLM (Keio)*.
Tadanori Inomata has worked for the Japanese Ministry of Foreign Affairs, the OECD and for various United Nations institutions. He has attended numerous MEA meetings and conferences and worked in the administration and review of the implementation of financial mechanisms of MEAs, especially that for the Montreal Protocol. For instance, he has served as Chairman of the Executive Committee of the Multilateral Fund for the Implementation of the Protocol. As an Inspector for the UN's Joint Inspection Unit, he prepared or participated in preparing a number of reports, the topics ranging from the review of management and administration in the International Maritime Organization to the review of environmental governance within the UN system. He has been honoured with the Orden Nacional Juan Mora Fernández en el grado de Gran Cruz Placa de Plata by the Republic of Costa Rica, in 2004; and a Montreal Protocol Implementers Award by UNEP, in 2007.

Shafqat Kakakhel Chairperson, Board of Governors, Sustainable Development Policy Institute, Pakistan. *BA, MA (Peshawar)*.
As a member of Pakistan's Foreign Service, Shafqat Kakakhel served (in a variety of positions) in Pakistani diplomatic missions in Beirut, Cairo, Bonn, New Delhi and Nairobi; held positions as a Desk Officer for the Middle East, Director of Policy Planning, and Director General for South Asia and SAARC in Pakistan's Ministry of Foreign Affairs; and served as a staff officer with the Secretary-General of the Organisation of the Islamic Conference. In the period 1994–1998, he served as Pakistan's High Commissioner/Ambassador to Kenya, Uganda and Ethiopia as well as Permanent Representative to UNEP and the UN Human Settlements Programme. In 1995, he was further elected as Chair of the G77 and China, and as President of the UNEP Governing Council; while in 1996 he served as chief negotiator for developing countries in the preparatory process for the UN Conference on Human Settlements (Habitat II) and chaired the main negotiating committee at the Conference. From 1998 until 2007, he was the Deputy Executive Director of UNEP, with the rank of UN Assistant Secretary-General. Since his retirement from the UN, he has tried to contribute to environmental protection and sustainable development in Pakistan through membership of, *inter alia*, the Task Force on Climate Change, the Advisory Group on Climate Change, and the Board of Governors of the Sustainable Development Policy Institute. He has also served as a member of the UNFCCC Executive Board of the Clean Development Mechanism and, in 2013, was elected as Co-Chair of the Climate Action Network-South Asia.

Donald W. Kaniaru Managing Partner, Kaniaru & Kaniaru Advocates. *LLB (East Africa), CLE Dip (Kenya School of Law)*.
Donald Kaniaru was Director of the Division of Environmental Policy Implementation and of the Division on Environmental Conventions with UNEP. He worked with UNEP for over 28 years, then served as Special Legal

Adviser to the Executive Director. He also served as Senior Consultant to UN bodies including UNEP, UN Habitat, UNDP and UNEP/WMO on climate issues. He is a member of the Law Society of Kenya; the East African Law Society; the IUCN Commission on Environmental Law; and the International Council of Environmental Lawyers (ICEL) as representative to the UN in Kenya. He was a trustee for ten years of the Center for International Environmental Law (CIEL) and still serves as Trustee of the Institute of Governance and Sustainable Development, both in Washington DC; and is an appointed member, since 2004, of the ICIPE Governing Council. He was involved in the preparatory processes of key environmental conferences including the UNCHE of 1972; the UNCED of 1992, the WSSD of 2002, and, also in 2002, the First Global Symposium of Judges. He has attended most UNEP Governing Council Sessions, from the first in 1973 to the first Session of the United Nations Environment Assembly (UNEA). He joined the Kenyan Ministry of Foreign Affairs in 1969 and still serves as a resource person for the Ministry. He served as Chair of the Kenya National Environmental Tribunal from 2005 to 2013; and is the recipient of an environmental award from CIEL (2010) and the Elizabeth Haub Prize for International Environmental Law (2009). He is also a member of the International Network on Environmental Compliance and Enforcement (INECE) Executive Committee.

Päivi Kaukoranta Director General for Legal Affairs, Ministry for Foreign Affairs, Finland. *LLM (Helsinki)*.
Since 1989, Päivi Kaukoranta has held various legal posts at the Finnish Ministry for Foreign Affairs. She has served as Director General since 2009. Before that she served as Director for the EU and Treaty Law Unit, Counsellor for Institutional and Legal Affairs at the Government Secretariat for EU Affairs at the Prime Minister's Office, and as Legal Counsellor at the Permanent Representation of Finland to the European Union. She is a member of the Permanent Court of Arbitration and Vice Chair of the Committee of Legal Advisers on Public International Law at the Council of Europe. She has participated as a member of the Finnish delegation in the negotiation of several international treaties and has prepared implementing legislation for such treaties. She has also published articles on public international law and European Union law.

Louis J. Kotzé Research Professor, North-West University, South Africa; Visiting Professor of Environmental Law, University of Lincoln, United Kingdom; Deputy-Director, Global Network for the Study of Human Rights and the Environment. *B. Comm LLB (PU for CHE), LLM LLD (NWU)*.
Louis Kotzé is the author, co-author, and co-editor of various publications on themes related to South African, regional and global environmental law. His recent books include: *Global Environmental Governance: Law and Regulation for the 21st Century* (2012); *Research Handbook on Human Rights and the Environment* (with Anna Grear [eds], 2015); and *Transboundary Governance of*

Biodiversity (with Thilo Marauhn [eds], 2014). His research focuses on environmental constitutionalism, human rights and the environment, and global environmental governance. He is co-editor of the *Journal of Human Rights and the Environment*. He is a member of, among others, the IUCN Commission on Environmental Law; the IUCN Academy of Environmental Law; the Volkswagen Foundation Global Young Faculty; the Global Ecological Integrity Group; the Environmental Law Association of South Africa; and the South African Young Academy of Science. He is an Alexander von Humboldt Foundation fellow; the Deputy-director of the Global Network for Human Rights and the Environment; and a National Research Foundation-rated researcher. He further represents the African continent on the International Law Association's Committee on the Role of Law in Sustainable Natural Resources Management for Development.

Tuomas Kuokkanen Ministerial Adviser, Ministry of Environment, Finland. *PhD (Helsinki)*.
In addition to working as a Ministerial Adviser with the Ministry of Environment, Finland, Tuomas Kuokkanen is a Part-time Professor of International Environmental Law at the University of Eastern Finland. Between 2004 and 2014, he has been a co-director for the University of Eastern Finland and UNEP Course on Multilateral Environmental Agreements. He has published a number of articles and chapters on international environmental law. He is the author of the book *International Law and the Environment: Variations on a Theme* (2002); and editor of the book *Seminal Cases of International Environmental Law* (1999). He has also participated as a member of the Finnish delegation in the negotiation of several multilateral environmental treaties and has prepared implementing legislation for such treaties.

Melissa Lewis PhD Researcher, Department of European and International Public Law, Tilburg University, the Netherlands; Honorary Research Fellow, School of Law, University of KwaZulu-Natal, South Africa. *LLB LLM (Rhodes), LLM (Lewis & Clark)*.
Melissa Lewis's research interests lie predominantly within the field of international environmental law, with a particular emphasis on the role of international law in protecting and regulating the use of biodiversity. She is the co-author, with Ed Couzens, of *Environmental Law: South Africa* (2013) and has been a co-editor of the University of Eastern Finland-UNEP *International Environmental Law-making and Diplomacy Review* since 2013. She has taught at Rhodes University, the University of KwaZulu-Natal and North-West University; spent time as a visiting researcher at Lewis and Clark Law School and the University of Toyama; and served on the Executive of the Environmental Law Association of South Africa. Since 2008, she has held the position of environmental law expert on the Technical Committee of the 1995 Agreement on the Conservation of African-Eurasian Migratory Waterbirds (AEWA). In this capacity, she has, *inter alia*, been involved in the drafting of amendments, resolutions and

guidelines for adoption by the Agreement's Meeting of the Parties, and attended meetings of the governing bodies of AEWA, the Convention on Migratory Species, and the Bern Convention on the Conservation of European Wildlife and Natural Habitats.

Elizabeth Maruma Mrema Principal Environmental Lawyer and Legal Counsel at UNEP; Director, Division of Environmental Law and Conventions at UNEP. *LLB (Hons) (Dar-es-Salaam), LLM (Dalhousie), PGDip. (Centre for Foreign Relations, Dar-es-Salaam).*
Elizabeth Mrema is a career diplomat, a principal environmental lawyer and legal counsel at UNEP with a particular focus on environmental policy implementation, international environmental law, compliance and enforcement of environmental conventions, and international environmental negotiations. She is currently the Director of UNEP's Division of Environmental Law and Conventions (DELC). Previously, she was the Deputy Director and Officer-in-Charge of the Division of Environmental Policy Implementation (DEPI), UNEP. She was responsible for conceptualizing and managing UNEP's activities in two of its core thematic areas of focus; ecosystem management (and services) and conflicts and disasters. She also managed the adaptation component of UNEP's climate change agenda. She has about twenty years of experience working with the United Nations in different portfolios. Between 2009 and 2014 she was the Executive Secretary of the Convention on Migratory Species. She has published several papers and articles on environmental law, compliance and enforcement of conventions, environmental negotiations and techniques and environmental conventions, as well as books currently being used by UNEP for its capacity building and training programmes.

Ville Niinistö Leader, Green Party, Finland. *MSocSc (Turku).*
Ville Niinistö has been a Member of the Finnish Parliament since 2007. He has been a member in several committees in the Parliament, including the Constitutional Law Committee, the Defence Committee, the Education and Culture Committee, and the Grand Committee. He was a member in the Finnish Delegation to the Nordic Council from 2007 to 2011. Between 2011 and 2014, he was the Minister of the Environment of the Finnish Government. During that period, he participated in a number of MEA and other international environmental meetings, including the Rio+20 Conference, the UNEP Governing Council meetings, and the Conferences of the Parties to the United Nations Framework Convention on Climate Change. In addition, he represented Finland in the meetings of the Environmental Council of the European Union. He has worked actively to promote synergies among MEAs, to improve the protection of the Baltic Sea, and to enhance the environmental protection of the Arctic region. He has also been involved in many national legislation processes. For instance, he led the drafting process for the enactment of the 2014 Climate Change Act in Finland.

Marc Pallemaerts *LLM (Harvard), PhD (Vrije Universiteit Brussel).*
Marc Pallemarts, who very sadly passed away in 2014, was a widely appreciated lawyer, academic, policy-maker and diplomat in the fields of international environmental protection and sustainable development. He played a key role in the development of international, European and Belgian climate policy. For instance, in 2001, he was the chief negotiator for the European Union and one of the architects of the so-called Marrakesh Accords for the international climate regime. He later served as a member of the Kyoto Protocol's Compliance Committee and in 2011 he was elected as Vice-Chairman of the Ad Hoc Working Group on Long Term Cooperative Action under the Convention (AWG-LCA). In addition to the climate regime, he was active in the fields of hazardous substances, environmental governance, and access to justice, to name but a few. From 2003 to 2005, he was Chairman of the Meeting of the Parties to the Aarhus Convention on Access to Information, Public Participation in Decision-making and Access to Justice in Environmental Matters. In 2012, he was appointed as Special Rapporteur on hazardous substances and wastes for the UN Human Rights Council. He was also a renowned academic, lecturer and researcher in the fields of international and European environmental law.

Kilaparti Ramakrishna Director and Head, Subregional Office for East and North-East Asia United Nations Economic and Social Commission for Asia and the Pacific. *PhD (Jawaharlal Nehru).*
Kilaparti Ramakrishna is currently the director of the UN Economic and Social Commission for Asia and the Pacific (UNESCAP) East and North-East Asia office in Incheon, South Korea. Before joining ESCAP, he was with the Woods Hole Research Center (WHRC) where he was the Sara Shallenberger Brown Chair in environmental law and policy, director of the WHRC policy programme and vice-president. He is a lead author of the current assessment (and many before it) by the Intergovernmental Panel on Climate Change. In addition, he has taught at a number of law schools, including at the Fletcher School of Law and Diplomacy, Harvard Law School, Boston University, Boston College and Yale University. For over five years, he worked for the UN in many capacities, including as the principal policy adviser to the Executive Director for UNEP; and as UNEP's chief of cross-sectoral environmental issues and Deputy Director in the Division of Policy Development and Law. He was special adviser to the United Nations in drafting the UN Framework Convention on Climate Change and also assisted with work on the Intergovernmental Negotiating Committee of the Convention on Biological Diversity. He also helped to establish the independent World Commission on Forests and Sustainable Development and served as its coordinator.

Niko Urho Senior Adviser, Ministry of the Environment, Finland. *MSc (Helsinki).*
Niko Urho has been involved in both research on international environmental affairs and in practical work on international environmental agreements and

diplomacy within the Finnish Ministry of the Environment. He has worked with the enhancement of synergies among biodiversity-related MEAs and participated, *inter alia*, in meetings of the Intergovernmental science-policy Platform on Biodiversity and Ecosystem Services (IPBES), the Convention on Biological Diversity (CBD) and the Ramsar Convention on Wetlands. He has participated in broader environment and development processes, including the United Nations Conference on Sustainable Development (Rio+20), and more recently the preparations for the United Nations Conference on Housing and Sustainable Urban Development (Habitat III). He works also with chemicals and waste instruments (the Basel, Rotterdam, and Stockholm Conventions, the Minamata Convention and SAICM) and Arctic issues.

Acronyms, abbreviations and initialisms

ACC	Administrative Committee on Coordination
AEWA	Agreement on the Conservation of African-Eurasian Migratory Waterbirds, 1995
AOSIS	Alliance of Small Island States
ASEAN	Association of Southeast Asian Nations
AU	African Union
BLG	Biodiversity Liaison Group
CBD	Convention on Biological Diversity, 1992
CBDR	common but differentiated responsibilities
CBO	community-based organization
CCA/UNDAF	Common Country Assessment and United Nations Development Assistance Framework
CCAMLR	Convention for the Conservation of Antarctic Marine Living Resources, 1980
CDM	clean development mechanism
CEB	United Nations Chief Executives Board
CEIT	country with economy in transition
CITES	Convention on International Trade in Endangered Species of Wild Fauna and Flora, 1973
CMS	Convention on the Conservation of Migratory Species of Wild Animals, 1979
CoP	Conference of the Parties
CoP/MoP	Conference of the Parties serving as the Meeting of the Parties
CRP	conference room paper
CSD	Commission on Sustainable Development
DDT	dichlorodiphenyltrichloroethane
EC	European Commission
ECOSOC	United Nations Economic and Social Commission
EEC	European Economic Community
EEG	Eastern European Group
EF	Environment Fund (of UNEP)
EMG	Environmental Management Group
ENGO	environmental non-governmental organization

EU	European Union
FAO	United Nations Food and Agriculture Organization
FTAA	Free Trade Area of the Americas
GC	Governing Council (of UNEP)
GDP	gross domestic product
GEF	Global Environment Facility
GEMS	Global Environment Monitoring System
GEO	Global Environment Outlook
GMF	Global Ministerial Environment Forum
GNI	gross national income
GPA	Global Programme of Action for the Protection of the Marine Environment from Land-based Activities
GRULAC	Latin American and Caribbean Group
HELCOM	Baltic Marine Environment Protection Commission (Helsinki Commission)
HLPF	High-level Political Forum
HLS	High-level Segment
IACSD	Inter-Agency Committee on Sustainable Development
IAEA	International Atomic Energy Agency
IAEG-SDG	Inter-agency Expert Group on the Sustainable Development Goals
ICBP	International Council for Bird Protection
ICCBD	Intergovernmental Committee on the Convention on Biological Diversity
ICESDF	Intergovernmental Committee of Experts on Sustainable Development Financing
ICJ	International Court of Justice
ICRW	International Convention for the Regulation of Whaling, 1946
IEA	International Energy Agency
IEG	international environmental governance
IGO	intergovernmental organization
ILC	International Law Commission
IMF	International Monetary Fund
IMO	International Maritime Organization
INC	Intergovernmental Negotiating Committee
IOPN	International Office for Documentation for the Protection of Nature
IPBES	Intergovernmental Platform on Biodiversity and Ecosystem Services
ITPGRFA	International Treaty on Plant Genetic Resources for Food and Agriculture, 2001
ITTA	International Tropical Timber Agreement, 1983
IUCN	International Union for Conservation of Nature and Natural Resources (World Conservation Union)
IUPN	International Union for the Protection of Nature

IWC	International Whaling Commission
IWRB	International Waterfowl Research Bureau
JIU	Joint Inspection Unit
L doc	limited/draft distribution document
LDC	Least Developed Countries
LMMC	Like-minded Megadiverse Countries
LMO	living modified organism
LRTAP	long-range transboundary air pollution
MARPOL	International Convention for the Prevention of Pollution from Ships, 1973
MDGs	Millennium Development Goals
MEA	Multilateral Environmental Agreement
MoP	Meeting of the Parties
MoU	Memorandum of Understanding
NAFTA	North American Free Trade Area
NCSD	National Commission on Sustainable Development (Finland)
NEMA	National Environmental Management Act 107 of 1998 (South Africa)
NGO	non-governmental organization
NIEO	New International Economic Order
OAU	Organization of African Unity
ODA	official development assistance
OECD	Organization for Economic Cooperation and Development
OILPOL	International Convention for the Prevention of Pollution of the Sea by Oil, 1954
OPEC	Organization of Petroleum Exporting Countries
OWG	Open-ended Working Group
PAGE	Partnership for Action on Green Economy
PPP	polluter pays principle
RBBM	results-based budgeting and management
RBM	results-based management
REIO	regional economic integration organization
RIO	regional integration organization
SADC	Southern African Development Community
SAICM	strategic approach to international chemicals management
SBI	Subsidiary Body for Implementation
SBSTA	Subsidiary Body for Scientific and Technological Advice
SDGs	sustainable development goals
SEEA	System of Environmental-Economic Accounting
SIDS	Small Island Developing States
SMART	specific, measurable, achievable, relevant and time-bound
UN	United Nations
UNCCD	United Nations Convention to Combat Desertification in those Countries Experiencing Serious Drought and/or Desertification, Particularly in Africa, 1994

UNCED	United Nations Conference on Environment and Development, 1992
UNCHE	United Nations Conference on the Human Environment, 1972
UNCLOS	United Nations Convention on the Law of the Sea, 1982
UNCSD	United Nations Conference on Sustainable Development, 2012
UNCTAD	United Nations Conference on Trade and Development
UNDP	United Nations Development Programme
UNEA	United Nations Environment Assembly
UNECE	United Nations Economic Commission for Europe
UNEP	United Nations Environment Programme
UNESCO	United Nations Educational, Scientific and Cultural Organization
UNESCWA	United Nations Economic and Social Commission for Western Asia
UNFCCC	United Nations Framework Convention on Climate Change, 1992
UNGA	United Nations General Assembly
UNHCR	United Nations High Commissioner for Refugees
UNICEF	United Nations Children's Fund
UNIDO	United Nations Industrial Development Organization
UNSC	United Nations Statistical Commission
US	United States of America
USSR	Union of Soviet Socialist Republics
WCED	World Commission on Environment and Development
WEHAB	water, energy, health, agriculture and biodiversity
WEOG	Western Europe and Others Group
WHC	Convention Concerning the Protection of the World Cultural and Natural Heritage, 1972
WSSD	World Summit on Sustainable Development, 2002
WTO	World Trade Organization
WWAP	World Water Assessment Programme
WWF	World Wildlife Fund
10YFP on SCP	10-Year Framework of Programmes on Sustainable Consumption and Production

List of treaties

1 Introduction

The substance and the structure of international environmental law-making and diplomacy

Ed Couzens, Tuula Honkonen, Melissa Lewis and Tuomas Kuokkanen

Introduction

What is presented in this collection of chapters is an amalgam of theory and practice – of the writings of academics studying international environmental law and governance; and the experiences of practitioners, diplomats and negotiators, working in the field. There are chapters on substance, descriptions and explanations of events; and chapters on procedure and technique as these have manifested themselves in multilateral negotiations. In an important sense, all of the chapters are on the evolution of international environmental law, be this overall or specific. Yet, the chapters are not historical studies as many of the issues discussed are still relevant, not merely 'history'. Furthermore, one thing that all of the chapters have in common is that ultimately they all look to the future, seeking to draw lessons from the past for the improvement of future practice.

It has been argued that through '[r]egional regimes and global accords, as well as nonbinding guidelines and principles', a 'body of legal instruments constituting a new area of international law: international environmental law' has begun to be formed (Tolba and Rummel-Bulska, 1998: 7). Through this process, the argument is made, 'a new form of multilateral diplomacy, environmental diplomacy, has emerged' (*ibid.*).

The authors assembled here vary from experienced diplomats who have been involved in the crafting, in the teeth of considerable opposition, of some of the world's most important international environmental conventions; to academics who have studied carefully the nuances of different regimes, governance structures and historical approaches.

The content of the chapters

International environmental law is not currently composed of a fixed set of principles and concepts. Rather, it is a dynamic construct that is constantly developing. In his chapter, Marc Pallemaerts outlines the sources of international environmental law. He then argues that a number of general principles can be identified as having developed – with these having emerged from both national and international law and practice – and outlines the content and international recognition of several of the most important of these principles. Regimes, he says, then develop from the sources and principles as a response to environmental problems in specific issue-areas, and themselves play an important role in further developing the sources, and articulating the general principles, of international environmental law. Regimes, according to Pallemaerts (who uses the climate change regime as an illustration), bring forward the dynamic nature of law as a product of continuous interplay between principles, rules and institutions – 'hardening' over time.

Sadly, Marc Pallemaerts passed away during the editing process for the present book. His death was a great loss to the international environmental community. The editors have the honour of commemorating his academic and professional work by including his ideas here as one of his last contributions, although his insights will continue to live on through the students he taught, colleagues he worked with and the people he knew.

After considering the sources and principles of international environmental law, it would be an omission not to consider the nature of, and the rules applicable to, treaties. To fill this need, Päivi Kaukoranta presents a brief overview of the essential elements of a treaty (as defined by the Vienna Convention on the Law of Treaties, 1969) and the basic concepts of the treaty-making process. While it is in the nature of international law that exceptional circumstances and exceptions to rules will always arise, it is important to embed understanding of international law-making firmly in the rules that provide the foundation of the system.

Treaties do not simply 'arrive' in their final forms *ad hoc*. They are necessarily products of their times and of their particular circumstances, and broad historical trends can be identified as international negotiators have set about solving the evolving environmental problems in different ways through the crafting of international conventions and the building of international regimes. With attention throughout the chapter to water issues as a touchstone, Tuomas Kuokkanen tracks the development of different phases of international environmental law-making from the approach of applying general international law without distinguishing specifically between protecting natural resources and protecting the environment; through the approach of distinguishing between substantive regulation dealing with protecting the environment and substantive regulation dealing with the exploitation of natural resources; to the approach of recognizing that these issues are interlinked and dealing with the relationship in an integrated manner. Kuokkanen argues that, even though each of these approaches has dominated a different period in history, they all remain applicable today and continue to be reflected in the ways in which the international community attempts to solve the world's environmental problems.

International environmental law-making and diplomacy needs to be understood in its entirety. This requires understanding both the practical 'on the ground' issues of actual negotiations, the 'micro' view, on the one hand; and the overall picture, the 'macro' view, on the other. Louis Kotzé provides an overall perspective of international environmental governance, explicating links between the environment, governance and law. The chapter then attempts to define environmental governance, considering the various definitional and interpretive challenges that arise, as well as difficulties with understanding the very concept of 'governance' itself and how this might be distinguished from the related but distinct concept of 'environmental governance'. The chapter then explores the principal objective of environmental governance as manifested in the judicial domain.

While multilateral international environmental agreements remain in principle treaties between sovereign states, it needs to be understood that increasingly these treaties are negotiated, adopted and then administered in the context of a framework regime provided by the United Nations system. As such it is important to have an understanding of this system. Tadanori Inomata's chapter deals with building a foundation for environmental governance *with*, but not (or at least not necessarily) *within*, the UN system. It is consequently about both managerial and democratic accountability. The first of these two aspects of accountability relates to the setting of objectives and policy and to management of resources within UN intergovernmental fora; and the second aspect to delivery of output from the UN to the global community, including ways in which to make UN objectives and policies conform to global public interests. Inomata's chapter explains current management and governance frameworks; identifies salient features and considers gaps and weaknesses, including specifically within the environmental field; and then concludes with a consideration of possible future administrative and managerial foundations and institutional arrangements.

Effective international environmental laws are not adopted, and regimes crafted, by accident. In the modern world there is a bewildering array of institutions to understand the involvement of, meetings to attend, documentation to read and internalize, and formal and informal networks to consider. At the time of publication, the database project on international environmental agreements of the University of Oregon (see iea.uoregon.edu) listed over 1,190 multilateral, over 1,500 bilateral, and over 250 'other', international environmental agreements. The relationships between these instruments, and between these and other instruments that are not considered to be 'environmental' in character – as well as the relationships between environmental and 'non-environmental' but cross-cutting issue-areas – necessitate considerable study.

All of these things create an increasingly complex maze of issues and processes that negotiators – whether representing governments or other stakeholders – need to be apprised of and need to be prepared to deliberate upon. Sylvia Bankobeza, Elizabeth Maruma Mrema and Kilaparti Ramakrishna provide an overview of the nature of international environmental diplomacy, considering how this has developed over the years to differ from 'traditional' diplomacy. They then consider the mechanisms, processes and systems used in the organization of the work of intergovernmental meetings; offer advice on measures that might usefully be taken in the planning for and preparation toward participation in international environmental negotiations; outline some of the challenges commonly experienced with negotiations; and offer suggestions that should enhance negotiating skills.

Diplomats, negotiators and scholars working in the field of international environmental law-making and diplomacy face increasingly complicated challenges related to understanding the overall picture of environmental problems and proffered solutions. They also need to understand how actors, ranging from intergovernmental organizations through governmental and non-governmental entities to individuals, have in the past and will in the future influence the course of environmental protection. Ed Couzens and Melissa Lewis piece together the jigsaw that is the history of environmental concern and law by considering the roles of different people and organizations in the areas of law-making generally; consideration of forestry, fisheries, biodiversity, and pollution; and the drawing of lessons from history.

Regimes cannot be created overnight. It takes time for multifarious interests to be accommodated and for a governance system that is broadly acceptable to be fashioned. Creating a single multilateral environmental agreement is not easy – and nor is creating, and defining the role of, an organization. The history of the creation of the United Nations Environment Programme (UNEP) displays both many of the vagaries of negotiating single treaties and also some special issues related to defining the place within the international system of a new organization. Donald Kaniaru explains how UNEP came into being, and how its special character as an international governance body located in a developing country came into being – a valuable subject for the understanding of international diplomacy and the relative bargaining strengths of states. He then locates this within a discussion of the concept of sustainable development, which Kaniaru believes is able to provide a common agenda for both developed and developing countries. He explains how the foundations for the international community's acceptance of this concept were laid in 1972, at the UN Conference on the Human Environment; and examines the concept's subsequent development in international environmental law and the role that UNEP has played in its promotion.

Successful diplomacy needs to be informed by an understanding of the past, if lessons are to be learned and mistakes are not to be repeated. While the everyday minutiae cannot be ignored, there are certain milestones in the history of international environmental law-making that stand out and need to be understood in the overall context. Inevitably, it is these markers that diplomats and scholars alike look to in seeking to understand the international system. After canvassing these, Shafqat Kakakhel briefly reviews states' responses to environmental challenges over the past six decades, concluding that, although positive signals can be seen, this is nevertheless in the face of overall degradation of the environment. He then looks to the future, making recommendations for how more effective governance might be achieved.

One of the most important features of the development of international environmental law-making and diplomacy has been the shift over time from treaties being created by small groups of law-makers to treaties, and wider regimes, being influenced and promoted by multiple actors, roleplayers and stakeholders. Within this evolution, few changes have been as significant as the rise of the influence of developing countries, the increased understanding of the differences in needs and interests between these and developed countries, and of the ways in which these differences need to be dealt with if poverty is to be alleviated and the environment protected. Debate over these differences and needs has become a feature of most recent negotiations, as is illustrated in several chapters of this book. Tuula Honkonen explains the history of the concept of common but differentiated responsibilities, with examples from different regimes; then canvasses the implications for negotiations of different aspects of the principle that might arise in negotiations; considers how divisions might be overcome; and then concludes with comments on the ultimate importance of the principle.

Mere reading of the texts of international conventions conveys little of the dramas, compromises, concessions and diplomatic skills that go into successful negotiations – nor the dashed hopes, realized fears, optimistic efforts and quiet satisfactions that result. In many cases the adoption of a convention is the beginning rather than the end of truly difficult negotiations. This is especially the case where the convention is in the nature of a framework treaty and some of the most difficult issues are left unresolved, to be the subject of future protocols. One such case was the issue of biosafety under the 1992 Convention on Biological Diversity. Arguably raising issues of the practical application of the principle of common but differentiated responsibilities, alongside practical issues of relative bargaining strengths, the eventual text – although inevitably a compromise – reflects a considerable victory for both the developing world and the nascent precautionary principle. Tewolde Egziabher provides general lessons for international environmental law-making and diplomacy in recounting the difficulties and tensions of the negotiations toward the eventual adoption of the Protocol.

As important as is understanding of the past, it is ultimately toward the future that international environmental negotiators must look. The most recent global international conference was the United Nations Conference on Sustainable Development in 2012 – the 'Rio+20 Summit'. Although many commentators have expressed disappointment with the results of the Conference, Niko Urho and Ville Niinistö express optimism toward the future and consider how the main achievements of the Conference have initiated various processes that might lead to a more balanced relationship between the different dimensions of sustainable development, especially as even since the Conference, headway has been made toward crafting an agenda for change. Key issues examined by the authors include measures to strengthen the international environmental governance system; the development of a Post-2015 Agenda that both satisfies human needs and respects nature; and the use of 'green economy' policies to ensure that the environment and natural resources are a central part of economic decision-making.

Conclusion

The editors of this collection believe firmly that the reader of this book, be that reader an experienced diplomat or a negotiator in training, a professor of international law or a student of legal studies, will benefit from the range of historical episodes and nuances presented and the lessons imparted from the depth of experience. As Tolba and Rummel-Bulska have suggested, the 'global environment is complex, and those who attempt to formulate international environmental law must perforce be specialists, each dealing in depth with a limited range of problems' – with the laws these people shape often requiring 'delicate negotiations and skilful diplomacy to find compromise solutions that satisfy the different political and economic motives of the states they represent' (Tolba and Rummel-Bulska, 1998: 14). Ultimately, says Bodansky, international environmental law 'aims to find, not the optimal outcome, but rather the skilful compromise that bridges the gap between competing positions and advances the ball, even if only a little' – he advocates seeing 'the discipline of international environmental law, not as a panacea, but rather as an art and a craft' (Bodansky, 2010: 271).

The collection of chapters is intended to give the reader understanding of the principles of international law, of formal treaty-making requirements, of negotiation techniques, of theoretical explanations, of actual negotiation nuances, and of the history of the development of the law and philosophy of the rise of environmental concern and of efforts to address environmental problems through international law-making – in short, to bring theory and practice, and academic insight and practical experience, together.

Issues canvassed in these chapters include the identification of sources of international environmental law, and the development of its principles and regimes; understanding of the complexity of negotiating in the modern world, and the imparting of practical negotiation skills; the differences between developed and developing countries and how the principle of common but differentiated responsibilities might be used to bring these together. The building of effective international regimes is considered; together with the creation of effective individual treaties; and the different stages of international environmental governance. Further, the importance of learning lessons from history is an ongoing theme, with some chapters focusing on clear explanations of how different historical matters and trends have related to each other; and other chapters explaining single events. Ultimately, however, all of the chapters can be said to have the same theme – finding different ways to explain the past in order to make prognoses and recommendations for the future, in the hope of improving the protection of the environment and the lives of people through better, and better understood, international environmental law-making and diplomacy.

Acknowledgements

The history of this collection of chapters is to be found in the holding in 2004 of the first University of Eastern Finland (previously the University of Joensuu) and United Nations Environment Programme Course on Multilateral Environmental Agreements (see www2.uef.fi/en/unep). The Course has been an annual event since 2004 and has to date seen the training of more than 350 participants (most of these being civil servants or diplomats already negotiating international environmental legal instruments on behalf of governments) from more than 120 countries – a significant network of alumni is being built. The success of the Course would not have been possible without the strong support of the United Nations Environment Programme, the Ministry for Foreign Affairs of Finland and the Ministry of the Environment of Finland, and the University of Eastern Finland – as well as the tireless efforts of numerous individuals and organizations.

In addition to the training of early to mid-career diplomats in negotiation techniques in the environmental field, the organizers of the Course have sought to make a permanent contribution to knowledge through the publication, by the University of Eastern Finland, of an annual book – the *International Environmental Law-making and Diplomacy Review*. Under the guidance of an Editorial Board comprising experienced and senior academics and diplomats, the first two issues of the *Review* were edited by Marko Berglund, to whom the subsequent editors owe much; the next six by Ed Couzens and Tuula Honkonen (formerly Kolari); and the ninth and tenth by Couzens, Honkonen and Melissa Lewis. The chapters in the current collection emanate from the *Review*, but have been considerably reconsidered, revised, reworked and updated.

References

Bodansky, D. (2010) *The Art and Craft of International Environmental Law*, Harvard University Press, Cambridge, MA.

Tolba, M.K. and Rummel-Bulska, I. (1998) *Global Environmental Diplomacy: Negotiating Environmental Agreements for the World, 1973–1992*, MIT Press, Cambridge, MA.

2 An introduction to the sources, principles and regimes of international environmental law

Marc Pallemaerts[1]

Introduction

International environmental law is a dynamic construct that is constantly developing. This brief synopsis will look at some of the ways in which international environmental law is born and changes. The chapter begins by addressing the different sources of international environmental law in order to understand the various forms in which this law takes shape. The second part of the chapter, gives particular attention to a number of general principles of international environmental law, and the last part addresses the creation and growth of international environmental regimes. Developing from the various sources of law, not least the aforementioned principles of international environmental law, regimes are developed as a response to environmental problems in specific issue areas. Regimes bring forward the dynamic nature of law in this area as it emerges from the continuous interplay between principles, rules and institutions.

Sources of international environmental law

General remarks

Several sources of international environmental law exist. Since international environmental law is a particular branch of international law, the theory of its sources mirrors that of the sources of international law generally. Treaties, both bilateral and multilateral, are the source of international law par excellence. These are supplemented by binding decisions of international organizations or other intergovernmental bodies established by treaties. In the environmental sphere, some decisions of the Conferences or Meetings of the Parties (CoP or MoP) of multilateral environmental agreements (MEAs) fall into this category. Customary international law has developed from state practice, while international judicial decisions form yet another source of international law. General principles of international law have been developed, often reflecting principles

---

1 Marc Pallemaerts specifically thanked Marko Berglund (Senior Officer, Ministry for Foreign Affairs, Finland) for his assistance with the preparation of this chapter, as originally written.

found in national legal systems. Soft law, in the form of non-binding decisions, declarations and resolutions of intergovernmental organizations and meetings, forms another important source of international environmental law. Though such instruments are, strictly speaking, legally non-binding, they are not devoid of normative content and help to shape the expectations of the international community.

Treaties

Multilateral environmental treaties, conventions or agreements form the backbone of international environmental law. Prior to 1960, some 42 multilateral treaties (which today are considered to be part of international environmental law) already existed. These mainly related to the management of living natural resources. The first MEA on marine pollution was concluded in 1954. During the 1960s, MEAs began addressing emerging transboundary environmental risks. A few treaties concerning radioactive, marine and freshwater pollution were concluded. As the international community was incited to further normative efforts by the first United Nations environmental conference held in Stockholm in 1972, the 1970s saw the adoption of no less than 75 new MEAs, more than during the entire period before 1970.

The development of MEAs clearly accelerated and both the substantive and geographical scope of these agreements expanded. In the 1980s, the growth of international environmental law slowed down somewhat, but 40 additional MEAs were nevertheless concluded during this decade. The scope of multilateral law-making was again extended, this time to start addressing environmental threats that were not merely transboundary, but truly global in their nature. In the 1990s, international environmental law-making again increased in speed as, exploiting the positive impetus generated by the 1992 Rio Summit, the international community concluded another 75 MEAs (CIESIN: ENTRI database).

Several different motives underlie the development of international environmental law. An MEA can be designed for the management and conservation of environmental resources situated beyond the limits of national jurisdiction. This is apparent in treaties, such as fisheries agreements, which deal with the so-called 'global commons'. Prevention and control of transboundary environmental interferences is another catalyst for international environmental law-making. This can lead to agreements to control various forms of cross-border pollution or to ensure cooperative management of environmental resources that are under the jurisdiction of several states, and are therefore sometimes referred to as shared natural resources. International environmental law can also be developed with a view to minimize or otherwise manage the transboundary economic effects, such as trade barriers and distortions of competition, resulting from unilateral, national environmental policies and laws. Finally, MEAs can be aimed at scientific, technological and financial cooperation to enhance the effectiveness of national environmental policies.

Soft law

Within the overall process of international environmental law-making, soft law has emerged as an important source of law. Although not legally binding, soft law can have a direct influence on the behaviour of both states and non-state actors. In this respect, it can act either as a complement to or as a substitute for hard law. Soft law often provides a consensual basis for the subsequent development of legally binding international norms. It then functions as a precursor of hard law, and the gradual transformation of soft law into hard law can be seen as a process of juridification of international environmental policy (Lang, 1984: 283). In this context, soft law has also been described as 'the thin end of the normative wedge of international environmental law' (Handl, 1990: 3).

General principles

The traditional theory of the sources of international law holds that general principles of law are derived by induction from the national legal systems of the so-called civilized nations. Indeed, Article 38(1) of the Statute of the International Court of Justice (1945) refers to 'the general principles of law recognized by civilized nations' as one of the sources of international law. According to a more modern view, general principles are derived from positive rules of international law. They can be seen as a reflection of a general legal conviction of the international community or as a type of 'formless interstate consent' (see generally van Hoof, 1983). A synthetic view, bringing together these two approaches, would hold that general principles emerge from both national law, and soft and hard international law. Principles are generally distinguished from rules of law. Rules are precise prescriptions for specific factual situations. They determine specific action by clearly identifiable subjects. Rules have a determinate content and provide a specific behavioural prescription, thus guaranteeing legal certainty. Principles, however, are flexible norms that help orient decision-making. There is a high degree of abstraction and a low measure of determinacy in principles and no automatic legal consequences can be derived from them. A principle can be seen as a kind of rule with indeterminate content, as addressees enjoy a wide margin of discretion in its implementation. The difference between rules and principles, in this view, appears more like a question of degree of determinacy rather than a clear-cut dichotomy (see generally de Sadeleer, 2002).

Principles of international environmental law

Introduction

It can be argued that several general principles of international environmental law have emerged from both national and international environmental law. In this overview, it is impossible to address all of them. Therefore, a few important examples will be focused on. These include the polluter pays principle and the precautionary principle, which were first developed at the regional level before arguably gaining near-universal recognition. The principle of common but differentiated responsibilities addresses the differences between developed and developing countries in their capacities to act. The participatory principle addresses the legal position of individuals and civil society organizations by affirming procedural rights of access to information, public participation and access to justice in environmental policy.

Polluter pays principle

The polluter pays principle (PPP) was developed in the 1970s as an economic principle within the frameworks of the Organization for Economic Co-operation and Development (OECD) and the then European Economic Community (EEC). Its aim was to internalize external costs in order to avoid distortions of trade and competition. The principle was initially recognized in regional soft law instruments of these two organizations. In 1972, the OECD Guiding Principles Concerning the International Economic Aspects of Environmental Policies first articulated the PPP as a principle 'to be used for allocating costs of pollution prevention and control measures to encourage rational use of scarce environmental resources and to avoid distortions in international trade and investment' (OECD, 1972).

The principle implies that 'the polluter should bear the expenses of carrying out the measures decided by public authorities to ensure that the environment is in an acceptable state' and that 'the cost of these measures should be reflected in the cost of goods and services which cause pollution in production and/or consumption' (*ibid.*: Art. 4). The EEC also advocated PPP in its first Environmental Action Programme of 1973, which included in its statement of the general principles of EEC environmental policy, *inter alia*, that 'the cost of preventing and eliminating nuisances must in principle be borne by the polluter' (EEC, 1973: 1). This principle was further elaborated in a Recommendation of 3 March 1975 regarding cost allocation and action by public authorities on environmental matters, which stated that 'the European Communities at Community level and the Member States in their national legislation on environmental protection must apply the "polluter pays" principle' (EEC, 1975: 1).

After being developed in soft law instruments, the PPP was subsequently recognized in regional hard law in 1986 with the Single European Act, which amended the EEC Treaty and inserted in it specific provisions on environmental policy. One of those provisions, Article 130R(2) of the Treaty, listed the general principles of the Community's environmental policy, including the PPP. In 1992, the PPP was eventually recognized in a universal soft law instrument. Principle 16 of the Rio Declaration provides that '[n]ational authorities should endeavour to promote the internalization of environmental costs and the use of economic instruments, taking into account the approach that the polluter should, in principle, bear the cost of pollution' (Rio Declaration, 1992). It is noteworthy that this universal formulation is weaker than that contained in the aforementioned European instruments.

So far, there has been scarce recognition of the principle in universal hard law instruments, as the PPP is most generally to be found in the preambles of various MEAs, rather than in their operative provisions. For example, the 1990 IMO Convention on Oil Pollution Preparedness, Response and Co-operation refers to the PPP in its preamble as 'a general principle of international environmental law'. One exception to this rather muted recognition is the 1992 OSPAR Convention, a regional MEA for the protection of the marine environment, Article 2(2)(b) of which states in a straightforward way that 'Contracting Parties shall apply the polluter pays principle'. Other instruments call on their Parties to be 'guided by' or to 'take into account' the polluter pays principle (Helsinki Convention, 1992: Art. 2(5); Civil Liability Protocol, 2003: preamble).

Precautionary principle

The precautionary principle evolved from the earlier principle of preventive action. It addresses problems of environmental decision-making under conditions of scientific uncertainty. Whereas the principle of preventive action was based on the recognition of the need to act to prevent certain harm, the precautionary principle is coupled with the idea of risk avoidance. The mere existence of a risk of harm is considered a sufficient basis for the adoption of preventive measures. While the principle is now widely referred to in national and international law and policy, it remains highly controversial in its interpretation and application. It is disputed, for example, whether the principle actually reverses the burden of proof, in other words whether it puts actors under an obligation to prove that the activities in which they are engaged do not cause harm. Moreover, there has been much debate over terminology. The United States, for example, has preferred to refer to the 'precautionary approach' (see, for example, Fitzmaurice, 2009: 24), while other countries have opted to speak of the 'precautionary principle', a term that potentially carries more normative weight. Also, the scope of application of the precautionary principle is unclear, as some states, most notably the members of the European Union, claim that it extends to issues of human health and consumer protection, whereas others maintain that it applies only to the prevention of environmental harm.

From national law, the principle made its way in Europe into regional soft law and regional MEAs in the late 1980s. However, the World Charter for Nature, a universal soft law instrument, already contained a precursor of the principle in 1982. It held that 'where potential adverse effects are not fully understood, the activities should not proceed' (UNGA, 1982, 'World Charter for Nature': para. 11). The principle was recognized more explicitly in the 1992 Rio Declaration. Principle 15 states that '[i]n order to protect the environment, the precautionary approach shall be widely applied by states according to their capabilities'. It is noteworthy, however, given the dispute over terminology raised above, that while clause 15 is headed a 'principle', there is a retreat in the text and the word 'approach' is then used. The status of the principle in universal MEAs is disputed. Some conventions include hortatory provisions encouraging Parties to take 'precautionary measures' (UNFCCC, 1992: Art. 3(3)), while others require their Parties to be 'guided by' the precautionary principle (Helsinki Convention, 1992: Art. 2(5)) or even to 'apply it' (Revised African Convention, 2003: Art. IV). Other instruments still refer to the precautionary approach in their preamble (Cartagena Protocol, 2000). In only a few international instruments are Parties specifically directed to apply the 'precautionary principle', as opposed to the 'approach'. Even the Bamako Convention on Hazardous Wastes within Africa, which takes a mandatory approach to prohibiting the entry into Africa of hazardous wastes, 'hedges' in providing that:

> [e]ach Party shall strive to adopt and implement the preventive, precautionary approach to pollution problems which entails, inter alia, preventing the release into the environment of substances which may cause harm to humans or the environment without waiting for scientific proof regarding such harm. The Parties shall cooperate with each other in taking the appropriate measures to implement the precautionary principle to pollution prevention through the application of clean production methods, rather than the pursuit of a permissible emissions approach based on assimilative capacity assumptions.
>
> (Bamako Convention, 1991: Art. 4(f))

In a judicial context, the precautionary principle has been applied by the International Tribunal for the Law of the Sea in disputes concerning the management of fish stocks (*Southern Bluefin Tuna Cases*, 1999: para. 80), radioactive pollution of the marine environment (*The MOX Plant Case*, 2001: para. 84) and land reclamation works (*Case concerning Land Reclamation by Singapore in and around the Straits of Johor*, 2003a: paras 95–99).

It should be noted that states are not always consistent in their positions with respect to the precautionary principle. In the latter case, for instance, Malaysia, which in some multilateral negotiations has sided with the US in opposing recognition of precaution as a general principle, as a claimant state whose environmental interests were threatened by land reclamation activities carried out by its neighbour Singapore, argued in its request for provisional measures:

> [t]he rights of Malaysia ... relating to the maintenance of the marine and coastal environment ... are guaranteed by ... the precautionary principle, which, under international law, must direct any State party [to UNCLOS] in the application and implementation of [its] obligations.
>
> (*Case concerning Land Reclamation by Singapore in and around the Straits of Johor*, 2003b: para. 18)

Principle of common but differentiated responsibilities

The influence of international development law and the New International Economic Order principles of the 1970s and 1980s, advocating differential treatment of developing countries in economic matters, led to the advent of the principle of common but differentiated responsibilities (CBDR) in international environmental law in the late 1980s and early 1990s. The principle was first applied *avant la lettre* in an MEA in the late 1980s, namely in the Montreal Protocol's provisions granting differential treatment to developing country Parties with respect to the phase-out of ozone-depleting substances. It was later formally recognized in general terms in Principle 7 of the Rio Declaration, which states that '[i]n view of the different contributions to global environmental degradation, States have common but differentiated responsibilities'. The developed countries acknowledge the responsibility that they bear in the international pursuit of sustainable development in view of the pressures their societies place on the global environment and of the technologies and financial resources they command.

Since the Rio Declaration, the principle has been enshrined in a number of universal MEAs. For instance, the 1997 Kyoto Protocol to the International Framework Convention on Climate Change reaffirmed the CBDR principle as stated in the Framework Convention and applied it in the design of the emissions reduction obligations. A more common approach, however, has been to urge the Parties to recent MEAs to 'take into account the circumstances and particular requirements of developing countries' (for example, the Rotterdam Convention, 1998: preamble; Stockholm Convention, 2001: preamble). Parties to the Convention on Mercury acknowledge, in the context of CBDR, 'States' respective circumstances and capabilities and the need for global action' (Minamata Convention, 2013: preamble), affirming thus the different dimensions of the principle.

The principle of common but differentiated responsibilities is a two-pronged concept. It allocates responsibility differently between countries and at the same time provides for a universal duty of cooperation common to all states. Thus, its substantive content is based on the twin principles of partnership and of differential treatment. There is an economic as well as a temporal dimension to the principle, with reference, respectively, to the different economic capacities of developed and developing states and to their different historical and current contributions to the causes of environmental degradation. States should be held accountable in different measure according to their respective contributions to the creation of global environmental problems and to their respective financial and technological capabilities to address those problems (see generally, Cullet, 2003).

However, the exact status and scope of application of the principle remain contested. Developed countries consider it relevant only to environmental issues that are truly global in nature, whereas developing countries argue that the principle of common but differentiated responsibilities should be applied in all areas of international environmental cooperation. The latter view made some headway at the Johannesburg World Summit on Sustainable Development (WSSD) in 2002. The WSSD Plan of Implementation contains the following statement:

> We commit ourselves to undertaking concrete actions and measures at all levels and to enhancing international co-operation, taking into account the Rio principles, including, inter alia, the principle of common but differentiated responsibilities as set out in principle 7 of the Rio Declaration on Environment and Development.
>
> (Plan of Implementation of the WSSD, 2002: para. 2)

Also relevant is the Outcome Document of the Rio+20 Conference, which reaffirmed 'all the principles of the Rio Declaration on Environment and Development, including, *inter alia*, the principle of common but differentiated responsibilities, as set out in Principle 7 of the Rio Declaration' (UNGA, 2012, 'The Future We Want': para. 15).

Participatory principle

The increasing articulation of procedural environmental rights at both national and international level has gradually led to the emergence of what the author would refer to as the 'participatory principle'. Access to information, public participation and access to justice have long been recognized in many national legal systems. Moreover, such participatory rights have also been recognized in international soft law instruments such as the World Charter for Nature (UNGA, 1982, 'World Charter for Nature'), the Rio Declaration on Environment and Development (Rio Declaration, 1992) and the Malmö Ministerial Declaration (2000).

The classic statement of the participatory principle at the universal level is to be found in Principle 10 of the Rio Declaration, which states that:

> [e]nvironmental issues are best handled with the participation of all concerned citizens, at the relevant level. At the national level, each individual shall have appropriate access to information concerning the environment that is held by public authorities, including information on hazardous materials and activities in their communities, and the opportunity to participate in decision-making processes. States shall facilitate and encourage public awareness and participation by making information widely available. Effective access to judicial and administrative proceedings, including redress and remedy, shall be provided.

An increasing number of hard law instruments of a regional nature also contain provisions based on this principle. The first was the 1985 ASEAN Agreement on the Conservation of Nature and Natural Resources, which unfortunately has not entered into force thirty years after its adoption and signing. The most well-known instrument implementing the participatory principle is a pan-European MEA, the 1998 Aarhus Convention on Access to Information, Public Participation in Decision-Making and Access to Justice in Environmental Matters (see further, Pallemaerts, 2004b: 14–22). One of the most recent is the African Union's 2003 African Convention on the Conservation of Nature and Natural Resources.

The participatory principle essentially calls for environmental information to be made public and disseminated as widely as possible, for public participation to be guaranteed in decision-making on projects, plans and programmes with significant environmental implications, and for access to justice to be granted to the public in environmental matters.

International environmental regimes

General remarks

States draw on international environmental law principles and other sources of international environmental law in creating international environmental regimes. Such regimes are the response of an international community still composed of a multitude of sovereign states to the challenge of international environmental governance. International environmental governance is one of the many forms of emerging processes of global governance, which can generally be described as a process of interest accommodation and cooperative action to address global issues beyond the control of individual state and non-state actors and to cope with the absence of centralized authority in the international community. It is increasingly involving not only governments but also a variety of other, non-state actors or stakeholders. It includes both formal institutions and informal arrangements. International regimes are a means of organizing the international community for the collective pursuit of common interests and for the management of interdependence in specific issue areas, such as, *inter alia*, environmental issues. Regimes tend to establish stable patterns of relationships, permanent lines of communication, interaction and collective decision-making and governance mechanisms among state and non-state actors.

The notion of regimes was first conceptualized by international relations scholars. From an international relations theory perspective, international regimes have been defined as 'a set of implicit or explicit principles, norms, rules and decision-making procedures around which actors' expectations converge in a given area of international relations' (Krasner, 1982: 186). According to another definition, international regimes are 'a form of collective action by states, based on shared principles, norms, rules and decision-making procedures which constrain the behaviour of individual states in specific issue areas' (List and Rittberger, 1992: 86). From a legal-institutionalist perspective, international regimes have been defined as 'a conglomerate of hard law rules, soft law instruments and institutions that are indispensable for the effective working of hard and soft law' (Lang, 1992: 108–122). The latter definition highlights the dynamic relationship between the various types of norms and institutions, because often the creation and development of international environmental regimes starts with soft law and eventually leads to hard law in the form of an MEA, for example. Even regimes based on a binding treaty framework continue, however, to generate soft law, for example in the form of CoP decisions. Regimes are also instrumental in entrenching and operationalizing principles of international environmental law.

An international regime is typically composed of several characteristic elements. Functional roles are attributed to state and non-state actors. Specific roles are associated with specific rights and entitlements and with specific behavioural norms and prescriptions. Social choice mechanisms and institutional frameworks and procedures for collective decision-making about the operation and transformation of the regime norms in question are also an indispensable component of any regime. These conceptualizations can easily be illustrated by reference to a typical global environmental regime.

The climate change regime as an illustration

The climate change regime provides an example of an international regime in the field of the environment. The regime unites several categories of actors. These are the contracting Parties to the 1992 United Nations Framework Convention on Climate Change, which are divided into developed – referred to as Annex I Parties in UNFCCC jargon – and developing country Parties, as well as regional economic integration organizations (REIOs) of which in actual fact there is only one in the regime: the European Union. Developed countries are further divided into member countries of the Organization for Economic Co-operation and Development (OECD) – referred to as Annex II Parties in UNFCCC jargon – and countries with economies in transition (CEITs). Other actors included in the climate change regime include intergovernmental organizations (IGOs), non-governmental organizations (NGOs) representing a wide variety of civil society and business interests, the various intergovernmental bodies established under the Convention itself (the CoP and its subsidiary bodies), the Global Environment Facility (GEF) and other financial mechanisms operating under the Convention, and the UNFCCC Secretariat.

The climate change regime functions according to agreed principles, laid down in key provisions of the Framework Convention. The ultimate objective of the regime, as set out in Article 2 of the Convention, is to achieve 'stabilization of greenhouse gas concentrations in the atmosphere at a level that would prevent dangerous anthropogenic interference with the climate system'. The guiding principles of the Convention are laid down in Article 3 and include promoting sustainable development and the principle of common but differentiated responsibilities (UNFCCC, 1992: Arts 3(4) and 3(1)). Although worded in slightly different terms from those of the Rio Declaration, the precautionary principle also features in the Climate Change Convention, Article 3(3) of which provides that '[t]he Parties should take precautionary measures to anticipate, prevent or minimize the causes of climate change and mitigate its adverse effects. Where there are threats of serious or irreversible damage, lack of full scientific certainty should not be used as a reason for postponing such measures, ...'. Article 3 includes economic principles too, such as the principle that measures taken by the Parties 'should not constitute a means of arbitrary or unjustifiable discrimination or a disguised restriction on international trade' (*ibid.*: Art. 3(5)).

The climate change regime lays down specific rules relating to the differentiated obligations and entitlements of the Parties (see further Pallemaerts, 2004a). Reporting obligations exist for all Parties but the different groups of countries need to report with different frequencies and have different data requirements. The national programmes that need to be set up by all Parties to address climate change require different levels of detail and purpose. In the Kyoto Protocol, an additional legally binding instrument, which was developed pursuant to the Framework Convention and adopted in 1997, quantified emissions limitation and reduction commitments have been undertaken by developed countries only.

Developing country Parties enjoy certain preferential rights. Their reporting obligations are conditioned on financial assistance. They are also entitled to benefit from technology transfer and the clean development mechanism (CDM), from which only developing countries are eligible to benefit as host Parties, has been established under the Kyoto Protocol in part to further this goal. Financial assistance is provided to meet the incremental costs of certain national measures and special financial assistance is provided to meet the costs of adaptation to climate change of those developing countries, such as small island states, that are most vulnerable to its adverse effects.

Finally, the climate change regime includes elaborate decision-making procedures. Within the CoP, decisions are made by consensus, as Parties did not manage to agree on any other decision-making rule. The specialized subsidiary bodies, the Subsidiary Body for Implementation (SBI) and the Subsidiary Body for Scientific and Technological Advice (SBSTA), have an advisory role. Other, more specialized regime bodies have been established under the Kyoto Protocol and the Marrakesh Accords (Report of the CoP, 2001), which lay down the detailed rules for the implementation of both the Protocol and certain provisions of the Framework Convention. The climate change regime is subject to continuous further development through decisions of the CoP, which can also adopt additional protocols, such as the Kyoto Protocol, and formal amendments to the Convention itself.

Conclusion

This chapter has aimed to shed light on the dynamic and varied nature of the norms of international environmental law. While it must be admitted that the hard law status of many ‘principles’ remains in doubt, it certainly appears that these are at least ‘hardening’ and provide an important pool for international environmental law-makers to draw upon in the process of establishing complex regimes. The development of international environmental law can then be seen as cyclical as, in turn, these regimes, which deal with the governance of specific issue areas, play a central role in further developing the sources of international environmental law, from hard law MEAs to soft law decisions and resolutions. They also provide a fertile ground for the articulation and implementation of general principles of international environmental law.

References

Case concerning Land Reclamation by Singapore in and around the Straits of Johor (Malaysia v. Singapore) (2003a) International Tribunal for the Law of the Sea, Order of 8 October 2003.

Case concerning Land Reclamation by Singapore in and around the Straits of Johor (Malaysia v. Singapore) (2003b) International Tribunal for the Law of the Sea, Request for provisional measures, 4 September 2003.

Center for International Earth Science Information Network (CIESIN), Columbia University, ENTRI database, www.sedac.ciesin.columbia.edu/entri/ (accessed 24 May 2015).

Cullet, P. (2003) *Differential Treatment in International Environmental Law*, Ashgate Publishing, Aldershot.

Declaration of the United Nations Conference on Environment and Development, Rio de Janeiro, 3–14 June 1992, UN Doc. A/CONF.151/26 (Vol. I, 1992). (Rio Declaration)

de Sadeleer, N. (2002) *Environmental Principles: From Political Slogans to Legal Rules*, Oxford University Press, Oxford.

EEC (1973) *Declaration of the Council of the European Communities and of the Representatives of the Governments of the Member States meeting in the Council of 22 November 1973 on the programme of action of the European Communities on the environment*, OJ 1973 No. C112, 20 December 1973.

EEC (1975) *EEC Recommendation of 3 March 1975 regarding cost allocation and action by public authorities on environmental matters*, OJ 1975 No. L194, 25 July 1975.

Fitzmaurice, M. (2009) *Contemporary Issues International Environmental Law*, Edward Elgar, Cheltenham.

Handl, G. (1990) 'Environmental Security and Global Change: The Challenge to International Law', *Yearbook of International Environmental Law*, 1: 3–33.

Krasner, S. (1982) 'Structural Causes and Regime Consequences', *International Organization*, 36: 185–205.

Lang, W. (1984) 'Die Verrechtlichung des Internationalen Umweltschutzes: Vom "Soft Law" Zum "Hard Law"', *Archiv des Völkerrechts*, 22: 283–305.

Lang, W. (1992) 'Diplomacy and International Environmental Law-Making: Some Observations', *Yearbook of International Environmental Law*, 3: 108–122.

List, M. and Rittberger, V. (1992) 'Regime Theory and International Environmental Management' in Hurrell, A. and Kingsbury, B. (eds) *The International Politics of the Environment: Actors, Interests and Institutions*, Clarendon Press, Oxford, 85–109.

Malmö Ministerial Declaration (2000) Adopted by the Global Ministerial Environment Forum, Sixth Special Session of the UNEP Governing Council, 31 May 2000.

OECD Recommendation of 26 May 1972, *Guiding Principles Concerning International Economic Aspects of Environmental Policies*, sedac.ciesin.org/entri/texts/oecd/OECD-4.01.html (accessed 24 May 2015).

Pallemaerts, M. (2004a) 'Le Cadre International et Européen des Politiques de Lutte Contre les Changements Climatiques' 1858–1859 *Courrier hebdomadaire du CRISP* 1–61.

Pallemaerts, M. (2004b) 'Proceduralizing Environmental Rights: The Aarhus Convention on Access to Information, Public Participation in Decision-Making and Access to Justice in Environmental Matters in a Human Rights Context', Human Rights and the Environment, Proceedings of a Geneva Environment Network Roundtable, UNEP, Geneva.

Plan of Implementation of the World Summit on Sustainable Development, UN Doc. A/CONF.199/20 (2002).

Report of the Conference of the Parties to the UNFCCC on its seventh session, held at Marrakesh from 29 October to 10 November 2001. Addendum. Part two: Action taken by the Conference of the Parties, Volume I, UN Doc. FCCC/CP/2001/13/Add.1 (2001).
Southern Bluefin Tuna Cases (New Zealand v. Japan, Australia v. Japan) (1999) International Tribunal for the Law of the Sea, Order of 27 August 1999.
The MOX Plant Case (Ireland v. United Kingdom) (2001) International Tribunal for the Law of the Sea, Order of 3 December 2001.
UNGA (1982) 'World Charter for Nature', UNGA Res. 37/7, 28 October 1982.
UNGA (2012) 'The Future We Want' Outcome Document, UNGA Res. 66/288, 27 July 2012.
van Hoof, G.J.H. (1983) *Rethinking the Sources of International Law*, Kluwer, Deventer.

3 Basic concepts of treaty law and the treaty-making process

Päivi Kaukoranta[1]

Introduction

Inter-state actions and the rights and obligations incurred by states Parties are regulated by international treaties. International conventions are listed in the famous Article 38(1) of the Statute of the International Court of Justice among the primary sources of international law to be applied by the Court when deciding disputes submitted to it. Treaties form an important method of creating public international law. International environmental law as a rapidly developing field of law also relies heavily upon the framework of treaties. It is therefore essential for negotiators of multilateral environmental agreements (MEAs) to understand the basis and procedure of this system of inter-state relations. Knowledge of how these building blocks of international law function enable negotiators to concentrate on the important substantial issues in multilateral environmental negotiations (standard studies and commentaries on the subject matter of this chapter, which are also commonly used by the author as a source of guidance, include *inter alia*, Aust, 2000; Koskenniemi, 2007; Macleod *et al*, 1996; McGoldrick, 1997; Reuter, 1995; Sinclair, 1984).

This body of international law cannot be discussed without referring frequently to the Vienna Convention on the Law of Treaties, a living instrument for practitioners in treaty offices. It is, however, important to note that although the Vienna Convention is often considered to provide an important 'touchstone' for the law of, and interpretation of the law of treaties, it does not have universal membership. At the time of publication of the present chapter, there were 114 Parties to the Convention. Nevertheless, many, if not most, of the rules articulated by the Convention can be considered applicable even to non-Parties. This is not because the Convention is *directly* binding upon these states, but rather because many of its provisions were designed to codify existing rules of customary international law; while prolonged reference to other provisions arguably means that they are today generally considered to reflect international customary law (or at least to provide indication as to what international customary law is likely to be on a

1 The author thanks Marko Berglund (Senior Officer, Ministry for Foreign Affairs, Finland) for his assistance with the preparation of this chapter, as originally written.

particular point), even though they might not have constituted customary international law at the time of the Convention's adoption.

Elements of the definition of a treaty

The Vienna Convention on the Law of Treaties (1969) defines the term 'treaty' in Article 2(1)(a):

> 'Treaty' means an international agreement concluded between States in written form and governed by international law, whether embodied in a single instrument or in two or more related instruments and whatever its particular designation.

Several elements of this definition should be clarified here. A treaty is distinguishable from another contract due to its international character and the identity of its Parties as states. Treaties are firmly in the domain of international law and do not include international agreements governed by domestic law, such as those related to the lease or purchase of goods.

A treaty, under this definition, must be concluded between states. (State representation can be quite diverse and, although usually concluded by heads of state or by governments acting on behalf of states, treaties may be so expressed as to be concluded by ministries or other state agencies.) However, although the Vienna Convention does not apply to agreements entered into between states and other subjects of international law, this does not affect the legal force of such agreements. These can be legally binding and rules of international law codified in the Vienna Convention may apply to them independently – the provision implies simply that they do not fall within the Vienna Convention's definition of a treaty. Such agreements include, for example, host country agreements with international organizations.

The same is true if an agreement is not in written form. While such an agreement cannot be a treaty under the Vienna Convention, this again does not affect whether or not it is legally in force. Sometimes agreements binding in international law have been made orally. For instance, the prime ministers of Denmark and Finland settled the *Great Belt* case in September 1992 telephonically (Finland had lodged a case with the ICJ, alleging that a Danish plan to build a bridge over the 'Great Belt strait' would hamper Finnish navigation) (*Case Concerning Passage Through the Great Belt*, 1992; Hakapää, 1995: 22).

Treaties are aimed at creating obligations under international law. States' intentions can be derived from and interpreted by examining the terms of instruments and particular circumstances at hand at the time of conclusion. Furthermore, the full provisions of treaties need not be contained in single instruments. For instance, agreements are often supplemented by annexes. These can add considerable flexibility to a treaty regime provided that they are subject to less onerous amendment procedures than the provisions of the agreement text itself. It is thus fairly common for environmental treaties to be supplemented by annexes and for these to be periodically amended, thus allowing the regime to evolve over time to address additional threats. Examples include the Stockholm Convention on Persistent Organic Pollutants and the Convention on International Trade in Endangered Species of Wild Fauna and Flora (CITES). Agreements can also be supplemented by protocols, which elaborate upon the provisions of the original agreement (see, for instance, the Montreal Protocol to the Vienna Convention on the Protection of the Ozone Layer) and can even entirely supplant original agreements (as in the case of the 1996 Protocol to the London Convention on the Prevention of Marine Pollution by Dumping of Wastes and Other Matter). The 'exchanges of notes' and the 'double exchanges of notes' can also be mentioned here since a treaty is, in such cases, formed by the combination thereof. Finally, although it can be indicative, the specific designation of an agreement is not decisive as to its status. Names of treaties are often based on state practice or on the practice of international organizations.

Special issues

States may also agree on instruments labelled as Memoranda of Understanding (MoUs). Although such instruments are usually meant to be legally non-binding, they do create political obligations for their signatories. There are, however, different schools of thought on the legal status of obligations under MoUs (see, for instance, Aust, 2000: 26–46, 404; Klabbers, 1996) and it is important to distinguish between a treaty and an MoU through use of terminology specific to each instrument. Where a treaty uses the word 'shall', drafters of MoUs are more likely to opt for the word 'will'. Treaties have 'Parties'; MoUs have 'participants' (or 'signatories'). Finally, treaties 'enter into force'; while MoUs 'come into effect'. Contrary to many treaties, MoUs should not provide for compulsory, legally binding dispute settlement procedures as these would be contrary to the nature of such an instrument. Similarly, MoUs – unlike treaties – should not contain binding provisions on national reporting or financial contributions (though note that the absence of such binding provisions can make it difficult to monitor an MoU's implementation and to secure funding for its administration). When negotiating an MoU, express provisions defining its status should be included for the sake of clarity. For example, negotiators could simply state that the agreement is not legally binding; or that it does not qualify for registration under Article 102 of the Charter of the United Nations, which deals with the registration of treaties and international agreements with the UN Secretariat (see further Aust, 2000: 26–46, 404).

Sometimes states choose to conclude an MoU instead of a fully fledged treaty, as domestic procedures concomitant on the conclusion of treaties may require more time than is desired – for example, the Memorandum of Understanding for the Global Biodiversity Information Facility (GBIF), first signed in 1999 for 2001–2006, then renewed for 2007–2011 and from 2012. MoUs also potentially provide a more flexible framework than legally binding treaties, as well as a framework that is better suited for partnerships between governments and non-governmental stakeholders. A regime that provides an interesting mix of both treaties and MoUs is the 'family' of ancillary instruments that have been adopted under the framework of the Convention on Migratory Species (CMS). Interestingly, a 2009 review of the organization and activities of the CMS and CMS family concluded that 'the legal status of agreements does not appear to be a matter of great significance'; and that '[a]lthough it may be regretted that MoUs are not legally binding, in practice this is not a vital issue', with the more significant difference between the regime's treaties and MoUs being that the MoUs depend exclusively on voluntary financial contributions, while the treaties have the advantage of core funding (Lee *et al.*, 2010: para. 255).

In negotiating an international agreement, parties may also opt for an 'exchange of notes' or 'exchange of letters'. Using this mechanism is not free of complications, however, as such an exchange *may* actually constitute a treaty or an MoU; and signatories may hold differing views on the instrument's status. In the former case, one often finds language like 'shall constitute an agreement' in the note or letter; whereas in the latter case, when a note or letter merely 'records the understanding', it is intended to take the form of an MoU.

While treaties, in the meaning of the Vienna Convention, can only be concluded between states, other provisions exist for the conclusion of agreements between other subjects of international law. In 1986 a convention on the law of treaties governing these subjects was concluded, although this is not yet in force. While international organizations are entitled to become parties to the Convention, its entry into force hinges upon a minimum number of ratifications by *states* specifically and this number (35) has not yet been reached (Convention on Treaties between States and International Organizations or between International Organizations, 1986). Moreover, as per the 'Reparations for Injuries' case, an international organization has the capacity to conclude treaties if this is provided for in its constituent instrument or if it is indispensable for the fulfilment of its purposes (*Reparations for Injuries Suffered in the Service of the United Nations*, 1949). Further, multilateral treaties, including MEAs, have increasingly begun to provide that certain international organizations can become Parties thereto. A provision allowing 'regional economic integration organizations' (REIOs) to become Parties to international treaties has in practice been a pseudonym for European Communities and the European Union (EU) after the Treaty of Lisbon. A further innovation in 2006 in the context of human rights treaties was a 'regional integration organizations' (RIOs) clause. Within the EU, competence in the field of the environment is shared between the EU and its Member States. Therefore, often both the EU and its various Member States are Parties to the same convention; for instance, from 8 July 2015 the EU has been the 181st Party to CITES. For the reason of shared competences there is a need to allow the EU to become a Party to such international agreements, or to insert a disconnection clause (according to which certain of the Parties to the multilateral convention, in their relations *inter se*, would not apply the rules of the convention but rather specific rules agreed among themselves) or other kinds of clauses taking into account the competences of the EU.

Binding decisions of international organizations or treaty bodies form yet another special type of international agreement. They are normally based either on special provisions in the treaty establishing the organization or in a bilateral treaty, which provides that the body may take decisions that will be binding upon the Parties. As delegates to international organizations may be called upon to make such decisions, it must be ensured that they have the proper powers and competence. The nomenclature of decisions of international organizations may vary from 'decisions' to 'recommendations' and 'measures'. As the binding nature of such decisions will not always be self-evident, it is advisable to use clear terminology. Binding decisions of international organizations or treaty bodies, such as measures adopted by the Antarctic Treaty Consultative Meeting, HELCOM recommendations amending Annexes to the Convention on the Protection of the Marine Environment of the Baltic Sea or decisions of the Commission established by the Convention for the Protection of the Marine Environment of the North-East Atlantic, must go through similar procedures as treaties in relation to their adoption and implementation at the national level.

Concluding treaties and their entry into force

Treaties may be initiated by a state, a group of states or an international organization. In some cases, the 'true ownership' of the initiative behind a treaty may lie with other subjects of international law or increasingly with non-governmental organizations (NGOs). In all of these cases, prior to formal negotiations, it is advisable to consider the feasibility of an initiative through informal discussions. Yet, sometimes initiatives known to be non-realistic at that point are made in order to cultivate attitudes for later negotiations. If needed, negotiating directives can be produced setting out the mandate of each actor. In many cases such a need arises from constitutional provisions of the actor. For example, in the case of EU, negotiating directives is an established practice, as reflected in Article 218(4) of the Treaty on the Functioning of the European Union. As per Article 2(1)(c) of the Vienna Convention, negotiating powers may be delegated by the competent national authority in a document designating a person or persons to represent the state. These actors may have powers to negotiate, adopt or authenticate the text of a treaty and to express the consent of a state to be bound by a treaty. Article 7 of the Vienna Convention confirms that full powers to act on behalf of a state are assumed for heads of state or government or ministers of foreign affairs. Heads of diplomatic missions and accredited representatives can act without full powers in the adoption of the text of a treaty. For other persons, competence may be delegated through a document produced as evidence naming the person and confirming authorization to represent the state. Such credentials must be signed by one of the 'Big Three', i.e. the head of state, the prime minister or the foreign minister.

The rules relating to the adoption and authentication of a treaty are governed by Articles 9 and 10 of the Vienna Convention. With regard to bilateral treaties, this is often completed by initialling the lower corners of each page. Today, bilateral treaties are often finalized through electronic correspondence and formal adoption and authentication takes place only at the time of signature. States may, however, suggest changes before signature takes place – and errors may be corrected (Vienna Convention, 1969: Art. 79). A bilateral treaty is concluded at the time of signature of both Parties.

With multilateral treaties, decisions are made by each state to adopt and authenticate treaties. In international conferences, unless parties decide to apply a different rule, decisions have traditionally been adopted by a two-thirds majority of states present and voting. The use of consensus, which should not be confused with unanimity, has today become more common. Furthermore, international organizations may have specific rules concerning the adoption of treaties. Within the United Nations, for example, the authentication of texts takes the form of adoption of resolutions. The Food and Agriculture Organization (FAO), for its part, requires the certification of two copies, by the Chairman of the FAO Conference and by the FAO Director General. At the end of a conference, it is normal for negotiating states to sign the 'final act', which is an optional step and does not commit the state to sign or ratify the agreement in question. Multilateral treaties are normally deemed to be concluded with signature of the final act or at the date of opening for signature.

After a treaty is concluded, it is normally first signed but this is not compulsory. Treaties adopted by the FAO Conference, for example, are not signed. Some treaties are open for signature only for a specific time whilst others remain open indefinitely (see, for instance, the Ramsar Convention on Wetlands of International Importance, 1971: Art. 9(1)). In either case, it is essential that the person signing the agreement enjoys the full powers addressed in Article 7 of the Vienna Convention. Full powers authorizing the person to sign an agreement shall state the full name of the person concerned and a full title of the treaty to be signed and are given by one of the 'Big Three'. Full powers are furnished with a date and place and although an official seal is usually used, this is not compulsory. Once a treaty is signed, a state is, until it has made its intention clear not to become a Party, under an obligation to refrain from acts that would 'defeat the object and purpose of the treaty' (Vienna Convention, 1969: Art. 18).

The Vienna Convention provides for several alternative ways of expressing consent to be bound by a treaty. This can be done by signature (meaning 'definitive signature'), 'exchange of instruments', 'ratification', 'acceptance', 'approval', 'accession' or by any other means (*ibid.*: Art. 11). Resorting to these alternative means does not affect the legal implications of expressing consent. With each treaty, it is important to note any final provisions that define particular ways in which consent may be given.

Consent to be bound by signature is common in the case of bilateral treaties or of treaties that have only a few Parties. Giving consent to be bound by signature is normally only possible for treaties that do not require prior parliamentary approval. In rare cases, the procedure of 'ad referendum signature' coupled with confirmation by the state may be used. Consent can be given through an exchange of instruments such as the notes or letters discussed above. Again, this is common with bilateral instruments but can also be used for agreements between more than two countries. This is true for example for many of the Nordic Agreements concluded under the Treaty of Co-operation between Denmark, Finland, Iceland, Norway and Sweden, 1962 (the Helsinki Treaty).

Ratification is an international act so named, whereby a state establishes its consent to be bound by a treaty. Ratification normally follows signature of a treaty, although the two acts can take place together. It is important to be aware of the common misconception that ratification means approval by a national parliament. Although in national legislation this may be the case, as a concept of international law this is not correct. The date of ratification is the date of deposit of the instrument of ratification, not the date of a national decision to ratify. Instruments of ratification must be signed by one of the 'Big Three' within a state.

Consent to be bound by a treaty can be given by acceptance or approval, which should be given under similar conditions as with ratification (Vienna Convention, 1969: Art. 14(2)). The use of acceptance and approval was originally developed in order to enable some states to avoid constitutional requirements to obtain parliamentary authority to ratify. This was the case for states where the parliamentary process was described as ratification without making a distinction with the procedure under the same name at the international level. States can also give consent to be bound by a treaty through accession (*ibid.*: Art. 15). Accession is not preceded by signature and is used as a means for a state to become a Party if it is unable for some reason to sign the treaty. This may be because the time for signature has lapsed or because the treaty is open for signature only for certain states. Today, accession is often possible even before a treaty's entry into force. The other means of giving consent to be bound by a treaty provided for in Article 11 of the Vienna Convention are not commonly used, except in cases of giving consent to be bound by amendments to treaties.

The entry into force of treaties is governed by Article 24 of the Vienna Convention. Modern treaties normally include explicit provisions on how they will enter into force, and multilateral agreements often require a certain number of states to give their consent to be bound. It is often impractical to provide that a treaty enters into force immediately on the date of consenting to be bound by the treaty. Many states need to take certain implementing measures between giving their consent and entry into force. To avoid confusion, standard clauses developed in the practice of international organizations such as the United Nations are often used. Exceptions to such standards exist, however, as with the Kyoto Protocol of 1997 to the UN Framework Convention on Climate Change of 1992, which Protocol entered into force only after its ratification by at least 55 countries, with these accounting for 55 percent of 1990 levels of carbon dioxide emissions in Parties listed as 'Annex I countries' (Kyoto Protocol, 1997: Art. 25(1)).

Significant delays may occur between a treaty's adoption and its entry into force. An example is the United Nations Convention on the Law of the Non-Navigational Uses of International Watercourses, which was adopted in May 1997 but only entered into force in August 2014 (interestingly, however, most of this Convention's provisions have been applicable in southern Africa for over a decade, having been mirrored in the 2000 Revised Protocol on Shared Watercourse Systems in the SADC Region, which entered into force in 2003). In order to enable the application of treaties during eventual delays of the entry into force, provision is sometimes made for the provisional application of a treaty or a part thereof (Vienna Convention, 1969: Art. 25). For countries lacking simplified internal procedures for provisional application, such provisions do not bring relief. Although provisional application has become a rather common procedure in contemporary treaty making, the International Law Commission (ILC) decided in 2012, during its sixty-fourth session, to include the topic in its programme of work (ILC, 2012: Chapter IV).

It is common for a treaty's text to be authenticated in two or more languages, in which case Article 33(1) of the Vienna Convention provides that the text will be equally authoritative in each language, 'unless the treaty provides or the parties agree that, in the case of divergence, a particular text shall prevail'. Depending on the treaty's geographic scope, its authentication in more than one language can play a significant role in facilitating accession by certain states. For instance, in terms of the original version of the Ramsar Convention, only the English text was designated as authentic. The Convention's Conference of the Parties soon realized, however, that this approach presented a potential hurdle to increasing the number of Contracting Parties (Ramsar CoP Recommendation 1.7). The Convention was thus ultimately amended so as to give equal status to the English, French, German and Russian versions (Paris Protocol, 1982). Similarly, the Convention on Establishing the European Forest Institute was concluded in 2003 in English only; but in 2012 French and German, and in 2013 Spanish, were added as authentic languages of the Convention following the procedure under Article 33(2) of the Vienna Convention (see depositary notifications of 21 August 2012 and 10 July 2013).

Amendments and reservations

Amendments to a treaty may be made by agreement between the Parties (Vienna Convention, 1969: Art. 39). Explicit amendment clauses are often included in a treaty. Non-automatic amendment procedures require agreement between the Parties and are often subject to constitutional procedures. Automatically binding amendment mechanisms facilitate the entry into force of amendments that may be necessary for the effective functioning of an agreement, but these may be problematic for constitutional reasons. Moreover, opting out and contracting out procedures exist. Review clauses are also common and review is often initially undertaken by the Conference of the Parties of an MEA.

The Vienna Convention makes provision for reservations to treaties (*ibid.*: Arts 19–23). Reservations are permissible unless these are specifically prohibited, or would be contrary to the object and purpose of the agreement. These can be entered into either at the time of signature and confirmed at the time of expressing consent to be bound by a treaty; or at the time of expressing consent to be bound. Interpretative declarations or statements titled otherwise may constitute reservations. Although commonly provided for, many MEAs do specifically preclude reservations (or, alternatively, limit the types of reservations that are permissible) in hopes of furthering the effectiveness of the treaties. Reservations may be withdrawn but may not be reformulated in a manner that would amount to a new or wider reservation.

Reservations may be contentious, as allowing them might enable a state Party to escape obligations that other Parties see as fundamental to the object and purpose of a treaty. In such cases, other Parties may object to reservations they find to be contrary to the rules of the law of treaties or otherwise unacceptable. For example, under the United Nations Convention on the Law of the Sea this is common practice while in the case of MEAs, objections are rather rare. For example under the Basel Convention on the Control of Transboundary Movements of Hazardous Wastes and their Disposal objections have been expressed *vis-à-vis* the declarations that have been considered to amount to forbidden reservations, having been made late and been unacceptable in substance.

The argument for allowing reservations is that this increases the likelihood of a state ratifying a particular treaty where it would otherwise prefer to remain a non-Party; and, in the same vein, keeps states that have already ratified the treaty – with reservations – within its parameters, where such states might otherwise choose to withdraw completely. In addition, allowing reservations is one strategy through which to overcome significant disagreements during treaty negotiations, which jeopardize the treaty's very adoption.

Another issue that arises is that of third states. Although a treaty will not create either rights or obligations for a third state without its consent (Vienna Convention: Art. 34), it is possible for the treaty to regulate the manner in which its Parties interact with third states (for instance, by prohibiting Parties to trade in certain substances with non-Parties, as is done by Articles 4 of the Montreal Protocol and 4(5) of the Basel Convention) and this may, in turn, provide an effective incentive for non-Parties to accede to the treaty.

Conclusion

This chapter has provided a mere overview of the treaty-making process and the basic concepts of treaty law. The modern law of treaties is arguably akin to that set out in the Vienna Convention on the Law of Treaties, which provides a good starting point for a negotiator working with the provisions of treaties. International environmental agreements have multiplied during the past decades and developed into a specialist system of law with its own principles, treaty bodies and institutional practices – a good testimony of fragmentation of international law. The emergence of international environmental law is a natural development or necessity as a reaction to the concern of the state of the environment. No legal regime is, however, isolated from general international law. As referred to above, the Vienna Convention is generally considered to reflect international customary law and therefore regulates everything that happens in the regime-building and regime-administration. By understanding and taking into consideration the regime applicable to international treaty-making, negotiators are more likely to achieve their desired outcomes in multilateral environmental negotiations. At the very least these rules provide an important element to be included in environmental treaty makers' tool-boxes.

References

'A Protocol on Amendment Procedures', Ramsar Convention Resolution 1.7 (1980).

Aust, A. (2000) *Modern Treaty Law and Practice*, Cambridge University Press, Cambridge.

Case Concerning Passage Through the Great Belt (Finland v. Denmark), Order of 10 September 1992 (Discontinuance), ICJ Reports (1992) 348.

Hakapää, K. (1995) *Uusi Kansainvälinen Oikeus* ['*New International Law*'], Lakimiesliiton Kustannus, Helsinki.

International Law Commission Report on the work of its sixty-fourth session (2012), legal.un.org/ilc/sessions/64/64sess.htm (accessed 24 May 2015).

Klabbers, J. (1996) *The Concept of Treaty in International Law*, Martinus Nijhoff, Brill Academic Publishers, Leiden.

Koskenniemi, M, (2007) *Fragmentation of International Law: Difficulties Arising from the Diversification and Expansion of International Law*, Report of the Study of the International Law Commission, Publications of the Erik Castrén Institute of International Law and Human Rights, Hakapaino Oy, Helsinki.

Lee, R., Filgueira, B., Caddell, R. and Frater, L. (2010) *Review of the current organization and activities of CMS and the CMS Family: First step of the Inter-Sessional Future Shape Process*, UNEP/CMS/Inf.10.14.8.

Macleod, I., Hendry, I.D. and Hyett, S. (1996) *The External Relations of the European Communities*, Clarendon Press, Oxford.

McGoldrick, D. (1997) *International Relations Law of the European Union*, Addison Wesley Longman, London.

Memorandum of Understanding for the Global Biodiversity Information Facility (2012), www.gbif.org/resource/80661 (accessed 24 May 2015).

Reparations for Injuries Suffered in the Service of the United Nations, Advisory Opinion of 1949, ICJ Reports (1949) 174.

Reuter, P. (1995) *Introduction to the Law of Treaties* (2nd ed.), Kegan Paul International Ltd, London.

Sinclair, I. (1984) *The Vienna Convention on the Law of Treaties* (2nd ed.), Manchester University Press, Manchester.

4 The problem-solving role of international environmental law, with special reference to water-related problems

Tuomas Kuokkanen[1]

Introduction

One of the functions of international law is to solve and manage problems in the international system (Heiskanen, 2004: 271). In the environmental context, one would list various environmental issues as problems, such as climate change, depletion of the ozone layer, acidification, and marine pollution. Whilst these surely represent environmental problems, they are not necessarily legal problems. Take, for example, unilateral trade restrictions that are motivated by environmental concerns. Despite being based on good environmental intentions, such measures might, from the trade law point of view, turn out to be problematic and eventually create legal problems. Therefore, there is a difference between a legal and an environmental problem. The concept of a problem is, thus, not a black and white question; but rather is one to be determined in a particular context.

A number of problems, both environmental and legal, in the environmental field boil down to the relationship between the protection of the environment and the utilization of natural resources. That relationship, which in many instances might be termed as tension, is not a monolithic but rather a complex, polynomial topic (Higgins, 1995: 129). Indeed, international law has, over the last hundred years or so, struggled to solve or manage various problems relating to the environment and natural resources.

At first sight, the distinction between natural resources and the environment might seem to be artificial, as natural resources can be regarded as part of the environment. For instance, Article 2(10) of the 1993 Convention on Civil Liability for Damage Resulting from Activities Dangerous to the Environment, defines 'environment' in the following way: '"[e]nvironment" includes: …natural resources, both abiotic and biotic, such as air, water, soil, fauna and flora and their interaction between the same factors…'. Yet, this distinction illustrates two aspects of the human relationship to nature: the exploitation of natural resources and the protection of the environment. While the former tends to underline the economic or beneficial side of nature, the latter emphasizes conservation and protection.

---

1 The author has participated in the research project 'Legal framework to promote water security' (WATSEC), financed by the Academy of Finland (268151). The chapter is also partly based on the book: Kuokkanen (2002) *International Law and the Environment: Variations on a Theme*.

The dual character outlined above is reflected in many natural resources: on one hand, they serve as natural resources subject to human consumption and exploitation and, on the other, they have a particular ecosystem function. Water is a good example of such a natural resource. While it has several uses, such as navigation and irrigation, it also has an essential ecosystem role.

This chapter will distinguish three main approaches taken in international law to the relationship between the exploitation of natural resources and the protection of the environment, using examples relating to water. First, the chapter examines the approach of simply applying general international law and thus not giving a specific legal meaning to the relationship between the two. Second, the chapter explores an approach according to which a differentiation is made between substantive regulation dealing with the protection of the environment and that dealing with the exploitation of natural resources. Third, the chapter considers the approach of dealing with the relationship in an integrated manner, recognizing that the issues are interlinked. Even though the three approaches have dominated different periods in history (roughly, the undifferentiated approach from 1850 to 1939; the separated approach between 1950 and 1980; and the integrated approach from 1980 onwards), they all remain applicable today. Indeed, the three approaches are reflected in the manner in which the international community addresses many current environmental issues.

Recourse to general international law

Undifferentiated approach to the utilization of natural resources and the protection of the environment

As early environment-related problems were of a sporadic and bilateral nature, it seemed sufficient to solve them retroactively through the settlement of disputes (a 'dispute' being defined by Merrils as 'a disagreement about something' and an 'international dispute' being 'a disagreement, typically but not exclusively between States, with consequences on the international plane' (Merrils, 2003: 529–530). The function of arbitration tribunals in the latter part of nineteenth century represented a landmark in the evolution of international law by demonstrating that international law can have professional, not merely academic or philosophical, value. From arbitration, international dispute settlement evolved to the Permanent Court of Arbitration, to the Permanent Court of International Justice and to the International Court of Justice. All of these fora have resolved environment-related cases by applying general international law.

The distinction between exploitation of natural resources and protection of the environment is not relevant from the perspective of general international law. Indeed, general doctrines and techniques are neutral in the sense that they apply to both. For instance, state sovereignty, abuse of rights, good faith, and dispute settlement are neutral doctrines and techniques as they can be applied in a general way (Kuokkanen, 2002: 52–67, 93–97). This does not mean that from the factual point of view there would not be any difference between the exploitation of natural resources and the protection of the environment. The point is rather that, legally, such issues can be addressed without drawing a distinction between the two. Thus, general doctrines are neither pro- nor anti-doctrines *per se*. Depending on the specific factual scenario and the applicable law, they can, however, lead to either a pro- or anti-result from the point of view of exploitation of natural resources or protection of the environment.

As issues relating to the environment and natural resources became increasingly relevant, it became necessary to begin to develop substantive regulations to deal with both protection and utilization. These new rules did not altogether replace general rules. Rather, general rules were gradually pushed into the background. They remained, nevertheless, relevant and applicable.

Dealing with water-related disputes

At the time when water conflicts were relatively infrequent, it was sufficient to deal with such issues by applying general international law. Moreover, if such disputes occurred, they were predominantly bilateral in nature. It was therefore adequate to resolve them retrospectively through traditional international dispute settlement techniques by applying general international law to the facts.

Traditionally, water issues reflect the tension between an upstream and a downstream country. From a legal point of view, the starting point in considering the applicable law is the abandonment of the doctrine of absolute sovereignty. That doctrine would allow an upstream country to use waters in its territory without limitations and a downstream country to prohibit the causing of any harm. As both the upstream and downstream country could rely on their territorial sovereignty in an absolute manner, the doctrine is self-contradictory. In the water context, the doctrine of absolute territorial sovereignty propounded by Judson Harmon in his legal opinion of 1895 has become known as the 'Harmon doctrine' (Opinion by Judson Harmon, 1895). The doctrine is based on a philosophical approach supported by early scholars, rather than an application of international law in an adjudicative context. In view of this lack of professional value, the Harmon doctrine revealed a need to develop more functional and analytical ways to deal with water disputes.

The *Lac Lanoux* arbitral decision (*Affaire du Lac Lanoux*, 1957) is a seminal case relating to water in which the arbitral tribunal managed to settle the dispute by applying judicial techniques. The case illustrates how a resort to third-party adjudication may prevent stalemates and promote a more constructive solution (Laylin and Bianchi, 1959: 37). By distinguishing between the formal and substantive aspects of sovereignty, a method capable of resolving concrete issues, unlike the Harmon doctrine, was applied by the tribunal. To supplement this method, the tribunal used procedural techniques involving the allocation of burden of proof. From the environmental point of view, the ruling recognized that a state has a right to use its natural resources as it sees fit; but must take into account the interests of other states and therefore has a corresponding duty to consult with other states before taking steps that might affect them.

The dispute in *Lac Lanoux* related to the exploitation of natural resources rather than to the protection of the environment. In effect, a clash between hydroelectric and agricultural interests formed the background to the dispute. While the French government planned to divert water to generate electric power, the Spanish government was concerned about the possible adverse impact of such a diversion on Spanish agriculture. From the legal point of view, France relied on its right to use its natural resources, while Spain argued that the French project required prior agreement between the two governments. The tribunal stated that there existed a principle prohibiting an upper riparian state from altering the waters of a river in such a fashion as seriously to prejudice the downstream state (*Affaire du Lac Lanoux*, 1957: 129). As Spain was not able to submit evidence showing any injury, there was no need for the tribunal to consider what would amount to so-called serious injury.

The outcome of the *Lac Lanoux* arbitration did not shed much light on the issue of serious injury as that threshold was left undecided. Rather, the award recognized a state's legitimate right to use its natural resources while taking into account the interests of other states. However, as environmental problems gradually increased there was a need to agree, for example, on the pollution loads and toleration thresholds in order to strike a balance between upstream and downstream states. As the difference between serious and non-serious injury is a difference in degree as opposed to a conceptual distinction, general international law could not by judicial means give a satisfactory answer on where and how to draw the line. Therefore, there was a need to elaborate more functional rules and methods to deal with water-related problems.

Recourse to a regulatory approach

Separating the utilization of natural resources and the protection of the environment

In an article published in 1908, Oppenheim argued strongly in favour of conventional law and noted that the future of international law belongs to conventional rather than customary law (Oppenheim, 1908: 348). In the same vein, Kelsen noted that '[t]here are no matters which cannot be regulated by international law' (Kelsen, 1966: 300–301). As the interdependence of states increased, it appeared, along the lines of Oppenheim's and Kelsen's statements, that there was a need to regulate international activities to balance the various interests and concerns. As a result, the sphere of international jurisdiction was bound gradually to expand. Parallel to international regulation, international institutions were established. The role of international institutions further increased after World War II along with the establishment of the United Nations and other international organizations.

It is against this background that one can approach the development of international regulations. However, as opposed to a unified regime, two distinct branches of law developed: international environmental law and the law of natural resources. These branches are based on different starting points. The law of natural resources tends to view natural resources as property subject to national sovereignty; while international environmental law appears to regard the environment as a common good and concern and thus subject to international regulation.

With regard to environmental protection, a move to a regulatory approach entailed a shift from the application of general international law to a substance-oriented approach, as there was (because of the specific nature of environmental issues) a need to develop substantive rules concerning the environment. The process had already started to evolve, although in a limited form, in the nineteenth century, and continued to develop in the first half of the twentieth century. Early agreements were introduced to conserve useful species, such as birds and wildlife, for hunting, agriculture, commerce and other similar needs – for example, in 1902, eleven European states concluded the Convention on Birds Useful to Agriculture. Controversies that arose related predominantly to the use of those natural resources that were shared internationally, in particular in a border area, or that were in the global commons. As such areas were subject to differing jurisdictions, or to none at all, their use tended to give rise to disputes. Therefore, international cooperation became necessary to avoid such disputes by regulating the use of boundary waters and the exploitation of species in areas beyond national jurisdiction. Finally, the process of internationalization was extended to transboundary relations. This phase began to develop in the 1960s and 1970s as the need to protect the human environment against pollution emerged. Thus, international environmental regulations, and thereby international jurisdiction, developed gradually.

The law relating to natural resources began to develop in another context. It was a reaction against the classical doctrine of international law, pursuant to which the expropriation of foreign property was unlawful unless justified by international law. The new approach began to develop after World War II when a number of colonies became independent. Despite their independence, natural resources in these newly independent states were, to a large extent, still owned or exploited by foreigners through concession agreements. Newly independent countries regarded the traditional rules of international law as an obstacle to their development. A demand for a more just era appeared, for example, from the following declaration by the non-aligned countries adopted in Belgrade in 1961:

> [T]here are crises that lead towards a world conflict in the transition from an old order based on domination to a new order based on co-operation between nations, founded on freedom, equality and social justice for the promotion of prosperity … the dynamic processes and forms of social change often result in or represent a conflict between the old established and the new emerging nationalist forces … a lasting peace can be achieved only if this confrontation leads to a world where the domination of colonialism-imperialism and neo-colonialism in all their manifestations is radically eliminated…
>
> (Belgrade Declaration, 1961: 6)

Criticizing the prevailing colonial influence, they pushed for economic self-determination and the establishment of conditions in which they could freely exploit their own natural resources. Accordingly, the former colonies initiated the process to amend the traditional doctrine on the protection of foreign property under the auspices of the United Nations.

The underlying theme of the process of decolonization was the desire to return sovereignty over natural resources to the newly independent states. Broms notes that the fact that the colonial powers felt no obligation to grant control over natural resources to the local population led to deep dissatisfaction among the local leaders, who understood the value of natural resources (Broms, 1997: 520). In 1962, the UN General Assembly adopted a Resolution (UNGA, 1962: Res. 1803) on Permanent Sovereignty over Natural Resources (on the development of the principle through the political organs of the United Nations in the period up to 1962 see, generally, Gess, 1964: 398–449; Hyde, 1956: 854–867; Elian, 1979: 83–100; and Schrijver, 1997: 36–81). According to principle 1 of this Resolution, 'the right of peoples and nations to permanent sovereignty over their natural wealth and resources must be exercised in the interest of their national development and of the well-being of the people of the State concerned'.

In the 1960s, the process was further extended by the New International Economic Order (NIEO), whereby developing countries began to criticize traditional trade principles and international economic institutions. From their point of view, international economic order favoured strong Western countries and multinational companies, and did not sufficiently take into account the special circumstances of developing countries. NIEO was a 1970s initiative of developing countries to establish what would, from their point of view, be a more just economic order. However, the significance of the NIEO was reduced by the fact that many developed states were reluctant to recognize its legal authority. In contrast, the 1962 Resolution on the Permanent Sovereignty over Natural Resources appeared to be generally accepted. In fact, the principle was integrated into Principle 21 of the Stockholm Declaration (1972) which stated that 'States have, in accordance with the Charter of the United Nations and the principles of international law, the sovereign right to exploit their own resources pursuant to their own environmental policies…', and later into a number of international environmental instruments such as the London Dumping Convention of 1972 (Preamble), the LRTAP Convention of 1979 (Preamble), the UNCLOS of 1982, the Vienna Convention of 1985 (Preamble), the UNFCCC of 1992 (Preamble), the CBD of 1992 (Art. 4) and the Rio Declaration of 1992.

Gradually, the law of natural resources and international environmental law developed in divergent directions. On the one hand, the law of natural resources appeared to deregulate the exploitation of natural resources; on the other, international environmental law appeared to regulate the protection of the environment. While the former sought to maximize national jurisdiction, the latter strove to maximize international jurisdiction. Yet, both areas of law concerned both the exploitation of natural resources and the protection of the environment.

Regulating the utilization and protection of water

In order to regulate the various interests concerned, states concluded many watercourse treaties from the beginning of the nineteenth century until World War II. In view of the inherent international aspect of boundary waters, it was natural that states began to regulate the use of such waters through bilateral and multilateral agreements. The general purpose of boundary water treaties was to prevent disputes by reconciling the various interests of riparian states. This objective is explicitly stated in the Preamble of the 1909 Boundary Waters Treaty between Canada and the United States, according to which the aim of the treaty is 'to prevent disputes regarding the use of boundary waters'.

Smith emphasized the need for a regulatory approach in his famous work of 1931 (Smith, 1931: 1–13), pointing out that, in many cases, a river system can present complex questions because the use of its waters is demanded simultaneously for navigation, irrigation, electric power and the supply of large cities. He further specified that the function of law is 'to provide rules for settling the possible conflict of interests' (*ibid.*: 13) by aiming to strike an equitable balance between them. Berber too argued in favour of treaty-making, which, according to him, represents the highest form of political wisdom. He noted that 'the conclusion of specific and specialized water treaties remains far and away the best solution' (Berber, 1959: 270).

States have been particularly eager to conclude agreements to safeguard the freedom of navigation. Furthermore, states established international bodies to deal especially with navigational interests. The first international waterway administration was established in 1804 to deal with navigation on the Rhine River (Rhine Convention, 1804). In 1814, a general declaration on the freedom of navigation was made by the Treaty of Paris (1814). Subsequently, in 1821, a river commission was established to oversee navigation of the Elbe (Elbe Convention, 1821). Internationalization was pushed further by the 1856 Treaty of Paris, which established the European Danube Commission, consisting not only of representatives of riparian but also of non-riparian states. Following the model of the Danube administration, the International Commission for the Navigation of the Congo was established in 1885 (Congo General Act, 1885). After World War I, the freedom of navigation of the important European rivers was confirmed by the Treaty of Versailles, 1919. For example, Article 291 declares the Danube an international river. Finally, under the auspices of the League of Nations, the Statute on the Régime of Navigable Waterways of International Concern was adopted at Barcelona in 1921. The Statute defined as navigable waterways of international concern all parts of a waterway which separate or traverse different states and which are naturally navigable to and from the sea.

With regard to non-navigational uses of boundary waters, states had, prior to World War II, already concluded a number of bilateral and multilateral treaties. While some of the treaties regulated utilization in general terms, others regulated such traditional uses as irrigation, fishing and the floating of timber. After the industrial revolution, it was recognized that regulations should be extended to also cover modern uses of boundary waters. To this end, bilateral agreements were concluded in order to impose detailed regulations on, for example, the use of hydroelectric power, the size of a dam to be constructed in a boundary water, or the volume of water to be diverted for mining or industrial purposes. Moreover, in 1923, a multilateral treaty called the Convention Relating to the Development of Hydraulic Power Affecting More than One State was concluded.

During the late nineteenth and early twentieth centuries, environmental issues and problems were not perceived to be very important and only a few boundary water treaties imposed regulations upon the use of waters aimed at preventing pollution. One example was the 1909 Boundary Waters Treaty (Art. IV, para. 2): '[i]t is further agreed that the waters herein defined as boundary waters and waters flowing across the boundary shall not be polluted on either side to the injury of health or property on the other'. As the recognition of freshwater pollution problems increased, there was a need to widen the scope of water agreements. Furthermore, it was understood that there was a need comprehensively to regulate a hydrologic unit. The process of internationalization was thus broadened from only regulating boundary waters to controlling watercourses of international concern also.

In the 1960s and 1970s, several bilateral and multilateral treaties were concluded to protect regional watercourses. For example, regulations were issued to protect Lake Constance (Lake Constance Convention, 1960), the Mosel (Mosel Convention, 1961), the Rhine (Rhine Agreement, 1963; Rhine Convention, 1976) and the Great Lakes (Great Lakes Agreement, 1978). These regulations set specific water quality objectives or emission limits or, alternatively, established joint bodies under which specific regulations could be determined. Thus, the emphasis was placed upon waters crossing boundaries rather than waters forming boundaries. To emphasize this aspect, international instruments began to refer to transboundary or international waters rather than to boundary or frontier waters.

Recourse to the management approach

The integrated approach to the utilization of natural resources and the protection of the environment

As the regulatory approach eventually proved unable to solve pollution problems, it was regarded as ineffective and overoptimistic. It was ineffective in the sense that its approach was mainly a reaction against problems that already existed. Rather than preventing environmental problems from appearing, states were forced into a crisis management approach when dealing with pollution problems that had already arisen. The regulatory approach appeared to be overoptimistic as it assumed that the emergence of environmental problems could be precluded through international regulations. Thereafter, it was pointed out that environmental policy should be complemented by a 'forecast and prevent' approach 'to ensure timely intervention' (in the World Charter for Nature, it was stated that '[t]he status of natural processes, ecosystems and species shall be closely monitored to enable early detection of degradation or threat, ensure timely intervention and facilitate the evaluation of conservation policies and methods' (UNGA, 1982, 'World Charter for Nature': para. 19)) so that potential environmental problems could be identified at an earlier stage and managed before they reached crisis proportions.

Optimization of short-term and long-term economic interests and environmental concerns began to develop, in a limited form, in connection with early environmental agreements on the use of boundary waters and the conservation of marine living resources.

With regard to marine living resources, the 1911 Fur Seals Convention represents an early agreement reflecting reconciliation between economic and conservation interests. The optimization approach was also used in regulating fishing and whaling. For instance, the 1946 International Convention for the Regulation of Whaling refers in its Preamble to the 'optimum level of whale stocks' while many fishing agreements used the concept of 'maximum sustainable yield' (see, for instance, the Convention on High Seas Fisheries of the North Pacific, 1952: Art. IV: '...for the purpose of maintaining or increasing its maximum sustained productivity'). This approach, with slight variations, was extended to marine living resources in general. The 1958 Convention on the Living Resources of the High Seas was based on the concept of 'the optimum sustainable yield'. Finally, optimal utilization was extended to the 1982 UN Convention on the Law of the Sea and to the 1995 Convention on Straddling and Highly Migratory Fish Stocks. As a consequence, the optimization approach replaced the freedom of exploitation. Referring to this evolution, the International Court of Justice stated in the *Fisheries Jurisdiction* case that 'the former *laissez faire* treatment of the living resources of the sea in the high seas has been replaced by a recognition of a duty to have due regard to the rights of other states and the need of conservation for the benefits of all' (*Fisheries Jurisdiction Case (UK v Iceland)*, 1974: 31; *Fisheries Jurisdiction Case (Germany v Iceland)*, 1975: 200).

At the end of the 1970s and the beginning of the 1980s, it was gradually acknowledged that protection of the environment had, until then, focused too narrowly on environmental effects; rather than on the primary causes of those effects. The European Community, in recognizing the insufficiency of this approach, pointed out that environmental problems ought to be addressed 'not so much as problems, but as symptoms of mismanagement and abuse' (Resolution of the Council..., 1 February 1993).

The purpose of the proactive method was, as André Nollkaemper notes, to move from 'end-of-pipe' solutions to a prescription of processes and clean production methods that prevented harmful effects from occurring in the first place (Nollkaemper, 1993: 128). Freestone and Hay have suggested that

> [t]he first element implies a shift of focus away from trying to determine the level of pollution which the environment can assimilate to technologies which will eliminate or at least reduce the input of pollutants to the environment. A shift away from policies based on 'dilute and disperse' towards policies based on 'minimization and containment' of substances harmful to the environment.
>
> (Freestone and Hay, 1996: 13)

The World Commission on Environment and Development (WCED) said in *Our Common Future* in 1987 that '[t]oday, the sources of [the] effects must be tackled' (WCED, 1987: 311). In the Bamako Convention on Hazardous Wastes of 1991 the obligation is laid down that '[t]he Parties shall co-operate with each other in taking the appropriate measures to implement the precautionary principle to pollution prevention through the application of clean production methods, rather than the pursuit of a permissible emissions approach based on assimilative capacity assumptions' (Bamako Convention, 1991: Art. 4(3f)).

To that end, policy-makers introduced the criteria 'Best Environmental Technology' and 'Best Environmental Practices' for pollution sources. These criteria were based on dynamic techniques rather than unified solutions. Moreover, it was recognized that, in fact, pollution sources often affected several environmental media; and that, therefore, it was more appropriate to consider impacts on the environment as a whole (see, for instance, the OECD Council Recommendation, 1991: Preamble), rather than focusing on each environmental element (that is air, water, and soil) separately. Environmental policy-makers thus adopted a dynamic approach to environmental media.

Next, the optimization process was extended to natural resources in general. In 1980, the International Union for Conservation of Nature and Natural Resources (IUCN) published the World Conservation Strategy, which defines the concept of sustainable utilization by noting that '[s]ustainable utilization is somewhat analogous to spending the interest while keeping the capital' (IUCN *et al.*, 1980: 10). In 1982, the UN General Assembly adopted the World Charter for Nature, according to which 'ecosystems and organisms, as well as the land, marine and atmospheric resources that are utilized by man, shall be managed to achieve and maintain optimum sustainable productivity' (UNGA, 1982, 'World Charter for Nature': para. 1(4)). Furthermore, the 1992 Convention on Biological Diversity covers both biological diversity and biological resources. The Convention requires that biological diversity is conserved and biological resources are used in a sustainable manner ('sustainable use' is defined in the Convention as follows: 'the use of components of biological diversity in a way and at a rate that does not lead to the long-term decline of biological diversity, thereby maintaining its potential to meet the need and aspirations of present and future generations' (Art. 2)). The concepts of 'green economy' (see, for instance, UNEP, 2011) and 'ecosystem services' (see, for instance, *Millennium Ecosystem Assessment*, 2005; Suvantola, 2011) also reflect the integrated approach.

The reconciliation between the environment and the economy was achieved through the emergence of the doctrine of sustainable development at the global level to bridge the gap between developed and developing countries. The WCED, chaired by Gro Harlem Brundtland, focused on the reconciliation of the environment and development in its report, which was titled 'Our Common Future'. The report stated that 'the "environment" is where we all live; and "development" is what we all do in attempting to improve our lot within that abode. The two are inseparable' (WCED, 1987: 20).

Through the 1992 United Nations Conference on Environment and Development (UNCED), convened in Rio de Janeiro, Brazil, 'sustainable development' became the dominant doctrine. Sustainable utilization was extended to cover different forms of utilization of natural resources, such as sustainable agriculture, sustainable land use, sustainable mountain development, sustainable use of biological resources, sustainable use of marine living resources, sustainable water utilization, and so on. Twenty years later, at the 2012 United Nations Conference on Sustainable Development (UNCSD), the same approach continued. The final Outcome Document, 'The Future We Want', reaffirmed the need to achieve sustainable development by, *inter alia*:

> promoting integrated and sustainable management of natural resources and ecosystems that supports *inter alia* economic, social and human development while facilitating ecosystem conservation, regeneration and restoration and resilience in the face of new and emerging challenges.
>
> (UNGA, 2012, 'The Future We Want': I.4)

Consequently, environmental concerns and exploitation interests were finally integrated. However, this does not mean that the doctrine of sustainable development has produced a harmonious outcome. Rather it has provided a framework under which the tension between the environment and the economy can potentially be coordinated and managed.

Management of international watercourses

The principle of reasonable and equitable utilization of waters began to develop at the beginning of the twentieth century. Realizing the indeterminacy of absolute sovereignty in the settlement of international disputes led to bilateral and multilateral agreements on the use of boundary waters based on the principle of equitable utilization (see, for example, the Treaty on Utilization of the Waters of the Rio Grande, 1944). The development of the principle highlighted a need to manage international watercourses by optimizing long-term interests and short-term needs and by taking into account all relevant factors and reaching a conclusion on the basis of the whole. Smith noted that, in view of various interests, it may be complex in a concrete case to determine which of these prevail (Smith, 1931: 3–4). He pointed out that conflicts of interests between states should be appraised taking into account the wider community to which states belong. In the same vein, when considering the principles governing international fluvial law, the Permanent Court of International Justice in the *River Oder* case stated as follows:

> [the] community of interest in a navigable river becomes the basis of a common legal right, the essential features of which are the perfect equality of all riparian States in the use of the whole course of the river and the exclusion of any preferential privilege of any one riparian State in relation to the others.
>
> (*Case Relating to the … River Oder*, 1929: 27)

From the doctrinal point of view, the concept of equitable utilization did not necessarily mean equal division or 'mathematical equality' (Koskenniemi, 1984: 154), but rather equality of rights. Schwebel notes that disputes over the right to use waters flowing across sovereign lines must be adjusted on the basis of 'equality of rights', but that 'such equality does not necessarily mean equal division' (Schwebel, 1982: 76, para. 47). According to Lipper, the principle of equitable utilization means that a riparian state cannot deprive another riparian state's right to an equitable share of the natural resources of an international watercourse (Lipper, 1967: 43).

In 1966, the International Law Association adopted the Helsinki Rules on the Uses of the Waters of International Rivers as a statement of existing rules of international law. Pursuant to the rules: '[e]ach basin State is entitled, within its territory, to a reasonable and equitable share in the beneficial uses of the waters of an international drainage basin' (Helsinki Rules, 1966: Art. IV).

What amounts to a reasonable and equitable share is, pursuant to the Helsinki Rules, 'to be determined in the light of all the relevant factors in each particular case' (*ibid.*: Art. V(1)). The rules specify relevant factors by providing a non-exhaustive list. For instance, the economic and social needs of each basin state as well as the avoidance of unnecessary waste in the utilization of waters of the basin shall be considered (*ibid.*: Art. V(2)). Also, use of the waters by a basin state that causes pollution resulting in injury in a co-basin state must be considered from the overall perspective of what constitutes equitable utilization (*ibid.*: Art. X). Thus, the idea of equitable utilization is not to provide an identical share but rather 'to provide the maximum benefit to each State from the uses of the waters with the minimum detriment to each' (*ibid.*: Art. IV).

The principle of equitable and reasonable utilization was subsequently codified in the 1997 Convention on the Law of the Non-navigational Uses of International Watercourses. According to the key provision in Article 5:

> [w]atercourse States shall in their respective territories utilize an international watercourse in an equitable and reasonable manner. In particular, an international watercourse shall be used and developed by watercourse States with a view to attaining optimal and sustainable utilization thereof and benefits therefrom consistent with adequate protection of the watercourse.

Along with the emergence of the doctrine of sustainable development, the concept of sustainable use of international watercourses was generally accepted. Chapter 18 of Agenda 21 deals with integrated approaches for the development, management and use of water resources (Agenda 21, 1992: chapter 18). Furthermore, as observed by Birnie *et al.*, since the 1990s, most of the new freshwater agreements recognize 'in some form the importance of sustainable development, sustainable use, or sustainable management as an aim or objective' (Birnie *et al.*, 2009: 562). Several regional conventions serve as examples of this, such as the Convention on Transboundary Watercourses, 1992; the Convention on the Danube River, 1994; the Agreement on Development of the Mekong River Basin,

1995; the Rhine Convention, 1999; and the Revised SADC Protocol on Shared Watercourses, 2000.

Another important development relates to environmental regime-building. In pursuit of long-term environmental goals, many regimes began from the 1970s onwards to design step-by-step interim objectives, usually through separate annexes or protocols. The same development occurred also in the water field. Several watercourse agreements include detailed annexes, which are subject to constant amendments. In addition, some watercourse agreements serve as framework conventions in two different ways. First, some agreements have adopted separate protocols on particular subjects, such as the UNECE Convention of 1992, to which two Protocols have been adopted: the Protocol on Water and Health (1999) and the Protocol on Civil Liability and Compensation (2003). Second, some conventions give an incentive, or even oblige riparian states, to conclude bilateral or regional agreements – see, for instance, the UNECE Convention, 1992 (Art. 9) and the 1997 UN Convention on International Watercourses (Arts 3-4).

The purpose of regime-building in the water sector has been to establish dynamic processes and frameworks under which normative regulations and scientific expertise would develop in synchronism. Through the partnership between policy and science, water regimes seek to manage potential adverse effects on a long-term basis and to reconcile economic interests and environmental concerns.

With the emergence of the doctrine of sustainable development, water protection and the utilization of waters are sought to be managed under the same framework. However, even though the doctrine of sustainable management is able to reconcile the protection and utilization of watercourses, the tension between them remains.

Conclusion

In light of the above, it is arguable that two opposing approaches have driven the development of the relationship between international law and the environment: protection of the environment and exploitation of natural resources. In the undifferentiated approach, the methods and techniques of general international law were applied to environmental problems as opposed to developing substantial environmental norms. Those methods and techniques were undifferentiated also in the sense that there was no clear-cut separation between issues concerning the protection of the environment and the utilization of natural resources. Conversely, during the separated approach, the two sides did not have much in common with each other. While the law of natural resources focused on deregulation, international environmental law involved international regulations. Finally, through the development of the integrated approach, the two found each other and began to fuse.

Even though the integrated approach is able to reconcile protection and exploitation at the level of legal principle, the tension between them remains. Indeed, the question of how the tension between internationalization and nationalization, between exploitation and protection, between man and nature, and between the environment and economy is to be resolved and reconciled in any particular instance is left open.

Moreover, even though the doctrines were discussed separately above, this does not mean that the doctrines are also functionally separate. Consider, for instance, the *Case Concerning the Gabčíkovo-Nagymaros Project* (1997) in the International Court of Justice. The case concerned a dispute between Hungary and Slovakia over the construction and operation of dams on the River Danube. When one state (Hungary) withdrew from the original agreement to construct the dam, and the other (Slovakia) proceeded, the Court found both states to be in breach of their legal obligations (see, for instance, Sands *et al.*, 2012: 313–319). With regard to the three approaches discussed in this paper, the case reflects *prima facie* the undifferentiated approach, because Hungary and Slovakia had recourse to classical dispute settlement in order to solve their bilateral dispute retrospectively.

Looking at the case more closely, one can, however, also discern themes relating to natural resources and the environment. For example, the case concerned, *inter alia*, a 1977 boundary waters treaty between the two states. That agreement was concluded for the development of 'water resources, energy, transport, agriculture and other sectors of the national economy' (*Case Concerning the Gabčíkovo-Nagymaros Project*, 1997: para. 15). Furthermore, the Parties committed themselves 'to ensure that the quality of water in the Danube was not impaired as a result of the Project' (*ibid.*). However, it seems that exploitation interests and environmental concerns were not fully integrated; but, rather, dealt with separately. Nevertheless, one can label many arguments by the two Parties as reflecting the integrated approach. For instance, the Parties referred to ecological risks, scientific evidence and the precautionary principle. Moreover, the Court noted that the need to reconcile economic development with the protection of the environment 'is aptly expressed in the concept of sustainable development' (*ibid.*: para. 140).

Thus, the *Case Concerning the Gabčíkovo-Nagymaros Project* illustrated that the three approaches are interlinked. This is the case in a number of instances. Indeed, the three approaches reflect three contextually different but interlinked ways to construe the relationship between the exploitation of natural resources and the protection of the environment.

Even though international environmental law has been able to provide tools to solve or manage problems, this does not mean that all problems have been or will be solved. The functionality of problem-solving tools depends on the specific context. While it is important to seek to develop new, or to apply existing, methods; it is equally important to assess whether such methods work effectively or whether they are merely symbolic (Pallemaerts, 2003: 701–727). On the basis of such reviews, one should, if necessary, adjust existing problem-solving methods, and consider developing further methods.

Moreover, environmental regulators and managers appear to have a Sisyphean task – once some problems have been dealt with, new problems have meanwhile emerged. Many agreed solutions, for example, have fallen short in addressing adequately the problems in question. In some instances, a problem has been identified but states have not been able to agree whether to use hard or soft measures to tackle the problem. In other instances, specific rules have represented unhelpful fragmentation from previously set ones. While some regimes do represent clear success stories, other regimes have turned out to be ineffective. For environmental regulators and policy-makers all these issues form new problems, which ask for new answers or solutions.

References

Affaire du Lac Lanoux, (1957) XII *UNRIAA*, 285–317; *Lake Lanoux Arbitration* (English translation), *International Law Reports*, 24: 105–142.

Agenda 21 (1992) UN Conference on Environment and Development, Rio de Janeiro, 13 June 1992, UN Doc. A/CONF.151/26/Rev.1.

Belgrade Declaration of Non-Aligned Countries, adopted at the First Conference of Heads of State or Governments of Non-Aligned Countries, Belgrade, 6 September 1961, UNITAR (Selected Documents 1945–1975) Vol. I, 6.

Berber, F.J. (1959) *Rivers in International Law*, Stevens & Sons, London.

Birnie, P., Boyle, A. and Redgwell, C. (2009) *International Law and the Environment* (3rd ed.), Oxford University Press, Oxford.

Broms, B. (1997) 'Natural Resources, Sovereignty over', *Encyclopedia of Public International Law*, III: 520–524.

Case Concerning the Gabčíkovo–Nagymaros Project (Hungary/Slovakia), Judgement of the International Court of Justice of 25 September 1997, *ICJ Reports* 7.

Case Relating to the Territorial Jurisdiction of the International Commission of the River Oder, 1929 Permanent Court of Justice, Series A, No. 23, 27.

Elian, G. (1979) *The Principle of Sovereignty over Natural Resources*, Martinus Nijhoff, Alphen aan den Rijn.

Fisheries Jurisdiction Case (United Kingdom v. Iceland) (Merits), Judgement of the International Court of Justice of 25 July 1974, *ICJ Reports* 3.

Fisheries Jurisdiction Case (Federal Republic of Germany v. Iceland) (Merits), Judgement of the International Court of Justice of 25 July 1974, *ICJ Reports* (1974) 175.

Freestone, D. and Hay, E. (1996) 'Origins and Development of the Precautionary Principle' in Freestone, D. and Hay, E. (eds), *Implementing the Precautionary Principle: Challenges and Opportunities*, Kluwer Law International, the Hague, 3–15.

Gess, K.N. (1964) 'Permanent Sovereignty over Natural Resources. An Analytical Review of the United Nations Declaration and Its Genesis', *International and Comparative Law Quarterly*, 13: 398–449.

Heiskanen, V. (2004) 'Death of the Layman: The Legacy of Deconstruction and the Philosophy of International Law', *Finnish Yearbook of International Law*, XV: 233–272.

Helsinki Rules on the Uses of the Waters of International Rivers (1966), Fifty-Second Report of the International Law Association (1967): 484.

Higgins, R. (1995) *Problems and Processes: International Law and How We Use It*, Oxford University Press, Oxford.

Hyde, J.N. (1956) 'Permanent Sovereignty over Natural Wealth and Resources', *American Journal of International Law*, 50: 854–867.

'Institutional Arrangements to follow up the United Nations Conference on Environment and Development', UNGA Res. 47/191, 29 January 1993.

IUCN, UNEP, WWF, FAO and UNESCO (1980) *World Conservation Strategy, Living Resource Conservation for Sustainable Development*.

Kelsen, H. (1966) *Principles of International Law* (2nd ed., rev. and ed. by Tucker, R.W.), Holt, Rinehart and Winston Inc., New York.

Koskenniemi, M. (1984) 'International Pollution in the System of International Law', *Oikeustiede-Jurisprudentia*, XVII: 91–181.

Kuokkanen, T. (2002) *International Law and the Environment: Variations on a Theme*, Erik Castrén Institute of International Law and Human Rights (Vol. 4), Kluwer Law International, the Hague.

Laylin, J.G. and Bianchi, R.L. (1959) 'The Rôle of Adjudication in International River Disputes. The Lake Lanoux Case' *American Journal of International Law*, 53: 30–49.

Lipper, J. (1967) 'Equitable Utilization' in Garretson, A.H., Hayton, R.D. and Olmstead, C.J. (eds) *The Law of International Drainage Basins*, Oceana Publications, New York, 15–88.

Merrils, J. (2003) 'The Means of Dispute Settlement' in Evans, M.D. (ed.) *International Law*, Oxford University Press, Oxford, 529–557.

Millennium Ecosystem Assessment: Ecosystems and Human Well-being. Synthesis (2005), Island Press, Washington D.C.

Nollkaemper, A. (1993) *The Legal Regime for Transboundary Water Pollution: between Discretion and Constraint*, Kluwer Law International, the Hague.

OECD Council Recommendation on Integrated Pollution Prevention and Control, 31 January 1991, OECD Doc. C(90)164/FINAL.

Opinion by Judson Harmon (1895), *Official Opinions of the Attorneys-General of the United States, Advising the President and Heads of Departments in Relation to Their Official Duties* (1895) Vol. XXI, Treaty of Guadalupe Hidalgo – International Law, 274–283.

Oppenheim, L. (1908) 'The Science of International Law: Its Task and Method', *American Journal of International Law*, 2: 313–356.

Pallemaerts, M. (2003) *Toxics and Transnational Law. International and European Regulation of Toxic Substances as Legal Symbolism*, Hart Publishing, Oxford.

Resolution of the Council and the Representatives of the Governments of the Member States, Meeting within the Council of 1 February 1993 on a Community Programme of Policy and Action in Relation to the Environment and Sustainable Development (93/C 138/01) (EC's fifth Environmental Programme), OJ 1993 No. C138, 17 May 1993.

Sands, P., Peel, J., Fabra, A. and MacKenzie, R. (2012) *Principles of International Environmental Law* (3rd ed.), Cambridge University Press, Cambridge.

Schrijver, N. (1997) *Sovereignty over Natural Resources. Balancing Rights and Duties*, Cambridge University Press, Cambridge.

Schwebel, S.M. (1982) Third report of the law of the non-navigational uses of international watercourses, Special Rapporteur, Document A/CN.4/348, *Yearbook of International Law*, 1982, Vol. II (Part One).

Smith, H.A. (1931) *The Economic Uses of International Rivers*, P.S. King & Son, London.

Stockholm Declaration of the United Nations Conference on the Human Environment, Stockholm, 16 June 1972, UN Doc. A/CONF.48/14/Rev.1 (1973), *International Legal Materials*, 11: 1416.

Suvantola, L. (2011) 'Ecosystem Services and Climate Change' in Couzens, E. and Honkonen, T. (eds) *International Environmental Law-making and Diplomacy Review 2010*, UEF-UNEP Course Series 10, University of Eastern Finland, Joensuu: 245–254.

UNEP (2011) *Towards a Green Economy – Pathways to Sustainable Development and Poverty Eradication* (UNEP), www.unep.org/greeneconomy/Portals/88/documents/ger/ger_final_dec_2011/Green%20EconomyReport_Final_Dec2011.pdf (accessed 24 May 2015).

UNGA (1962) 'Permanent sovereignty over natural resources', UNGA Res. 1803(XVII), 14 December 1962.

UNGA (1982) 'World Charter for Nature', UNGA Res. 37/7, 28 October 1982.
UNGA (2012) 'The Future We Want' Outcome Document, UNGA Res. 66/288, 27 July 2012.
United Nations Declaration on Environment and Development, Rio de Janeiro, 14 June 1992, UN Doc. A/CONF.151/5/Rev.1 (1992), 31 *International Legal Materials* (1992) 876.
WCED [World Commission on Environment and Development] (1987) *Our Common Future*, Oxford University Press, Oxford.

5 A juridical-conceptual perspective on environmental governance

Louis J. Kotzé

Introduction

It is now generally accepted that human-induced environmental change and degradation are likely to lead to, or are already resulting in, amongst other things: irreversible depletion of renewable and non-renewable resources; destruction of whole ecosystems; displacement of people; armed conflicts; threats to state and human security; and threats to human well-being, societal stability, and good order. Within this context, it has recently been informally suggested that we have left the Holocene and entered a new geological epoch called the Anthropocene (Crutzen and Stoermer, 2000). Emphasizing the central role of mankind in geo-ecological systems, the word Anthropocene suggests that the Earth is rapidly moving into a critically unstable state, with Earth systems gradually becoming less predictable, non-stationary and less harmonious as a result of the global human imprint on the biosphere. The Anthropocene, as a powerful trope or cognitive framework, leaves little doubt that we will have to change our behaviour and the impact of our behaviour on the environment if we hope to continue life on Earth as we know it.

Humans have long sought to address environmental change and degradation by means of a host of social and institutional interventions, including the creation of environmental laws. Within environmental law, the concept of 'environmental governance' has emerged as a 'new' mode of intervention or strategy to regulate human behaviour and its effects on the environment – and is emerging as a field of study in its own right. Environmental governance is an extra-legal concept, but is increasingly used in the legal domain and its growing popularity is specifically evidenced by its increased use within environmental law literature.

Notwithstanding its frequent use, there has been comparatively little scholarly effort to formulate a general juridical theory of environmental governance. This is evidenced by the dearth of literature specifically dealing with the concept from a legal point of view. There seems to be no universally accepted definition, description or typology of the concept that should allow for consistent and universal application to environmental law problems. More particularly, despite their increased interest in and focus on the topic, environmental lawyers are apparently hesitant at best, or unable at worst to understand, systematically to describe, and justifiably to concretize the notion of environmental governance; if the latter achievement is at all possible. The reasons for this are many and varied. In 2009, Fisher *et al.* raised questions about the maturity, methodology, and quality of environmental law scholarship (Fisher *et al.*, 2009: 228). The authors identify a non-exhaustive list of four methodological challenges, which in their view contribute to the existing 'dearth of critical analysis' in environmental law scholarship. One of these challenges is 'the heavy reliance in environmental law on a diverse range of governance arrangements' – others in the range include the speed and scale of regulatory change; inter-disciplinarity; and the multi-jurisdictional nature of environmental law regimes (*ibid.*: 228–243). The authors explain that:

> [t]he methodological challenge raised by governance regimes is that such [governance] regimes require [environmental law] scholars to take a 'more diverse view of state authority and its exercise' but, in doing so, it is not clear what form such a 'diverse view' should take and how it differs from existing scholarly approaches. *Indeed, the concept of governance is much admired and referred to in worshipful tones but rarely scrutinised and deconstructed by environmental law scholars.*
>
> (*ibid.*: 235 [original emphasis])

Reasons for this state of affairs could be that governance is a catch-all term; it deals with legal and non-legal issues; it involves novel forms of authority; issues of environmental governance are not confined only to environmental law, but also require a broader trans-disciplinary legal view that straddles the traditional boundaries of environmental law; and environmental governance derives from a multi-disciplinary foundation, which suggests that while it contains some legal elements it also heavily relies on a range of other disciplines (for example, ecology, ethics, sociology, politics and economics) (*ibid.*: 235–239). The result is that it remains unclear what a legal theory of environmental governance entails; and what the content and meaning of the concept are for environmental lawyers.

Lawyers, especially law academics, frequently employ definitions in an effort to understand certain legal concepts. As a result, they also often seek themselves to formulate definitions of certain concepts. Even though such an approach (i.e. the desire to define) may rightly be criticized by some, for the purpose of this chapter, an attempt will be made to propose a tentative preliminary definition of environmental governance, insofar as the present author views the concept's function in the legal domain. This can, and will, never be the final word on the matter. However, in the absence of a current uniform explanation for the concept in terms of a legal setting, it is hoped that this contribution may contribute to initiating the debate.

The chapter commences with a brief reflection on the scope and scale in terms of which environmental governance currently is used. The discussion then attempts to summarize some of the challenges resulting from definitional and interpretative deficiencies. The concept of 'governance' is then explored; and the chapter endeavours also to explain the link between the environment, governance and law. In the final instance, the chapter proposes a tentative definition of environmental governance and also attempts to explain the principal objective of environmental governance as it manifests in the juridical domain.

Scope and scale of use

While environmental governance is a trite term in the political sciences (see, for example, Young, 1997; Norichika and Haas, 2004; Chambers and Green, 2005), it has only recently emerged on the law scene. Most lawyers use environmental governance as a broad contextual setting for discussion of specific environmental law-related issues including, among others, the functioning of environmental law regimes in the European Union (EU) and elsewhere; the operation and administration of international environmental law regimes; the role of courts in resolving environmental disputes; the role of environmental governance in protecting biodiversity and conservation; good environmental governance, including issues such as public participation and access to justice; and governance for sustainable development (this not being a closed list). It seems as though environmental governance has become an umbrella concept which has itself not yet been fully described, but which is frequently used by lawyers to accommodate environment and/or sustainability-related issues.

Apart from these varying contexts, the concept is also used at various levels, including, the international, the national, the regional and the local. Its origins can be traced back to developments at the international level including, among others, the work of the World Bank and other international organizations such as the United Nations (UN) and the United Nations Environment Programme (UNEP) (to name but a few); the development of multilateral environmental agreements on a very extensive range of issues; various treaty regimes and the work of treaty secretariats; the influential work of non-state actors such as the scientific community and the World Conservation Union (IUCN); and a host of other environmental and developmental organizations (Sands, 2003: 70–122; Iwama, 2004: 15–34; Kingsbury, 2007: 64–83; Dunoff, 2007: 86–106). In this sense, environmental governance is a generic concept and its influence has filtered down from the international level to regional and national levels, and back, where it is currently widely used in, for example, the EU and various country-specific contexts.

Definitional and interpretative challenges

While many environmental lawyers employ the concept of environmental governance, it is clear from the available literature that the concept has different meanings to different people and that it is variously understood by different sectors within the environmental law domain itself. Moreover, it is evident from the literature that, because 'governance' could potentially broaden legal perspectives on law-making, implementation, enforcement and regulation, while lawyers are increasingly recognizing the importance of environmental governance they remain hesitant about engaging fully with the theory of environmental governance.

Like one of its parent concepts, sustainability, the meaning of the concept seems to depend on the context in and the purpose for which it is used, as well as the scientific discipline in terms of which it is used (Sands, 1994: 303–381; Boer, 1995: 101–125; Redclift, 1995: 17–34). More importantly for present purposes, there has been to date no comprehensive analysis and synthesis that aims to advance a theoretical description of environmental governance in the context of environmental law. In the words of Fisher *et al.*: '[i]ndeed, the concept of [environmental] governance is much admired and referred to in worshipful tones but rarely scrutinised and deconstructed by environmental law scholars' (Fisher *et al.*, 2009: 23). In short: while the popularity of environmental governance appears to be mounting, the concept suffers from diversity and inconsistency in application and interpretation; it remains subject to frequent but imprecise use; it fits awkwardly within the environmental law domain; and, because it is an amorphous concept, for environmental lawyers, it remains at best clouded and vague.

In addition to the broader theoretical uncertainty related to the concept itself, various other very specific, but related, issues arise, namely: (a) the issue of the origins of environmental governance, the context in which it is used, and, more importantly, the issue of why it has become such a popular concept in current discourse; (b) whether environmental governance is an ideal or an objective, a means to achieve an ideal or objective, a regime, a process or processes, a principle, an institution or institutions, or all, or a combination of the foregoing; (c) what the dimensions, object(s), objectives, purpose and scope of environmental governance are; (d) what comprise the basic fundamental elements, institutions, mechanisms and stakeholders of environmental governance in the environmental law domain; (e) the ways in which lawyers perceive environmental governance, its value and its use for environmental law discourse, and what the relationship or link between environmental governance and environmental law may be; and finally, (f) what a theory of environmental governance might entail in the environmental law context.

This chapter provides some initial thoughts that may serve as a starting point for further exploration of some of these issues (for a fuller discussion, see Kotzé, 2012).

Considering the concept of governance

The word 'governance' invokes a certain sense of familiarity. It is often encountered in daily life; for example in the media, corporate boardrooms, the world of politics and power, in dealings with governments, state departments and government officials; in almost all instances where regulation occurs and where authority, in whatever form and whether emanating from state or non-state sources, is present and exercised. Despite its popularity, governance is a vague and amorphous concept, which is bedevilled by inconsistent use in a plural and multi-disciplinary setting. Governance is also multi-contextual and could be viewed, for example, from a geo-political perspective, a corporate perspective, a micro perspective such as project governance, and the governance of specific functional areas such as water governance and financial governance. The term 'governance' is often political and value laden and therefore deliberately vague, fluid and non-committal. It is open to interpretation and has even been described as a fad, an Anglicism that is often used to add to the complex social science repertoire (what Benz calls a *Modeausdruck* or fashionable term) (Benz, 2004: 12).

Much of the uncertainty surrounding environmental governance can be attributed to the non-existence of a uniform understanding of the concept 'governance' itself. This is so because 'governance' remains a vague and transcendent concept subject to frequent but imprecise use despite numerous attempts to define it. One of the reasons for the illusiveness and ambiguity of the concept may be that, as Ocheje puts it: '[i]n a divided and multicultural world, "governance" is a value-laden concept, and this invariably militates against the emergence of a single universally acceptable definition' (Ocheje, 1999: 165).

Nevertheless, any effort that seeks to attribute some meaning to the concept of governance, must, as a point of departure, acknowledge that the concept is ambiguous and illusive and that it may be defined differently depending on one's scientific perspective and discipline. The aim of this chapter requires a definition of 'governance' from a legal perspective.

In 1995, the United Nations Commission for Global Governance defined governance very broadly as: '...the sum of the many ways individuals and institutions, public and private, manage their common affairs'. It is a continuing process through which conflicting or diverse interests may be accommodated and cooperative action may be taken. It includes formal institutions and regimes empowered to enforce compliance, as well as informal arrangements that people and institutions either have agreed to or perceive to be in their interests (Commission for Global Governance, 1995: 2).

Curtin and Dekker point to the all-inclusive nature of this definition and to the fact that the definition emphasizes certain characteristics of governance as a legal institution, i.e. the actors and subjects that are part of the governance regime have legal powers in relation to one another and in relation to other subjects (Curtin and Dekker, 2005: 9).

The Governance Group of the World Bank Institute defines 'governance' more constrictively as follows:

> [g]overnance consists of the traditions and institutions by which authority in a country is exercised. This includes the process by which governments are selected, monitored and replaced; the capacity of the government to effectively formulate and implement sound policies; and the respect of citizens and the state for the institutions that govern economic and social interactions among them.
>
> (World Bank, 2007)

A United Nations (UN) study on good governance in the UN Economic and Social Commission for Western Asia (UNESCWA) defines governance as: '...the existence of institutions, processes and mechanisms by which authority is exercised in an economy' (ESCWA, 2000: 1). According to the study, governance also includes formal institutions and regimes that are responsible to ensure and enforce compliance. Apart from these formal arrangements, it includes more informal arrangements between citizens, institutions and the state. It suggests that the main actors in governance are actors at the global level (global governance), state or national actors, and civil society governance (grass-roots or local government level) (*ibid.*: 4). According to UNESCWA, governance includes three aspects: political governance (policy formulation); economic governance; and administrative governance (policy implementation or enforcement) (*ibid.*: 9).

Another synthesizing view on governance is that it can be seen as an institutional response to collective problems. Young states that:

> [a]t the most general level, governance involves the establishment and operation of social institutions (in the sense of rules of the game that serve to define social practices, assign roles, and guide interactions among the occupants of these roles) capable of resolving conflicts, facilitating cooperation, or, more generally, alleviating collective-action problems in a world of interdependent actors.
>
> (Young, 1994: 15)

Any effort to understand governance must also distinguish between the concepts of 'government' and governance. The definitive difference between the two concepts seems to be that government usually relates to institutional structures and governance to a process and/or an analytical perspective that is used to understand regulation in an age of globalization. Vidačak and Božić highlight the procedural characteristics of governance when they state that governance is:

> … the capacity of the formal and informal institutional environment (in which individuals, social groups, civil associations and government officials and employees interact) to apply and carry through a given government policy and to improve coordination in the private sector.
>
> (Vidačak and Božić, 2006: 57)

Their description, coincidentally, also points to the various relationships and organizational patterns inherent to governance.

Grant and Barker define government from an international law point of view as:

> …the organization of public power within any given territory. In this sense, it is said that a government is an essential element of the State. The term is further used to connote the executive organs of States in their relationships with one another.
>
> (Grant and Barker, 2004: 206)

In this view government is a necessary element/ingredient or actor to realize governance, which, in turn, involves various relationships and postulates a certain organizational pattern (UN DESA, 2000: 6).

Reinalda's explanation of the governance theory for the purpose of the theoretical analysis appears suitable for the purposes of the present enquiry because it encapsulates the essence of governance as derived from the various authorities above. Reinalda states that:

> [t]he governance perspective … is grounded in the normalcy of continuous change. It departs from the 'social engineering' thesis that society is always malleable by governmental policies and institutions ('steered' or 'managed' social change). …Governments can manipulate long-term processes and, with these in mind, they are willing to perform various tasks. …In this context, legislation has obtained a steering effect. It has become more and more instrumental, in particular in combination with research into the impact of legislative measures. …Non-governmental or private actors are also involved in this social engineering. The idea that private groups can initiate social and political change is not new. …Governance thus refers to the solving of collective problems in a continuously changing public and private realm, stressing processes and institutional procedures and practices.
>
> (Reinalda, 1999: 116–117)

This brief selective analysis suggests that governance is a continually changing process principally aimed at directing the behaviour of people for the purpose of promoting common interests including, among others, the mutual well-being of all. This process is executed by way of institutional structures (governments), although government is not the sole actor in the process of governance. The private sector, including, *inter alia*, non-governmental organizations (NGOs), community-based organizations (CBOs), private individuals and the public at large, also (should) influence the outcome of the public sector driven process of governance. Governance is also facilitated by mechanisms and procedures that are, generally speaking, embedded in and mandated by law. Law thus emerges as a determinant, a justification and a source of governance.

Law, governance and the environment

In *The Concept of Law*, Hart refers to a 'simple society' and seems simultaneously to distinguish this from what one may call a 'complex society' (Hart, 1961/1994: 91–99). According to Kornhauser's estimation of Hart's treatise, the latter author considers a 'simple society' to be: small and closely knit; insulated from external shocks; free from the plagues of natural disasters; and homogenous. As such, a 'simple society' is easy to govern and would not require more complex societal constructs, such as law, to better facilitate governance. A society, however, becomes more complex in the absence of these 'ideal' conditions, and, as a result, '…law emerges as an instrument of governance of societies that are large and no longer closely knit or that face an external environment that changes too rapidly for social custom to adapt to these changes' (Kornhauser, 2004: 357–358). It goes without saying that, when viewed in terms of this typology, we live in complex societies rather than simple ones; and, as a consequence, our societies require law as an instrument of governance.

Ost generally describes complexity with reference to the 'game model' and self-responsibility of firms with respect to environmental governance thus:

> ...post-modern society and law quite clearly require the application of complex models. The paradigm of simplicity developed by Descartes has in fact become definitively obsolete, as have the associated ideas of linear causality, ontological dualism ... and of apodictic certainty. By contrast we need notions of multiple and circular causality, the interweaving of elements and involvement of the observer, and the idea of uncertainty. Order has henceforth to make compromises with disorder.
>
> (Ost, 1994: 339)

When viewed in the light of the Anthropocene's cognitive framework referred to above, it may even be fair to predict that our society on Earth, or life as we know it, will be subject to even greater complexities, external influences and 'shocks' as we prepare to suffer increased environmental impacts as a result of our own doing, and would accordingly in the future rely even more heavily on law to facilitate governance of these complexities (Kotzé, 2014: 121–156).

The question might be asked whether law *can* govern the environment? The present author holds the view that, speaking in the strictest sense, environmental governance cannot 'manage or govern the environment'. Governance is a human function directed at humans and, as such, humans can only govern humans, and the impact of human actions on the environment. Law is one of the societal constructs that humans use to govern themselves and their actions. Extrapolated to the environmental context, this would mean that humans can only indirectly 'govern the environment' in a strict sense insofar as they are able to influence/manipulate/direct/change the behaviour and actions of people that have impacts on the non-human environment.

In this respect it is also worth noting Kelsen's view (Kelsen, 1945) that while the object of law is human behaviour, law is not exclusively concerned *only* with human behaviour; it is also concerned with the objects of human behaviour and the results or effects of human behaviour on animate and inanimate objects. In other words, law could be seen as mediating the interactions within society and between society and non-human entities (Pelletier, 2010: 221). It is therefore not true that 'nothing but human behaviour enters into the contents of legal rules' (Kelsen, 1945: 3); law also concerns the effects of human behaviour on other non-human entities and the manner in which people behave towards and interact with these entities. Law is thus used as part of governance by humans who themselves 'stand out in relief against a world which is conceived as comprising a collection of mechanistic, causal and systematic processes, and discrete elements which are amenable by means of rational thought to human control and direction' (Godden and Peel, 2010: 58).

Bothe summarizes these ideas eloquently as follows:

> [n]one of these [environmental] problems can be addressed directly by [legal] prohibitions or orders. To give an example pertaining to the field of environmental protection: An 'order' given to a river to be clean is not a valid legal rule – it is devoid of a valid addressee. Law can only determine human behaviour, it cannot change nature. Thus, if law is to contribute to the solution ...it has to direct or induce human behaviour in a way that the problem is solved. As these are very complex problems, the behaviour of many actors must be determined in a coherent way so that the factual end result is the one which was desired. Thus, the impact of law on the solution of those problems will always be an indirect one. This being so, the question has to be asked where and how precisely law should trigger which type of human behaviour in order to solve a problem.
>
> (Bothe, 2007: 351)

For a law to be effective, and hence to achieve its desired outcome, Bothe argues that the law should trigger a '...causation process consisting of many steps' (*ibid.*); ultimately with the view to changing behaviour, influencing human actions and, hence, controlling the effect of these actions on the environment. In other words: environmental law should, *inter alia*, contain incentives, disincentives, and sanctions, which should 'force' or convince someone to do something, or to abstain from doing anything at all which may negatively affect the environment.

These sentiments are reiterated by DiMento, who states that:

> [l]aw aims to influence behavior in order to promote environmental quality. It works in parallel with other institutions. It also works according to dynamics that some theorists would not classify as institutional. Law interacts – sometimes effectively, sometimes awkwardly, sometimes counter productively – with other systems that seek to order behavior and achieve social control. In view of this explanation, environmental law could be described as an institution and social construct which aims to regulate/dictate/inform/guide humans or, more specifically, human behaviour which may affect environmental quality.
>
> (DiMento, 2003: 360)[1]

Further support for the role of law in influencing environmental quality through governance is derived from Godden and Peel's statement that:

> [t]ypically, the role of law in environmental governance has been to facilitate social change by influencing the decisions and behaviour of individuals, governments, businesses, organisations and the community to embrace more sustainable forms of living. Taking a very general perspective, the manner in

---

1 On this, it is worth seeing also the view of Boyd (2004: 360).

> which legal rules are used to achieve social reform is by setting standards for the behaviour of various actors and agents, and providing a range of sanctions and incentives to ensure compliance with that desired behaviour. Although this is only one possible interpretation of how law operates in a complex society, nonetheless many people typically associate law with the idea of rule setting ...this rule setting is multidimensional and now operates across several levels from the local to the global. From this perspective, law is about giving effect to (evolving) societal norms. These norms may derive from formal written sources, such as international treaties, national statues and case-law decisions made by judges within the court hierarchies, or from customary practices...
>
> (Godden and Peel, 2010: 80–81)

They continue by stating that:

> [i]n a context where the human-environment relationship was generally conceived in terms of the impact (often negative) of human activities upon the environment, a key role played by law and legal institutions in emerging form of environmental governance was in regulating the environmental effects of human activity and, where necessary, mediating or ameliorating those impacts in various ways. As our conception of the environment has evolved, this has created momentum for transformations in the broader frameworks of law, policy and social structures that for convenience, rather than more precise articulation, we have designated as governance. Different models of governance thus provide a significant framework affecting the manner in which the human-environment interrelationship is conceived. Yet describing different modes of environmental governance that have manifested in environmental law presents a significant challenge given the very dynamic and complex interactions involved.
>
> (*ibid.*: 83)

To be sure, the relationship between law, the environment, and governance is particularly complex, and in some instances also problematic. Richardson puts it as follows:

> [t]he sustainable development agenda poses major challenges for public law systems premised on administrative agencies' monopoly of decision powers and whose functionality and legitimacy traditionally has been grounded in jurisdictional and procedural rules. A regulatory agency conceived in the Weberian schema is controlled by inputs – by legislative directions, which are to be applied strictly and faithfully. However, what government promotion of sustainability presupposes is control primarily by outputs: an activity is 'adequate' not if it conforms to statutory rules and procedures, but primarily if it produces certain policy results.
>
> (Richardson, 2002: 48)

Nevertheless, what is clear is that there is a definite link between law, the environment and governance. Law (but not only law) provides the institution of governance with the means and legitimacy to regulate human behaviour and activities that affect the environment. In regulating human behaviour, law is therefore concerned with the effects of human behaviour on the environment, and it would seek to change, steer or influence human behaviour to such an extent that the impacts of this behaviour on the environment conform to a standard that is acceptable to society. 'Acceptable' could mean that human behaviour conforms to universally agreed standards or rules of behaviour set by society itself and it implies that the extent of the impact on the environment does not exceed the thresholds of what society deems to be acceptable. If the standards and rules of regulating behaviour and impact thresholds are provided in laws, so too are the means to achieve these standards. For example, in its efforts to ensure that people have clean drinking water, law will allow and prohibit certain human actions that might affect the water. Most usually by means of a statute (or a treaty at the supra-national level), law will provide rules of behaviour and it will contain minimum thresholds or requirements that are scientifically determined in terms of the carrying capacity of the environment. Whether environmental law is successful in realizing these elaborate goals within the governance paradigm is an altogether different matter which is not addressed in this chapter.

Environmental governance

If the foregoing describes, at least to some extent, what governance may entail and what the connection between law, governance and the environment is, then one could possibly apply this theory of governance and law to environmental issues with the view to formulating a definition of environmental governance. In other words, an admittedly simplistic explanation of environmental governance would be one that marries 'governance', 'law' and 'environment'. What, then, is 'environment' for the purpose of law and governance?

It hardly needs repeating that there have been many attempts to define 'environment'. For Redgwell, there is as yet no uniformly accepted definition of 'environment' in the realm of international environmental law (Redgwell, 2006: 658). Sprout and Sprout point to the 'semantic chaos' that is a result of the varied approaches, contextual differences, and varied priorities and expectations in this regard (Sprout and Sprout, 1972: 579). Generally speaking, 'environment' has historically been perceived to relate only to the natural, non-human environment, together with the physical man-made changes to this environment. However, scientists have increasingly come to realize the significance of human or social conditions and dimensions as also being important components of the environment.

In this sense, we have come to realize that the environment is a complex and integrated system where one element or condition is often dependent on others. The very nature of the environment as a holistic, integrated and interrelated whole requires us to part with our current fragmented, 'silo-based', and reductionist approach to the way we perceive and purport to regulate the effects of our activities in and on the environment. Dubos emphasizes the need for an integrated approach to the way we govern human behaviour by stating that:

> [t]he most pressing problems of humanity… involve relationships, communications, changes of trends – in other words, situations in which systems must be studied as a whole, in all the complexity of their interactions. This is particularly true of human life. When life is considered only in its specialized functions, the outcome is a world emptied of meaning. To be fully relevant to life, science must deal with the responses of the total organism to the total environment.
>
> (Dubos in *ibid.*: 575)

Kubasek and Silverman also point out that:

> …environment is not viewed primarily as a set of independent, strictly bounded territories but, rather, as one related unit, divided if at all, into natural components – air, water and land – each having interactive relationships with one another and with humans.
>
> (Kubasek and Silverman, 2008: 428)

What is clearly evident is that we need to use the sciences (legal, natural, political – to name but a few) to formulate strategies for solutions that should address the entire complex system of the *total* environment. In an attempt to do just this, this chapter will employ the definition of 'environment' as provided in the South African National Environmental Management Act 107 of 1998 (NEMA), which is one of the most comprehensive definitions of which the present author is to date aware; and because it exemplifies the integrated and holistic nature of the environment.

NEMA (s 1) defines 'environment' as:

> … the surroundings within which humans exist and that are made up of –
>
> (i) the land, water and atmosphere of the earth;
> (ii) micro-organisms, plant and animal life;
> (iii) any part or combination of (i) and (ii) and the interrelationships among and between them; and
> (iv) the physical, chemical, aesthetic and cultural properties and conditions of the foregoing that influence human health and well-being.

It has been illustrated above that 'governance' is a process that we can apply in order to formulate and implement strategies for solutions to regulate the effects of human activities, primarily by means of law. This implies that it would also be possible, therefore, to regulate the effects of human activities on the environment by means of governance and law.

In an age of globalization, governance is changing fundamentally the way that regulation, especially the way in which political control is exercised, occurs and is conceived (Kotzé, 2012: 95). The interactions between governance and law are changing as relationships between multiple different actors change – the traditional, strict, clear delineation between the state and society is becoming blurred as the requirements of governance increasingly cross the line (*ibid.*). While still unrealistic to suggest that state-derived political authority and private, non-political authorities are the same and have the same impacts, the inevitable result of their moving closer together is that the precise location and source of authority for regulation are becoming hybrid (*ibid.*: 96). This suggests that the conceptual manifestation of environmental governance is presently occurring in a non-static epistemic and fluid normative space.

Levy and Newell suggest that environmental governance:

> ...refers to the multiple channels through which human impacts on the natural environment are ordered and regulated. It implies rule creation, institution-building, and monitoring and enforcement. But it also implies a soft infrastructure of norms, expectations, and social understandings of acceptable behaviour towards the environment, in processes that engage the participation of a broad range of stakeholders.
>
> (Levy and Newell, 2005: 2, cited in Kotzé, 2012: 194)

Considering, 'environmental governance' as a process, the present author has previously suggested that it could be defined from a legal perspective as:

> a management process executed by institutions and individuals in the public and private sector holistically to regulate human activities and the effect of human activities on the total environment (including all environmental media, and biological, chemical, aesthetic and socio-economic processes and conditions) at international, regional, national and local levels; by means of formal and informal institutions, processes and mechanisms embedded in and mandated by law, so as to promote the common present and future interests human beings hold in the environment.
>
> (Kotzé, 2009: 107–108; and Kotzé, 2010: 3–20)

This definition, which is anthropocentric with its emphasis on human interests, suggests that law is the foundation for environmental governance and that environmental governance is a management process that would be illegitimate if not mandated by law (Kotzé, 2012: 199). The definition stresses that environmental governance is not aimed so much at governing (or managing) the environment itself, but rather focuses on governing human behaviour that might have impacts on the environment (*ibid.*). A revised definition might read:

> ...environmental governance is a normative institutional regulatory intervention and social construct that is predominantly based on law and that aims

> to influence how people interact with the environment. It entails a pluralistic, dynamic, multi-level, multi-actor response and process of change which pragmatically aims to change human behaviour *vis-à-vis* the environment, and idealistically to optimize environmental benefits and use, while at the same time seeking to protect and preserve sufficient environmental capital for present and future generations.
>
> (*ibid.*: 200)

Generic descriptions of environmental governance suggest that 'it is an institutional response and societal construct which could be formal, informal, or both'; and that it 'consists of many state and non-state actors that operate on various levels' – while environmental governance 'aims to influence human behaviour with respect to the environment and has sustainability as a central guiding motive or overarching goal' (*ibid.*: 223).

Environmental governance and sustainability

The above conceptualization of environmental governance is, admittedly, very broad. Such a broad or comprehensive understanding is convenient since it allows one the luxury to derive various objectives or purposes for which environmental governance could be used. The present author is convinced also that many other authors have already and will in the future identify and formulate various other specific objectives of environmental governance. Regardless of possible criticism that it may result in too superficial an analysis, this chapter, due to space constraints, focuses only on what, to the present author's mind, is the ultimate objective of environmental governance: namely, sustainability (see, among the many publications on the issue of sustainability, Beyerlin, 1996; Bosselmann, 2008).

Sustainability, like 'governance', is one of those terms that are clouded by uncertainty and vagueness. Pinto opines that the vagueness of terms like these can be attributed, among other factors, to international negotiation strategies that aim to achieve a certain 'constructive ambiguity' for the simple reason that '…often because the idea that first fired the collective imagination and mobilized legislative effort, was contained in some captivating phrase capable of widely different interpretations…' (Pinto, 1996: 250).

The most basic understanding of the concept suggests that sustainability has been developed, *inter alia*, to embed or articulate the increased realization that environmental issues cannot be viewed in isolation from various other considerations, including, *inter alia*: adaptation, infrastructural development, migration, protection of human rights, social development, and socio-economic development (on this, see also Fitzmaurice, 1996).

There are various approaches to sustainability. Each approach will, depending on its objectives and theoretical underpinnings, influence the manner in which sustainability will be understood and defined. One approach is to define sustainability as an 'opportunity'. According to Serageldin, '[s]ustainability is to leave future generations as many opportunities as, if not more than we have had ourselves' (Serageldin, 1998: 1349). The same author equates 'opportunity' with capital, which includes: human capital (taking into account, for example, education and health considerations); man-made capital (usually used in a financial or economic sense); natural capital (as used by environmental economists); and social capital (including institutional and cultural bases for allowing a society to function adequately as a society) (*ibid.*: 1349–1350). Depending on one's view of maintaining this 'capital', sustainability could be strong, sensible, or weak. Weak sustainability is '...maintaining total capital intact without regard to the composition of that capital between the different kinds of capital...' (*ibid.*: 1351). Sensible sustainability requires that '...in addition to maintaining the total level of capital intact, some concern should be given to the composition of that capital between natural, man-made, human and social'; while strong sustainability '...requires maintaining different kinds of capital intact separately' (*ibid.*: 1351–2). A second approach is to describe sustainability as a 'given stage of development of nations' (Ginther and De Waart, 1995: 9); and a third would entail viewing sustainability as a compromise between economic and environmental interests (Lang, 1995: 93). In this sense, its '...principal merit is that it modifies the previously unqualified development concept, insofar as development must possess both economic and ecological sustainability' (*ibid.*).

Another approach is to consider sustainability as an 'area' in which certain scientific activities take place, all of which aim to achieve certain beneficial outcomes (*ibid.*) – in the present author's view this is the most preferred approach.

By way of summary: sustainability requires the integration and harmonization of potentially conflicting concerns; it demands preservation of current capital for the use of present and future generations; and it means that ecological limits should restrict socio-economic activities. Mostly, though, sustainability requires a change in the way we think and act with respect to life, our existence on Earth and, specifically, the environment. Because law and governance (or environmental governance) can influence and mould the ways in which humans think and act with respect to the environment, one should be able to use environmental governance as a strategy for achieving sustainability. This is, admittedly, far easier said than done; partly because the many complexities espoused by sustainability also concomitantly increase the complexities that environmental governance needs to deal with. The success of environmental governance in tackling these challenges, with the view to achieving sustainability, will ultimately depend on the design, quality, quantity and effectiveness of environmental governance interventions.

Conclusion

The intention in this chapter was not comprehensively to elaborate on the environmental governance concept. The debate on the theoretical design and legal meaning of the environmental governance concept is in its early stages. What is clear, to the present author, is that this is the dawn of the 'governance', and more specifically the 'environmental governance', era. In addition, law and the environmental law sub-discipline, flawed as they may be, play an important part in the environmental governance paradigm, especially insofar as law aims to regulate human behaviour. It is also evident that the world is currently set on an unsustainable path; and that what is clearly required is that laws, legal institutions, mechanisms and processes, along with governance arrangements, insofar as they relate to environmental matters, must be continually revisited and improved if we are to achieve sustainability, in both its theoretical and its practical contexts.

The chapter has established that governance is clearly a social phenomenon because it involves people, it is institutional because it provides the rules of the game and material institutions such as government, and it is normative because it is based on and uses normative arrangements (or rules) to achieve a certain outcome. In terms of the normative basis of governance, and more specifically the rules of governance, law plays a critical role because law is the constitution of governance; law legitimizes governance; law creates agents of governance and allows them to govern; law provides the authority to these actors to govern; law prescribes how to govern and what to govern; and law provides the minimum thresholds for what is deemed acceptable or unacceptable behaviour in society. Law therefore ultimately fulfils a distinct constitutive, legitimizing, prescriptive, proscriptive, instrumentalist and guiding function in and of governance. In short, '[G]overnance can be accomplished by law' (Keohane and Nye, 2002: 203) and the regulative objectives of law are simultaneously accomplished through governance.

Understood in its broadest possible form, the environment relates to everything that people perceive to exist around them, including people themselves; the natural environment; the human-made environment; water, soil and air; all forms of life including biological and chemical processes; non-human living and non-living entities; and the manner in which people interact and experience the aesthetic (including the socio-cultural) and utilitarian aspects of the environment.

What is also clear is that human actions affect the environment. Human behaviour depletes environmental resources, it produces new environmental components and harms the environment. Environmental governance is a strategy that people use to alter human behaviour with a view to achieving a type of environment or environmental quality or level of environmental protection that they perceive to be more acceptable. People design institutions and act through them to change human behaviour with respect to the environment. For our present purposes it is unnecessary to reflect on the underlying motivations for people to do so: it could be to optimize economic benefits, to gain competitive advantage, to gain greater political power, or even for genuinely altruistic ecological purposes. A more important point is that human behaviour towards the environment can be changed: '[H]uman nature is somewhat malleable, its shape determined in limited but important ways by whether the prevailing social, economic, and political systems are designed to bring out cooperation or conflict, ecological awareness or consumer fetishism' (Hempel, 1996: 21).

Viewed thus, the pragmatic and idealistic objectives of environmental governance also become clear. Its pragmatic objective is to change human behaviour, often by means of law, with a view to addressing those environmental issues that society perceives to be problematic. If governance is an institutional response that seeks to change human behaviour, then environmental governance aims to change human behaviour with respect to a comprehensively conceived environment. The idealistic objective of environmental governance is the achievement of sustainability, and in this sense the pragmatic objective of changing human behaviour *vis-à-vis* the environment is a prerequisite and first step to be taken *en route* to that end. Yet, the achievement of sustainability (meaning an equal balance between social, financial and ecological capital) is arguably an impossible task, and instead of ever hoping to achieve it one can hope that the attempt to do so will play a guiding role in the performance of environmental governance. Thus, while the value and use of sustainability should not be unrealistically overstated, it remains an important conceptual framework or organizing principle for the design of those institutional responses through which people seek to influence behaviour with respect to the environment:

> [s]ustainability is ultimately about ideas and forms of human organization that cohere ecologically and that do not require linear notions of time for their validation – only a deep sense of harmony and connectedness. By providing the organizing framework for this sense to develop, sustainable development ...offers a means of collective hope and transcendence that help make the personal sacrifices required for future environmental improvement more worthwhile ...As with the postmaterialist notion of progress, sustainable development refers to development that is largely qualitative or self-limiting in nature. It can conceivably encompass most of the important objectives of global environmental governance. And despite suffering from abstraction and oversimplification in day-to-day usage, it offers a useful bridge for connecting environmental concerns with social and economic well-being.
>
> (*ibid.*: 40–41)

While this chapter has attempted to provide a tentative theoretical formulation of environmental governance from a legal perspective, it is hoped that many more will follow and, more importantly, that the theory will be implemented in practice to change behaviour and ultimately to achieve sustainability.

In conclusion, and by way of summary, this chapter sought to point out that: (a) environmental governance is an amorphous extra-legal concept, which has an unclear meaning and/or inadequate content for environmental lawyers; (b) environmental governance should be accommodated in law, given its increased popularity in the legal domain; (c) environmental governance is used in many contexts and at various levels and originates from myriad international developments; (d) it is unclear what environmental governance means to lawyers; and that, (e), lawyers have only recently embarked on a process to apply and explore 'governance' in the environmental law domain, and this process is far from complete. Most importantly perhaps, the foregoing suggests that much work still needs to be done before the legal fraternity's appetite for legal clarification by means of definition is satisfied in this respect.

References

Benz, A. (2004) 'Governance – Modebegriff oder nützliches sozialwissenschaftliches Konzept?', in Benz, A. and Dose, N. (eds) *Governance – Regieren in komplexen Regelsystemen: Eine Einführung*, VS Verlag für Sozialwissenschaften, Wiesbaden, 13–36.

Beyerlin, U. (1996) 'The Concept of Sustainable Development', in Wolfrum, R. (ed.), *Enforcing Environmental Standards: Economic Mechanisms as Viable Means?*, Springer, Berlin, 95–121.

Boer, B. (1995) 'The Globalisation of Environmental Law: The Role of the United Nations', *Melbourne University Law Review*, 20(1): 101–125.

Bosselmann, K. (2008) *The Principle of Sustainability: Transforming Law and Governance*, Ashgate, Aldershot.

Bothe, M. (2007) *Environment, Development, Resources Offprint: Volume* 318, Martinus Nijhoff Publishers, Leiden, 337–516.

Boyd, D.R. (2004) 'Sustainability Law: (R)Evolutionary Directions for the Future of Environmental Law', *Journal of Environmental Law and Practice*, 14: 357–385.

Chambers, B.W. and Green, J.F. (eds) (2005) *Reforming International Environmental Governance: From Institutional Limits to Innovative Reforms*, United Nations University Press, Tokyo.

Commission for Global Governance (1995) *Our Global Neighbourhood*, Oxford University Press, Oxford.

Crutzen, P. and Stoermer, E. (2000) 'The "Anthropocene"' *IGBP Global Change Newsletter*, 41: 17–18.

Curtin, D.M. and Dekker, I. (2005) 'Good Governance: the Concept and its Application by the European Union', in Curtin, D.M. and Wessels, R.A. (eds) *Good Governance and the European Union: Reflections on Concepts, Institutions and Substance*, Intersentia, Antwerpen, 3–20.

DiMento, J.F.C. (2003) *The Global Environment and International Law*, University of Texas Press, Austin.

Dubos, R. (1968) *So Human an Animal*, Scribner, New York.

Dunoff, J.L. (2007) 'Levels of Environmental Governance', in Bodansky, D., Brunnee, J. and Hey, E. (eds) *The Oxford Handbook of International Environmental Law*, Oxford University Press, Oxford.

ESCWA (2000) 'Good Governance: Enhancing Macro-Management in the ESCWA Region', UN Doc. E/ESCWA/ ED/2000/7.

Fisher, E., Lange, B., Scotford, E. and Carlarne, C. (2009) 'Maturity and Methodology: Starting a Debate about Environmental Law Scholarship', *Journal of Environmental Law*, 21(2): 213–250

Fitzmaurice, M. (1996) 'The Contribution of Environmental Law to the Development of Modern International Law', in Makarczyk, J. (ed.) *Theory of International Law at the Threshold of the 21st Century: Essays in Honour of Krzysztof Skubiszewski*, Kluwer Law International, the Hague, 909–926.

Ginther, K. and De Waart, P.I.J.M. (1995) 'Sustainable Development as a Matter of Good Governance: An Introductory View', in Ginther, K., Denters, E. and De Waart, P.J.I.M. (eds) *Sustainable Development and Good Governance*, Martinus Nijhoff, Boston.

Godden, L. and Peel, J. (2010) *Environmental Law: Scientific, Policy and Regulatory Dimensions*, Oxford University Press, Melbourne.
Grant, J.P. and Barker, C.J. (eds) (2004) *Parry and Grant Encyclopaedic Dictionary of International Law*, Oceana Publications, Dobbs Ferry.
Hart, H.L.A. (1961/1994) *The Concept of Law* (2nd ed.), Clarendon Press, Oxford.
Hempel, L.C. (1996) *Environmental Governance: The Global Challenge*, Island Press, Washington.
Iwama, T. (2004) 'Multilateral Environmental Institutions and Coordinating Mechanisms', in Norichika, K. and Haas, P.M. (eds) *Emerging Forces in Environmental Governance*, United Nations University Press, Tokyo, 15–33.
Kelsen, H. (1945) *General Theory of Law and State*, Harvard University Press, Cambridge, MA.
Keohane, R.O. and Nye, J.S. (2002) 'Governance in a Globalizing World', in Keohane, R.O. (ed.) *Power and Governance in a Partially Globalized World*, Routledge, London, 193–218.
Kingsbury, B. (2007) 'Global Environmental Governance as Administration: Implications for International Law', in Bodansky, D., Brunnee, J. and Hey, E. (eds), *The Oxford Handbook of International Environmental Law*, Oxford University Press, Oxford.
Kornhauser, L.A. (2004) 'Governance Structures, Legal Systems, and the Concept of Law', *Chicago-Kent Law Review*, 79(2): 355–381.
Kotzé, L.J. (2009) 'Environmental Governance', in Paterson, A. and Kotzé, L.J. (eds) *Environmental Compliance and Enforcement in South Africa: Legal Perspectives*, Juta, Cape Town, 296–335.
Kotzé, L.J. (2012) *Global Environmental Governance: Law and Regulation for the 21st Century*, Edward Elgar, Cheltenham.
Kotzé, L.J. (2014) 'Rethinking Global Environmental Law and Governance in the Anthropocene' *Journal of Energy and Natural Resources Law*, 33(2): 121–156.
Kotzé, L.J. (2010) 'Towards a Tentative Legal Formulation of Environmental Governance', in Honkonen, T. and Couzens, E. (eds) *International Environmental Law-making and Diplomacy Review 2009*, University of Eastern Finland, Joensuu, 3–20.
Kubasek, N.K. and Silverman, G.S. (2008) *Environmental Law* (6th ed.), Pearson Prentice Hall, Upper Saddle River, NJ.
Lang, W. (1995) 'How to Manage Sustainable Development', in Ginther, K., Denters, E. and De Waart, P.J.I.M. (eds) *Sustainable Development and Good Governance*, Martinus Nijhoff, Boston.
Levy, D.L. and Newell, P.J. (2005) 'Introduction', in Levy, D.L. and Newell, P.J. (eds) *The Business of Global Environmental Governance*, MIT Press, Cambridge, MA, 1–16.
Norichika, K. and Haas, P.M. (eds) (2004) *Emerging Forces in Environmental Governance*, United Nations University Press, Tokyo.
Ocheje, P. (1999) 'Exploring the Legal Dimensions of Political Legitimacy: A 'Rights' Approach to Governance in Africa', in Quashigah, E.K. and Okafor, O.C. (eds) *Legitimate Governance in Africa: International and Domestic Legal Perspectives*, Kluwer Law International, the Hague, 165–205.
Ost, F. (1994) 'A Game without Rules? The Ecological Self-Organization of Firms' in Teubner, G., Farmer, L. and Murphy, D. (eds), *Environmental Law and Ecological Responsibility: The Concept and Practice of Ecological Self-regulation*, John Wiley & Sons, Chichester, 337–361.
Pelletier, N. (2010) 'Of Laws and Limits: An Ecological Economic Perspective on Redressing the Failure of Contemporary Global Environmental Governance' *Global Environmental Change*, 20: 220–228.

Pinto, M.C.W. (1996) 'Common Heritage of Mankind': From Metaphor to Myth, and the Consequence of Constructive Ambiguity', in Makarczyk, J. (ed.) *Theory of International Law at the Threshold of the 21st Century: Essays in Honour of Krzysztof Skubiszewski*, Kluwer Law International, the Hague, 249–268.
Redclift, M. (1995) 'Sustainable Development: Economics and the Environment', in Redclift, M. and Sage, C. (eds) *Strategies for Sustainable Development: Local Agendas for the South*, Wiley, Chichester, 17–34.
Redgewell, C. (2006) 'International Environmental Law', in Evans, M.D. (ed) *International Law* (2nd ed.), Oxford University Press, Oxford, 657–688.
Reinalda, B. (1999) 'International Organizations as Sources of Political Change', in Van Kersbergen, K., Lieshout, R.H. and Lock, G. (eds) *Expansion and Fragmentation: Internationalization, Political Change and the Transformation of the Nation State*, Amsterdam University Press, Amsterdam, 107–124.
Richardson, B.J. (2002) 'Trends in North America and Europe', in Bosselmann, K. and Grinlinton, D. (eds) *Environmental Law for a Sustainable Society*, New Zealand Centre for Environmental Law, Auckland, 70–93.
Sands, P. (1994) 'International Law in the Field of Sustainable Development', *The British Yearbook of International Law*, 65(1): 303–381.
Sands, P. (2003) *Principles of International Environmental Law* (2nd ed.), Cambridge University Press, Cambridge.
Serageldin, I. (1998) 'The Formation of a Global Development Agenda', in 2 *Boutros Boutros-Ghali: Amicorum Discipulorumque Liber*, Bruylant, Bruxelles, 1345–1368.
Sprout, H. and Sprout, M. (1972) 'The Ecological Viewpoint-and Others', in Black, C.E. and Falk, R.A. (eds) *The Future of the International Legal Order Volume IV: The Structure of the International Environment*, Princeton University Press, Princeton, 569–605.
UN DESA [United Nations Department of Economic and Social Affairs, Division for Public Economics and Public Administration] (2000) *Building Partnerships for Good Governance: The Spirit and Reality of South-South Cooperation* (United Nations).
Vidačak, I. and Božić, J. (2006) 'Civil Society and Good Governance in Societies in Transition: The Case of Croatia', in Benedek, W. (ed.) *Civil Society and Good Governance in Societies in Transition*, euer Wissenschaftlicher Verlag, Vienna, 55–76.
World Bank (2007) 'Governance Matters 2007: Worldwide Governance Indicators, 1996–2006' www.info.worldbank.org/governance/wgi/index.aspx#home (accessed 26 March 2015).
Young, O.R. (1994) *International Governance: Protecting the Environment in a Stateless Society*, Cornell University Press, Ithaca.
Young, O.R. (ed.) (1997) *Global Governance: Drawing Insights from the Environmental Experience*, MIT Press, Cambridge, MA.

6 Building institutional and managerial foundations for a new structure for environmental governance with the United Nations system

Tadanori Inomata[1]

Introduction

In order fully to understand modern environmental governance, it is important to have an understanding of the United Nations system. Even more than that, before entering into any discussion of specific issues of international environmental governance (IEG), one should consider how the United Nations (UN) system, through its governance, can provide member states and their peoples with public accountability of its operations (for a comprehensive index of the United Nations system of Organizations, see www.unsceb.org/directory).

Public accountability within the UN system can be said to have two aspects: *managerial accountability* within the UN system; and *democratic accountability* of the UN system. The first of these aspects relates to objectives and policy setting, and to management of resources within the UN intergovernmental forums. The second concerns output delivery to the global community, with public scrutiny aimed at making the objectives and policies of the UN system conform to global public interests. A solid foundation for environmental governance needs to be laid *with*, but not *within*, the UN system.

Management and governance frameworks

For the sake of efficiency any organization should have in place a clearly defined governance framework for decision-making and a mechanism for setting its agenda and its objectives, goals and policies, as well as a management framework for the implementation of the decisions taken. National organizations, be these governmental or not, will usually have a single constitution, a body of law, by-laws, regulations and rules that are relevant to governance, organization, management and administration. What parameters apply to performance evaluation and accountability are therefore usually fairly easy to identify.

---

1 The contribution of Tita Korvenoja (Ministerial Adviser, Director for UNEP Affairs, Ministry of the Environment, Finland), by way of advice and editing on this chapter, is gratefully acknowledged.

The situation differs radically, however, for international organizations. In the UN system both objective setting and the execution and delivery by the administration of organizational decisions are subject to the will of intergovernmental entities usually composed of member states. States called upon to pay the expenses of the organization are inevitably reluctant to accept open-ended commitments to its activities unless assured of efficacy. Governments have long sought to establish an elaborate system of procedures for the governing body collectively to approve the programmes of organizations, to allocate appropriate funds to these, and to monitor their use and effects. An established system should provide delegated authority to the executive heads and administrations of the organizations, in return for their transparency and accountability.

The formation of international environmental regimes has been motivated by the need of states to find *in situ* solutions to inter-state problems, but the solutions found have tended to be rather *ad hoc*, short-term and often duplicative in the long run. The result has been that new independent regimes have often come into existence as and when new global issues have arisen – being reactive rather than proactive. The increasing proliferation of international regimes has increased member states' burdens, both in terms of efforts to manage individual regimes better and of providing effective governance to ensure coherence and coordination amongst them.

At the same time, the ever-growing interest in the environment by both member states and entities within the UN system has been confirmed in recent years by a 'phenomenal' growth (from US$1.8 billion in 2006 to US$4 billion in 2012) in the multilateral resources made available for activities (in both core and non-core budgets) – this growth has been 'significantly faster than the total level of resources devoted by the [UN] system to operational activities for development' (Inomata and Cazeau, 2014: iii). If money is to be used effectively, understanding of the system is needed.

Management and oversight lacunae

Introduction

Fragmentation of responsibilities and proliferation of institutions inhibit the decentralized UN system from setting up a single governance and management framework. A number of salient features in management methods and approaches militate against creating such a framework at the intergovernmental level. These features are partly a corollary of member states' reluctance to make long-term policy and resource commitments to durable and far-reaching systematic solutions; as well as increased reliance on voluntary contributions instead of assessed contributions; and, also, member states' preference for zero-growth budgeting. Confusion between normative and operational activities in the UN institutions is created by UN funds and programmes often funding the cost of activities of a normative nature from voluntary contributions. There are also built-in deficiencies in the methods and approaches employed in the management of the secretariats of various organizations. These include a dichotomy between programming and budgeting, the inadequacy of system-wide management frameworks and the lack of a mandatory framework for joint programming and financial appropriation among the organizations.

Various weaknesses in the UN governance system

Lack of a single governance and management framework

There are diverse independent entities within the UN system, each with its own governing body to set objectives and make management decisions. Inherent in the decentralized nature of the structure of international institutions is the problem that no single management and governance framework exists within the system.

Lack of coherent follow-up and implementation

Improvements in setting objectives and governance within the UN system have yet to achieve all that they could have. Various attempts have been made from the inception of the United Nations through the past seven decades, ranging from the adoption of global platforms and action programmes common to all institutions within the UN system through UN-sponsored world conferences, to the establishment of new funds, programmes and organizations. Often, new organizations have been established when coordinated follow-up was required to ensure the implementation of an adopted programme. However, monitoring and implementation of the agreed actions were often hortatory at best, relying upon the will of stakeholders and constituencies in the sectors concerned.

Dichotomy between programming and budgeting

Almost all normative bodies experience a dichotomy between programming and budgeting, with policy decisions being taken separately from resource considerations or *vice versa*. Member states only reluctantly accept additional financial obligations as a direct consequence of their programmatic decisions on the work of the organization; and so extra-budgetary and voluntary contributions in money, goods and services dominate in the economic, humanitarian and social sectors. The practice of the zero real growth principle in the budgeting of the regular programmes of international organizations has exacerbated this trend. The demarcation between voluntary contributions and regular core resources is blurred. It sometimes seems that there is no longer application of the concept that the expenses of the organization in the meaning of Article 17 of the UN Charter shall be considered and approved by the General Assembly (Art. 17(1)); that the expenses of the organization shall be borne by the Members as apportioned by the General Assembly (Art. 17(2)); and that the General Assembly shall consider and approve any financial and budgetary arrangements with specialized agencies (as referred to in Art. 57) and shall examine the administrative budgets of such specialized agencies with a view to making recommendations to the agencies concerned (Art. 17(3)). Instead, funding of the UN system organizations is assured according to the convenience of member states and donors.

Under the circumstances, the organizations' ability to deliver results from programmes depends heavily upon the ability of the programme managers to interact with contributors and donors for fundraising. This situation is detrimental to the UN organizations' public mission of ensuring their transparency and accountability for mobilizing the necessary regular resources, in order to achieve the officially mandated objectives and programmes.

Confusion between normative activities and operational activities

Normative and operational activities have also been blurred. For example, the regular core budget programmes of the UN Development Programme (UNDP), the UN Children's Fund (UNICEF), the UN High Commissioner for Refugees (UNHCR) and other UN funds and programmes cover research and policy development components with outputs very similar to research and policy-formulation activities that should be financed by the regular budget of the UN and its specialized agencies.

Lack of system-wide management tools

There are no reliable data and statistics available to inform the public of how much money is being spent by the UN system as a whole. Such information would seem fundamental to any systematic planning and management of international organizations, but, thus far, the UN system has never been able to establish a readily available system-wide accounting framework to measure total available resources and their use. Nor has it attempted to establish a process for common resource planning and allocation.

The results-based budgeting and management (RBBM) approach in force since 2002 has been instrumental in visualizing 'specific, measurable, achievable, relevant and time-bound' (SMART) objectives in the budgeting in the United Nations (UN Joint Inspection Unit, 2004). In May 2006, on the recommendations of the Committee for Programme and Coordination (UNGA, 2005: Corr. 1, para. 248), the General Assembly approved the benchmarking framework for results-based management (RBM) as a concept applicable to the United Nations and recommended consideration of its application in other UN system organizations (UNGA Res. 60/257: para. 2). However, it has not been possible to establish a system-wide RBBM resource management framework in the absence of commonly agreed intergovernmental objectives among all organizations within the UN system. Without such a global governance framework, the RBM approach has arguably even exacerbated fragmentation and compartmentalization of organizations' activities.

Currently being unrolled throughout the UN system is a programme called 'Umoja' (Swahili for 'unity'), which is a 'robust reporting and data visualization platform' that gives staff and managers the ability to 'search, view and analyze a variety of metrics, reports and key performance indicators' (see Umoja, n.d.). The intention is to give the UN the 'ability to conduct complex and real-time analyses of critical data' (*ibid.*).

Persistence of an archaic interagency coordination concept

The traditional concept of interagency coordination prevails; namely, that member states believe that the administrations of UN agencies tend to duplicate their activities despite the possibly contradictory wills of member states. To them, the only panacea has appeared to be a call for better interagency coordination at the administrative level. Obviously, there is an inherent limit to such coordination. Unless the governing bodies' decisions are coherent and clear in resource allocation on common ventures among agencies, effective coordination is unlikely. The current coordination framework of the UN Chief Executives Board (CEB), composed of executive heads of agencies under the chairship of the Secretary-General, is run mostly on a *post factum* basis, respecting the *fait accompli* committed by their governing bodies with respect to their own programmatic and financial decisions. There is no mandatory framework to enable the administrations to negotiate and agree *ex ante* on system-wide programmes and projects.

Management and oversight lacunae in the environmental field

Proliferation of environment-related initiatives

Examples of management and oversight *lacunae* can be found in environmental governance within the UN system. Concern about the deteriorating global environment led to the creation of the UN Environment Programme (UNEP) in 1972, followed by the establishment of other environment-related institutions, such as the Commission on Sustainable Development (CSD) (since replaced by the High-level Political Forum (HLPF) on Sustainable Development), numerous multilateral environmental agreements, the Multilateral Fund for the Implementation of the Montreal Protocol and the Global Environment Facility (GEF). UNEP, however, cannot be considered an 'authoritative body as regards ensuring programmatic and managerial synergies among multilateral environmental agreements' (Inomata and Cazeau, 2014: iv).

The environmental sector is characterized not only by diversity of environmental institutions but also by the overlap of activities between these institutions and global and regional cooperative programmes and frameworks that are involved more or less actively in environment-related activities. Furthermore, it has been accompanied by the existence of multiple intergovernmental and inter-secretariat coordinating bodies. There is not a clear division of labour between development organizations and environmental entities; and there are not 'clear-cut definitions of interfaces between environmental protection and sustainable development and between normative and operational activities' (*ibid.*: iii). As demands for resource-efficiency are growing, striving to retain strict division between normative and operational activities may become less feasible in the future. The environmental sector may increasingly experience arrangements in which operational activities are integrated into normative work. This is well reflected in, for instance, the Intergovernmental Platform on Biodiversity and Ecosystem Services (IPBES), which, in addition to its scientific work, also has a very strong capacity-building component intertwined into its programme of work. The fading boundaries between the normative and operational activities require a coordinated approach in order to avoid overlaps in activities and mandates.

As environmental concern has grown, and its cross-cutting nature has become better understood, every organization in the UN system has come to include environmental activities and projects within its activities. This also assists with attracting voluntary contributions from donors, thus helping to perpetuate the organizations' survival. Even though mainstreaming of the environmental dimension into development policies is a positive trend and is welcomed by donors, it may contribute to further fragmentation of the governance in a situation where overall coordination of the system is weak.

Resource management

Underfunding persists as a source of weakness within the UN system, as is often claimed by its bureaucrats. However, if funds were strategically used with better coherence, those available would enable the system to play a significant catalytic role in ensuring effective global governance within the environmental sector.

Something that hinders the UN system from managing resources efficiently is the competition and confusion of mandates between the environmental institutions and development organizations undertaking environment-related activities. The blurring of distinctions between environmental protection and sustainable development has exacerbated this confusion, even though this could also be interpreted as successful mainstreaming of environmental aspects into the development agenda. A clear trend during the 1990s was that normative activities promoted by UNEP and the multilateral agreements for environmental protection grew much faster than did operational activities for development devoted to the environment. However, in the early 2000s that trend was reversed in favour of operational activities. Nowadays, the primary growth is in developmental agencies such as the UNDP, UNICEF and specialized agencies undertaking environment-related activities as part of their work on sustainable development. In recent years, MEAs' core budgets have stagnated. This suggests that much of the MEAs' additional financial needs for normative activities had to be met by voluntary contributions under their non-core programmes.

Towards governance of sustainable development

Introduction

The year 2015 is likely to be seen, in retrospect, as a significant one for international environmental governance. It has been described as the year in which the future of the global development agenda will be set, with states, civil society and UN organizations all seeking a global Post-2015 Agenda that will 'embrace all aspects of sustainable development guided by a set of Sustainable Development Goals (SDGs)' (see www.unep.org/post2015/). The concept of the SDGs arose at the UNCSD (Rio+20) in 2012, with its objective being to produce 'a set of universally applicable goals that balances the three dimensions of sustainable development: the environmental, social, and economic'– to supersede the Millennium Development Goals of 2000 (*ibid.*). The task of designing a set of measurable targets and indicators is underway.

Lack of coordination

Adding to the problem of institutional fragmentation has been the lack of a *modus operandi* to govern and manage the relationship between sustainable development and environmental protection. In the context of agreements concluded at the 1992 UN Conference on Environment and Development (Rio de Janeiro) and the 2002 World Summit on Sustainable Development (Johannesburg), sustainable development is meant to be a development process that enables a meeting of the needs of present generations without compromising the ability of future generations to meet their own needs (this formulation of the term essentially being that suggested by the 1987 Brundtland Commission; WCED, 1987). Furthermore, integrating its three components – economic development, social equity and environmental protection – as interdependent and mutually reinforcing pillars should assist in achieving sustainable development (UNGA, 1987).

A variety of General Assembly and UN Economic and Social Council (ECOSOC) resolutions, most notably UNGA resolution S-19/2 (1997) on the programme for further implementation of Agenda 21, have stated that good governance for sustainable development consists of properly constructed strategies to enhance prospects for economic growth and employment while at the same time protecting the environment. On the other hand, the UNEP Governing Council/Global Ministerial Environment Forum (GC/GMEF) held in Cartagena in 2002 adopted the 'Cartagena Package' on international environmental governance (UNEP, 2002), according to which environmental governance consists of mainstreaming environmental protection into developmental and economic policies through the development of a system-wide coherent policy, as well as resources management for its implementation.

Theoretically, a consensus seems to exist within the UN system as to the definition of and relationship between the concepts of sustainable development and environmental protection. However, in practice, equitable governance between sustainable development and environmentally protective measures is not easy to achieve, as there is no consensus on how to reconcile the competing priorities of the three components of sustainable development.

The Rio Summit broadened the scope of governance far beyond the confines of UNEP, thus rendering coordination of multilateral policies and decisions more complex for the organization. In tandem with this new governance concept, a 'fading out' of certain of the Rio principles germane to international cooperation for environmental protection may arguably be observed: these including precautionary control measures based on scientific assessments; and the international community's bearing of incremental costs incurred to implement environmental measures by developing countries. 'Incremental costs' are changes in total costs arising from implementing additional environmentally protective measures; their measurement being a key to environmental financing that should not be confused with or substituted by ordinary developmental assistance as they are based on rigorous environmental assessments and identification of differential costs to implement MEAs in developing countries. It could be argued that the principle of common but differentiated responsibilities is another principle that has 'faded', although it continues to be placed high on the agendas of developing countries negotiating toward Post-2015 arrangements. At the national level, there exist long-term approaches and mechanisms to reconcile the interests. However, the UN system has never been able to establish such a process, nor implement a mechanism to ensure it. The ever-growing involvement of international organizations and bilateral donors in strengthening norms, capacity-building, networking and funding in the environmental field has exacerbated institutional fragmentation and duplication of policies and operations of international environmental initiatives. These initiatives, springing up after the Earth Summit in 1992 and the WSSD in 2002, have arguably eroded UNEP's embracing mandate for global environmental governance.

There are a number of salient features which can be derived from *lacunae* in UN accountability and environmental governance. Under the circumstances, such lacunae encompass a lack of coordination, coherence and cooperation at the global level; the absence of a programmatic and planning instrument for system-wide coordination; inadequate levels of implementation and coordination at national level; a lack of intergovernmental ownership in interagency coordination; a need for synergy of control measures among MEAs; and an absence of environmentally sound procurement policies in international organizations.

Coordination mechanisms

The UN system secretariats established the Environmental Management Group (EMG), with the support of the General Assembly (Res. 53/242, 1999), for the purpose of enhancing interagency coordination among UN agencies, funds and programmes and the secretariats of MEAs in the fields of environment and human settlements. The EMG meets under the chair of the UNEP executive director, who reports on its activities – formerly to the UNEP GC/GMEF, now to the United Nations Environment Assembly (UNEA). The most important goal of the EMG is to promote a so-called issue management approach to key areas of environmental and human settlements concern. The aim is to achieve, on an issue-by-issue basis, effective management, coordination, joint action, rational and cost-effective use of capacities and resources and to facilitate linkages among MEAs, and between the activities under the MEAs and relevant activities elsewhere in the international environmental governance system.

On the other hand, from 1993 until 2001 the Inter-Agency Committee on Sustainable Development (IACSD) existed for interagency coordination in the area of sustainable development. Its role was to identify major policy issues relating to the follow-up by the UN system and to advise the Administrative Committee on Coordination (ACC), which was a predecessor body to the CEB, on ways and means of addressing them to ensure effective system-wide cooperation and coordination in the implementation of Agenda 21, the Programme of Action for the Sustainable Development of Small Island Developing States (SIDS) and other UNCED outcomes. It provided coordinated policy positions as input to the Commission on Sustainable Development. In 2001, the CEB abandoned a holistic approach. It disbanded the IACSD and took steps through its High-level Committee on Programmes to establish or strengthen interagency collaborative arrangements in the key areas of freshwater, water and sanitation, energy, oceans and coastal areas, and consumption and production patterns. Specific actions taken included the establishment of various sector groups: UN-Water, UN-Oceans, the International Strategy for Disaster Reduction, the Marrakech Process on sustainable consumption and production patterns, and UN-Energy.

It is therefore obvious that there are two sets of coordinating mechanisms building up: one in UNEP on environmental protection; and another in the CEB purview on sustainable development. Irrespective of any theoretical or juridical explanation of their relationships, considerable overlapping of their tasks will remain.

At the country level, the UN agencies are yet to generalize the use of the Common Country Assessment and UN Development Assistance Framework (CCA/UNDAF) processes to mainstream environmental protection within development policy. The Common Country Assessment is, as defined by the General Assembly, the common instrument of the UN system for analysing national development situations and identifying key development issues. Although compliance with MEAs should take place at the country level as the responsibility of the Contracting Parties concerned, the UN resident coordinators and the secretariats of the MEAs have made few efforts to promote the implementation of MEAs in the CCA/UNDAF processes.

Programmatic and planning instrument for system-wide coordination

The UN system is still to develop a common fundamental programmatic instrument spelling out who does what and how their communalities of interests can be enhanced. The UN Medium-term Plan and UNEP's System-wide Medium-Term Environmental Programme ceased to be system-wide instruments in the 1990s.

These instruments had provided the UN system with a mandatory process to define system-wide strategic objectives and orientations of the UN system organizations based on legislation by the intergovernmental fora as well as the agreed programmes and activities of the organizations in 4- or 5-year medium terms.

Under the implementation frameworks of the Millennium Development Goals, the CEB identified 27 mechanisms for international cooperation to ensure environmental sustainability – including, for instance, the GEF, UN-Water, the World Water Assessment Programme (WWAP), the Global Environment Monitoring System (GEMS), Cities Alliance, UN-Oceans, the Global Programme of Action for the Protection of the Marine Environment from Land-based Activities (GPA), and the Millennium Ecosystem Assessment. On the other hand, UNEP has compiled a list of joint projects and programmes undertaken with other UN system organizations relevant for the activities of MEAs in the areas of biodiversity, chemicals and waste control, customs and illegal trade, education for sustainable development and advocacy, harmonization of reporting under MEAs, health and environmental initiatives, marine pollution, protection of regional seas, and world climate impacts assessment. However, how the UN system should integrate these networks and a series of joint programmes as a programmatic and planning instrument for system-wide coordination remains unclear.

At the first session of the UNEA, a draft resolution on a UN 'System-wide Strategy on the Environment' was tabled. Even though the content of the version of the resolution that was eventually adopted is considerably less ambitious than the original draft, it has enabled the Executive Director of UNEP to initiate discussions on the strategy in the EMG (www.unep.org/unea/docs/Compilation_of_decisions_and%20resolutions_advanced_unedited%20copy.pdf – Proceedings of the UNEA at its first session). The underlying aim of the strategy is to 'ensure the coherence of relevant policies' and 'effective coordination of the diverse [UN] services, activities and programmes' in the environmental field (*ibid.*). The idea is to provide a system-wide medium- and long-term vision; identify common and/or complementary approaches and policies; establish coordinating processes for planning and execution of UN system activities; and suggest a mechanism for assessing effectiveness of UN system-wide activities (*ibid.*).

Lack of intergovernmental ownership in interagency coordination

Most environmental management issues have been left to the discretion of various secretariats of international organizations, probably because of the often highly technical and scientific nature of understanding and approaching environmental problems. Many coordination-related weaknesses have been perceived at the administrative level and dealt with among the secretariats of UN system entities. The issue of promoting synergies amongst the various MEAs has also been approached with the aim of achieving coherence between the operations of the conventions' secretariats. The Environment Management Group and the CEB environmental sector groups are essentially secretariat bodies and subject to the 'principle of subsidiarity' for decision-making among them, meaning that these interagency bodies should make their decisions at the lowest possible levels. However, obviously, they cannot in principle take decisions contrary to the interests of any of their organizations.

Need for synergy of control measures among multilateral environmental agreements

The international community is not equipped with a regular mechanism for solving substantive contradictions in control measures between environmental conventions, for example between the Kyoto Protocol and the Montreal Protocol regarding the use of alternative substances and technology to replace chlorofluorocarbons and other ozone-depleting substances by hydrochlorofluorcarbons (and its by-product hydrofluorcarbons), which have high global-warming effects. Successive efforts within the Montreal Protocol at applying an environmentally responsible approach to its primary-rule system for the control of ozone-depleting substances (i.e., to use alternative substances taking into account environmental effects such as global warming) are yet to succeed in ensuring integrated implementation of that Protocol and the Kyoto Protocol on climate change.

This lack of coherence within governance is due both to the inadequate development of common criteria for environmentally responsible principles; and – perhaps more fundamentally – due to the absence of an overriding legal framework applicable to all environmental conventions ensuring environmentally sound and responsible policies and behaviours in the implementation of MEAs. Such a framework, which might need to be based on a 'world convention on the law of environmental treaties', has yet to be developed. Development of *jus cogens* in this field might include the principle that actions under multilateral environmental programmes and conventions must be harmonized to ensure that perceived benefits under one are not achieved at the expense of deleterious consequences for another (Report of the Secretary-General, Protection of the Atmosphere, 2000: para. 3; Inomata, 2001: 37).

Such a law of treaties should identify and assist in horizontally harmonizing principles and rules applicable to MEAs with respect to environmentally responsible principles, precautionary approaches, sharing of scientific assessments, mutual information and monitoring of transboundary hazards, compliance procedures and mechanisms of coordination of normative and operational actions. Without these principles and rules, it will always be difficult to achieve full and integrated accountability, in recognition that environmental issues dealt with by different MEAs are inextricably linked. Notwithstanding the increasing trend to call for more conventions and legally binding frameworks for environmental protection, there are serious and paradoxical *lacunae* in the rule of law that should govern the coherent application of different provisions of control measures under the MEAs.

In the absence of an overarching law of environmental treaties to ensure the harmonization of activities under different MEAs, efforts to synergize treaty implementation are becoming increasingly important. For instance, the synergies process among the Basel, Rotterdam and Stockholm Conventions has evolved through a series of decisions that culminated in omnibus decisions taken in 2011

(SC-5/27, RC-5/12, BC-10/29) and 2013 (BC.Ex-2/1, RC.Ex-2/1, SC.Ex-2/1). The synergies process has led to increased efficiency of secretariat activities through a joint secretariat, more coordinated decision-making through organization of back-to-back or simultaneous Conferences of the Parties (CoPs) and, finally, joint action on the ground through adoption of joint programmes of work. In 2015, the CoPs considered the possibility of establishing a joint trust fund, but the discussion on this important issue that could have sealed the synergies process was deferred to the next meeting. In 2017, an independent review of the synergies arrangements between 2005–2015 will be published with conclusions for follow-up action. The recent initiatives toward increased cooperation within the cluster of 'biodiversity-related' conventions are also promising, including decision XII/6 of the CoP12 of the Convention on the Biological Diversity, which initiates a Party-driven process on enhancing synergies among the biodiversity-related MEAs.

Possible future administrative and managerial foundations

From the foregoing, it is clear that at the headquarters level, MEA secretariats should not create further permanent interagency coordinating bodies, although some of the existing interagency bodies (such as the Biodiversity Liaison Group) might usefully be strengthened and made more responsive to guidance from relevant CoPs.

Rather, a bottom-up process of compiling needs in the field at the country level should be strengthened. To this end, active use should be made of the CCA/UN Development Assistance Framework processes to identify common country needs in sustainable development and environmental protection and map national and regional ecosystem problems, including compliance with MEAs. Such bottom-up processes will keep momentum for multilateral cooperation in the respective areas of environmental protection. Based on these processes, the global legislative forums, such as the UN General Assembly and the Economic and Social Council, should develop at field and headquarters levels a system-wide planning process for managing resources for results.

In this respect, with a view to enhancing the overall effectiveness of the environmental governance within the United Nations system, it may be recommended that the General Assembly establish a clear understanding on the division of labour between development agencies, UNEP and MEAs. This understanding should outline these entities' respective roles and competences for environmental protection and sustainable development (see Inomata, 2008).

The question is how the division of labour might be organized. The current framework of international environmental governance is undermined by the absence of a holistic approach to environmental issues and lack of clear operational linkages between development assistance on the one hand; and compliance and capacity-building assistance for environmental protection in developing countries, on the other.

The UN Conference on Sustainable Development (UNCSD, or Rio+20) in 2012 did not create a new organization, but reaffirmed UNEP's role as the leading global environmental authority and its role to promote the coherent implementation of the environmental dimension of sustainable development within the United Nations system. Further, based on the Conference's Outcome Document, the Governing Council of UNEP was upgraded into a universal body, the United Nations Environment Assembly, which is the highest conveying body on environment within the United Nations (see, further, Urho and Niinistö, this volume).

The Conference also suggested the formulation of UN system-wide strategies on the environment to fulfil the UNEP coordination mandate within the UN system, and that UNEP adopt a strategic planning and coordinating exercise of its governing body through an instrument applicable to all UN system organizations (as summarized by Inomata and Cazeau, 2014: 1). Further, that sustainable development be promoted through its three integrated dimensions (sustained and inclusive economic growth, social development, and environmental protection) to achieve internationally agreed development goals (*ibid.*: 1–2).

Further suggestions included that international environmental governance be achieved within the institutional framework for sustainable development by mainstreaming environmental protection into the sustainable development process; and that new institutional arrangements for sustainable development be provided, including the replacement of the CSD with a high-level political forum (*ibid.*: 2). Finally, that the 'need for strengthening coherence and coordination, avoiding duplication of efforts and reviewing progress in implementing sustainable development' be emphasized (*ibid.*).

It can be argued that Rio+20 'marked an inflection point in placing the integration of all three dimensions at the core of sustainable development policies' (*ibid.*: 5). In February 2013, the UNEP GC held its first universal session and agreed to invite the General Assembly, by resolution, to rename the GC the United Nations Environment Assembly of UNEP (*ibid.*: 6). The GC also decided that the UNEA would 'take strategic decisions and provide political guidance', including performing functions including, *inter alia*, 'setting [of] the global environmental agenda'; providing 'overarching political guidance and defining policy responses to address emerging environmental challenges'; undertaking 'policy reviews, dialogue and exchange of experiences'; setting the 'strategic guidance on the future direction of [UNEP]'; organizing 'multi-stakeholder dialogues'; and 'fostering partnerships for achieving environmental goals and resource mobilization' (*ibid.*).

Rio+20, it can be said, 'brought about a better understanding of and approach to international environmental governance' – it 'having been revealed that, in achieving an inclusive, transparent and effective development path, environmental protection and the other two dimensions of sustainable development [...] are inevitably intertwined' (*ibid.*).

Conclusion: future institutional arrangements

It can be argued confidently that there has been 'notable evolution in strengthening environmental governance since 2008' with Rio+20 bringing about 'a better understanding of and approach to international environmental governance' (Inomata and Cazeau, 2014: 6). This evolution has shown that, 'in achieving an inclusive, transparent and effective development path, environmental protection and the other two dimensions of sustainable development – economic growth and social development – are inevitably intertwined' (*ibid.*).

Future institutional overhauls of global environmental governance need to build on the reform of UNEP (especially by building on and strengthening the role of UNEA as the highest convening UN body on the environment) and good practices and lessons gleaned from successful international environmental regimes.

Reforms should always aim at laying a foundation for a new governance structure for environmental protection and sustainable development, which would consist in promoting synergies to assist in reconciling substantive differences and contradictions between MEAs; promoting and enforcing a system-wide strategic planning framework for the management and coordination of environmental activities; and promoting and enforcing a set of common guidelines for the provision and use of administrative, financial and technical support services to enhance synergies between United Nations system agencies and MEAs, as well as amongst MEAs.

In this regard, it will be important to monitor closely the political and normative role that UNEA plays – and to consider how the development of its role and its future prospects might be assisted. It is also important that UNEA is able to feed into the HLPF discussions to ensure that the voice of the world's environmental authority is heard in sustainable development debates. The Executive Director of UNEP suggested in 2015 that UENA is 'not just an expanded UNEP [GC], but [with each member state having a voice on environmental sustainability] symbolizes a fundamental change of scope' as 'the world's authoritative voice on environmental matters across' the UN system (www.unep.org/unea/ed_intro.asp). How authoritative this voice becomes will depend upon the member states themselves.

References

'Cooperation with Other Conventions, International Organizations and Initiatives', decision XII.6 of the Conference of the Parties to the Convention on Biological Diversity (2014).

'Enhancing Cooperation and Coordination Among the Basel, Rotterdam and Stockholm Donventions', Decisions of the Conferences of the Parties to the Basel (BC-10/29), Rotterdam (RC-5/12) and Stockholm (SC-5/27) Conventions (2011).

'Enhancing Cooperation and Coordination Among the Basel, Rotterdam and Stockholm conventions', Omnibus Decision of the Conferences of the Parties to the Basel (BC.Ex-2/1), Rotterdam (RC.Ex-2/1) and Stockholm (SC.Ex-2/1) Conventions (2013).

Inomata, T. (2001) 'Toward Integrating the Implementation of Multilateral Environmental Agreements – Reflection on the Harmonization of Measures to Protect the Ozone Layer and Global Climate System', *Gaimushou Chosa Geppou* [Ministry of Foreign Affairs Research Journal], 12: 1–41.

Inomata, T. (2008) 'Management Review of Environmental Governance within the United Nations system', JIU/REP/2008/3.

Inomata, T. and Cazeau, J.W. (2014) 'Post-Rio+20 Review of Environmental Governance within the United Nations System', (Geneva: United Nations Joint Inspection Unit), www.unjiu.org/en/reports-notes/JIU%20Products/JIU_REP_2014_4_English.pdf (accessed 24 May 2015).

Report of the Secretary-General (2000) Protection of the Atmosphere, UN Doc. E.CN.17/2001/2.

Umoja (n.d.), 'About Umoja', www.unumoja.net/display/public/About+Umoja (accessed 2 June 2015).

UN Administrative Committee on Coordination (1991) Addendum to the Annual Overview Report of the Administrative Committee on Coordination, Programme and Resources of the United Nations System, UN Doc. E/1991/42/Add. 1.

UN Administrative Committee on Coordination (1993) Programme and Resources of the United Nations System for the Biennium 1992–1993, UN Doc. E/1993/84.

UN Administrative Committee on Coordination (1995) Programme and Resources of the United Nations System for the Biennium 1994–1995, UN Doc. E/1995/64.

UNEP (2002) 'Cartagena Package on International Environmental Governance', UNEP GC/GMEF decision SS.VII/1 on international environmental governance.

UNGA (1987) Development and International Co-operation; Environment. Report of the World Commission on Environment and Development, Note by the Secretary-General, UN Doc. A/42/427.

UNGA (2005) Report of the Committee for Programme and Coordination, UN Doc. A/60/16.

UN Joint Inspection Unit (2004) 'Implementation of Results-based Management in the United Nations Organizations', UN Doc. JIU/REP/2004/6, www.unjiu.org/en/reports-notes/archive/JIU_REP_2004_6_English.pdf (accessed 24 June 2015).

Urho, N. and Niinistö, V. (2015) 'Future prospects for Enhancing Sustainable Use of Natural Resources: The Role of International Environmental Governance after Rio+20' in Kuokkanen, T., Couzens, E., Honkonen, T. and Lewis, M. (eds) *International Environmental Law-making and Diplomacy: Insights and Overviews*, Routledge, London, 2016: 201–215.

World Commission on Environment and Development (WCED). (1987) *Our Common Future*, Oxford: Oxford University Press.

7 International environmental diplomacy and negotiations

Sylvia Bankobeza, Elizabeth Maruma Mrema and Kilaparti Ramakrishna

Introduction

The world is faced with a diversity of environment-related issues and concerns of wide international significance, which can only be adequately addressed through international cooperation. International environmental diplomacy and negotiations bring together governments and related stakeholders in consultations and intergovernmental processes to address environmental issues at the global, regional and national levels. Many of the current issues that are being negotiated by states at various international environmental meetings, including in multilateral environmental agreements (MEAs) processes, are complex and technical in nature. The number of institutions, the number of meetings being convened, and the amount of documentation involved in international environmental negotiation and diplomacy have also grown over the years, creating a maze of issues and processes, which governments need to be apprised of, and need to be prepared to deliberate on.

This chapter focuses generally on the issue of international environmental diplomacy and negotiations. The chapter begins by providing an overview of what international environmental diplomacy is and how it differs from traditional diplomacy. It then proceeds to consider the systems, processes and mechanisms that are used to organize the work of intergovernmental meetings; to provide advice on the measures that should be taken to prepare and plan for effective participation in international environmental negotiations; to outline some of the common challenges and hindrances to negotiations; and to offer suggestions as to the attributes of a skilled negotiator.

International environmental diplomacy

International environmental diplomacy is the act and practice of conducting negotiations between nations in the field of the environment. Governments, through international environmental diplomacy and cooperation, consult and/or meet to deliberate on various environmental issues of a transboundary, regional or global nature and make decisions on the way forward. International environmental diplomacy is also used to develop standards through treaties and soft law instruments (these being non-legally binding agreements) so as to ensure sustainable development and protect the environment at all levels. International environmental diplomacy takes place in the course of conducting negotiations among countries in conferences and meetings, diplomatic consultations, and inter-state interactions. The practice involves government representatives and related stakeholders (such as civil society organizations and professional bodies), who consider environmental issues through consultations in the process of negotiations. Included in the practice are also the skills of, and roles played by, negotiators when handling and resolving issues diplomatically – that is, courteously and without acrimony.

International environmental diplomacy provides an opportunity for countries to deliberate on emerging issues and measures that can be taken to ensure sustainable use, management and protection of environmental resources at the national level. In recent years, this has included negotiations for the development not only of environmental treaties, but also of implementation mechanisms such as compliance mechanisms, financial mechanisms and technology support. All of these mechanisms provide tangible assistance for the implementation of MEAs to developing countries and countries with economies in transition.

International environmental diplomacy has developed over the years to include features that were not envisaged in traditional diplomacy. The unique features in environmental diplomacy include the diversity of actors, which include business leaders, diplomats, environmental action groups, government officials, journalists, politicians, scientists, and so forth. For instance, the negotiations toward the Kyoto Protocol at the 1997 third Conference of the Parties to the United Nations Framework Convention on Climate Change (UNFCCC) of 1992 were attended by over 10,000 participants, representing 159 states (153 being Parties to the UNFCCC), and including 2,211 states delegates, 282 observer delegates, 237 NGO delegations, 3,844 NGO delegates, 3,635 journalists, 455 media organizations and 400 UNFCCC Secretariat personnel. Another distinct feature of modern international environmental diplomacy is its complexity in terms of the kind of processes, segments, consultations and negotiation groups, the types of documentation, and size of meetings (including meetings within meetings) with which negotiators have to be familiar when navigating through the processes. There is diversity of fora, bilateral diplomacy and multilateral diplomacy. There are also meetings of intergovernmental organizations (IGOs), non-governmental organizations (NGOs) and civil society dialogues (UNEP, 2007a: 26–37).

Systems, processes and mechanisms

Introduction

International environmental meetings, depending on their size and scope, have over the years devised elaborate systems, processes and mechanisms to organize their work. These enhance efficiency and save time. Examples of relevant intergovernmental meetings include United Nations (UN) environmental conferences (for instance, the UN Conference on Sustainable Development (UNCSD) 2012, the

'Rio+20 Conference'), sub-regional and regional environmental conferences, Intergovernmental Negotiating Committee (INC) meetings, and MEA Conferences of the Parties (CoPs) and Meetings of the Parties (MoPs). The CoP/MoPs meet periodically to keep under review the implementation of MEAs or for further negotiations on a treaty. The outcome of these negotiations depends on the purpose of the meeting and the convener/s; and may include the adoption of legally binding or non-binding decisions, a negotiated text, a report, recommendations or an Outcome Document. Negotiations can take place in one setting or be convened in various segments and settings. For instance, negotiations may begin with a meeting of technical officials, who deliberate on all relevant issues, and subsequently progress to a high-level/ministerial segment where decisions are taken.

The format, preparation of agendas and provisional agendas, preparation of scenario notes, and the organization of work depends on the size of the meeting and the convener's practices. For instance, intergovernmental meetings with a global scope organized by the UN tend to have a clear format, with the rules of procedure for specific meetings/conferences guiding the conduct of business in meetings, election of officials, voting procedures, languages of meetings and so on. To manage the process, and depending on the rules of procedure, the Secretariat can convene a bureau meeting, which is normally constituted by several government officials (the Chair of the meeting/conference, Vice-Chairs and a rapporteur, who are selected based on geographical balance), to hold sessions behind the scenes to plan for the meeting, to monitor progress or to provide guidance to the Chair on the conduct of business of the meeting.

Negotiating formats

There are various negotiations formats, depending on the type, size and the organizers of a meeting. For example, in large intergovernmental meetings organized by the UN, there will normally be plenary sessions where general debates take place and decisions are taken. In the same meetings, opportunities are often given – through bloc negotiations – for countries in a particular bloc to converge with like-minded countries to deliberate on their positions, which are then fed to the plenary. The Chair of the plenary plays a very important role by identifying the areas of convergence and divergence, as well as calling for the establishment of different working groups (which may be open or comprise selected countries). Such break-away groups may include, *inter alia*, contact groups, Friends of the Chair consultations, formal and informal consultations, regional group consultations, and like-minded group consultations. A legal group and various drafting groups can be set up to draft clauses and harmonize agreed texts and decisions. These, and other types of groups not mentioned here, are established with defined mandates and limited working time, especially when the plenary cannot address all issues in detail (as a result of limited time) or needs to address unresolved issues in different sections of the agenda items/revised text, or when there is a need to address divergent views of some delegates. The results are normally presented back to the plenary for consideration.

All of the above sessions include multiple actors and have multiple roles intended to feed into the main meeting. Typical composition of delegations has, over the years, evolved to include the participation of government delegates, accredited civil society and major groups' representatives. Depending on the issue and the convener, these stakeholders will be given different opportunities to interact at various levels or segments.

Understanding terms referring to common UN documents

In multilateral environmental negotiations convened under the framework of the United Nations, a negotiator will come across terms that refer to common UN documents. For instance, in-session documents are documents containing new proposals or outcomes of in-session work, which are only used during the sessions concerned. Examples include conference room papers (CRPs) and limited/draft distribution documents (L docs), which may include draft decisions (documents prepared at the pre-session or in-session stage of the meeting, and which may become final decisions if the meeting's delegates so decide). Informal documents include a working paper and a non-paper. A working paper is more substantive and less ephemeral than a CRP and less specific to a particular delegation than a non-paper. The distribution of this paper is normally limited to participants in the conference. On the other hand, a non-paper is an informal text that is distributed to facilitate the process of negotiating an agreement. It is not a formal proposal, nor does it engage its author in multilateral environmental negotiations.

Other types of documents that a negotiator might come across during multilateral environmental negotiations meetings include a draft negotiation text, which is the main document being negotiated. A chair's summary is a draft text introduced by the presiding officer in an attempt to help the conference towards agreement; it can include some words or text in square brackets, indicating that the issues to which they relate are for later resolution. A chairman's draft is often an attempt at a final text that might secure consensus; it is a proposal prepared by the presiding officer of a meeting to assist in reaching consensus. A compilation text is a chairman's compilation, which puts together a number of competing proposals submitted by delegates; it is a text that lays out proposals made by delegations. An Outcome Document includes decisions, a set of recommendations or a plan of action adopted at major UN conferences and international agreements meetings. A Declaration, which is not normally binding, is a formal statement of aspirations issued by a meeting.

In recent years, the distribution of conference documents has been facilitated by the internet. Pre-session, in-session and post-session documents can be uploaded for delegates' online access, allowing negotiations to be 'paper smart' and environmentally friendly.

Managing synergies among instruments and processes

There is today such a proliferation of international environmental agreements that the University of Oregon's Database Project lists nearly 3,000 of these

(Couzens *et al.*, chapter 1 in this volume: 3). Even within conventions themselves it is sometimes the case that there are multiple negotiation tracks and splinter consultations, as outlined in the present chapter. It is becoming increasingly necessary in the face of this increasing complexity for an international environmental negotiator to understand how numerous other, related conventions and issues might affect the negotiating positions of his/her own delegation and those of other Parties.

Given the large number of MEAs and the sheer number of meetings, working groups, etc. under each of them, negotiators and delegates are increasingly addressing this complexity by clustering and synergizing agreements. When MEAs have related or even partly overlapping mandates, clustering them into one group for the purposes of enhancing cooperation can bring many benefits, including savings in time and in human, financial and environmental resources through realized synergies. The clustered MEAs may also develop entirely new modes of cooperation. A prime example of MEA clustering is the chemicals and hazardous wastes cluster, which includes the Basel Convention on the Control of Transboundary Movements of Hazardous Wastes and Their Disposal, the Stockholm Convention on Persistent Organic Pollutants and the Rotterdam Convention on Prior Informed Consent. These three MEAs have carefully institutionalized their cooperation and coordination on an administrative as well as operational level. The synergistic functions within the chemicals and hazardous wastes cluster include, among others, back-to-back meetings, financial management and resource mobilization, combating illegal traffic and trade in hazardous chemicals and wastes and technology transfer and transfer of know-how (see, for instance, Stendahl, 2008).

In developing a new instrument or deliberating on MEAs, it is important for a negotiator to have a clear understanding of the agreements that relate to each other, in terms of understanding the similarities between such agreements, the links in their mandates, and cross-cutting areas. Such an understanding is necessary when considering the need for MEAs within a particular cluster to cooperate and coordinate some of their work, and enables a negotiator to manage the complexity, inter-linkages and synergies among various instruments and processes.

To obtain a clear perspective, one can perform an analysis of the MEAs within the relevant cluster, focusing on their similarities, links, cross-cutting areas, areas of cooperation, joint working arrangements (if any), and coordination efforts. This information can also be important when determining the appropriate international response to a particular issue, as the best way to proceed might not always be by developing a new legal instrument.

Framework for effective negotiations

The framework conditions needed for effective negotiations to take place include clear rules of procedures; and negotiators/Parties who are willing to participate, ready to negotiate, and who have the necessary resources to negotiate. Desirable framework conditions also include experienced Chairs, who are skilled in the art of conducting negotiations; and negotiation blocs that can produce articulate, coherent and effective group positions. In addition, it is important that there be a sense of urgency in the process and deadlines be adhered to as the negotiations proceed. All negotiators also ought to have the ability and willingness to consult, bargain and compromise, and have a means of influence and leverage. The latter is most likely to be present when there is a level playing field between the negotiators in interacting and consulting continuously and when the Parties accept the moral authority of the Chair.

Preparing and planning for negotiations

Selecting delegations

A negotiation team should be identified and mobilized well in advance for negotiators to have sufficient time to become familiar with the agenda items and issues, and to brief other government policy-makers on important issues. In composing a country's delegation (and depending on the subject of the meeting), it is important to consider the mixture of talents and skills needed: technical/scientific, diplomatic, and legal.

If a delegation has more than one delegate, the head of delegation should be identified. The advantage of having a large delegation is to have greater human capital to attend parallel sessions. However, when the delegation is small, with few delegates, one delegate can 'wear many hats'. In such situations, some small delegations rely on regional groups and/or coalitions for their representation in parallel sessions.

In selecting delegations, continuity is critical for ongoing negotiation processes. This can be secured by having focal points/desk officers, if appropriate, to attend these sessions. However, this consideration of having the same person attend particular meetings has to be balanced with the ongoing need to train and empower new negotiators by exposing them to the negotiation process (UNEP, 2007b: 20–21).

National coordination

In view of the technicalities involved in, and the cross-cutting nature of, environmental issues, the preparation of negotiations requires prior cross-sectoral consultations and a variety of expertise among the negotiators. Prior to negotiations, it is important for government delegates to arrange for inter-ministerial coordination or a national stakeholder consultation. Such coordination/consultation enables the government position to take into account the role of other ministries and other relevant stakeholders (such as non-governmental organizations, industry, and so forth) in the area that is being negotiated. There may be coordination challenges (either vertical or horizontal) that need to be managed when handling issues that cut across the work and mandate of different government departments. Institutional, legislative and administrative conflicts may also need to be addressed where these arise. Issues may arise concerning the role of the environment ministry versus other ministries in managing aspects of the environment. For example, with regard to an issue such as biosafety, the MEA focal point of the Convention on Biological Diversity of 1992 (CBD) at the national level, who follows up on MEA meetings, is normally based in the ministry responsible for the environment, while biosafety experts may be based in the ministry of agriculture. Consequently, the issue may arise as to who will take the lead in biosafety related meetings. Issues may also be raised regarding policy-making versus implementing agencies: which department/ministry should be assigned the lead agency role with regard to a particular environmental issue.

Preparing for effective participation

In preparing for negotiations, a negotiator needs to understand his/her position, objectives, interests, strategy, bottom line (in terms of how far he/she can go to accommodate other negotiators' proposals on particular issues in the agenda), options and ambitions, as well as whether he/she has any alternatives. The negotiator also needs to understand his/her relationship with others, whether he/she will play a dominant role, and how to interact with negotiators from like-minded or opponent countries. It is important to have a good understanding of the national interest and position on the issues under negotiation, and those of other delegations or groups. This includes being able to identify the most significant agenda items of priority interest to the negotiator's country and to focus closely on these.

For a national delegation or delegate to prepare itself or oneself effectively for upcoming negotiations, the identified or composed delegations need to know, meet and consult with national colleagues who participated in the previous negotiating meetings or conferences. This is especially the case where the national delegation has a new team or individual but is participating in an ongoing negotiation process. National reports prepared after participation in previous conferences should be reviewed in order for delegates to acquaint themselves with, *inter alia*, the nature of the debate, the issues that were particularly significant and/or controversial at previous negotiations (and the reasons for such significance/controversy), different national and regional or block positions on various agenda items, their own national positions in past meetings, whether these positions were accepted or not, and the reasons for either outcome. Such information should enable the team to be consistent in their position and, if they intend to modify or change their position after further reflections at home, to ensure that they are cautious and strategic and do not embarrass their country during the negotiations.

In the event that there are still open texts, information as to which delegations supported which particular language or phrasing at the last or previous negotiations will be important for the national delegation to be aware of. It is crucial to be apprised ahead of the negotiations as to which countries shared the national delegation's position or views, and to be able to continue to ally and consult with these.

In view of the ever-increasing numbers of issues, and the corresponding increases in numbers of states and negotiators in multilateral negotiations, coalitions continue to emerge in response to the issues of the time. National delegations must be able to identify which of the many and overlapping coalitions they fit into in terms of membership – and how to utilize those groupings to fulfil their objectives. Negotiating groups may be formed on several bases. There are power-based groups and coalitions, including the Umbrella Group JUSCANNZ (developed, non-EU states); the European Union (currently 28 Member States forming an 'institutionalized' group); the G-77 and China, which currently has 134 members; and the Least Developed Counties (LDC) Group, which has 48 members. Some groups are clearly interest-based, such as the Small Island Developing States/Alliance of Small Island States (SIDS/AOSIS) group, and like-minded groups (for instance, the Like-minded Megadiverse Countries (LMMC)). In addition, there are UN regional groupings: the African Group; the Western Europe and Others Group (WEOG, including the EU, United States, New Zealand, Canada and Australia); the Latin American and Caribbean Group (GRULAC); the Eastern European Group (EEG, or Countries with Economies in Transition); and the Asia Pacific Group (formerly the Asian Group) (see UNEP, 2007b: 23–29).

In a particular meeting, it is possible for a country to associate with more than one group, depending on the issue at hand. A national delegation needs to identify its coalitions and use these platforms to sell some of their country positions. Members of the delegation must participate in all of the bloc and coalition meetings in order to ensure that their country's position is represented appropriately. In the event that the delegation is a member of more than one coalition, it will also need to ensure that there are no inconsistencies between the positions taken by different coalition groups. During negotiations, a negotiator must avoid contradicting statements made by the representative of a coalition to which he/she belongs because these statements are made on his/her behalf. A negotiator is expected to use his/her intervention to support statements made by the coalition spokesperson; to elaborate upon that statement or present additional arguments; and to explain why the issue is of particular concern to his/her delegation.

Many times during negotiations, specific issues may be referred for further deliberation and compromise to a smaller contact group, informal working group, or Friends of the Chair group, etc. In such a situation, the delegation needs to ensure that there is somebody (either a spokesperson from their own delegation or a specific coalition spokesperson) to represent their interests in such smaller negotiating groups. After all, it is in such smaller groups that issues are often digested, discussed and agreed upon for formal presentation and adoption by the negotiation conference. Delegations need equally to know where and when such groups will meet to ensure that their concerns are well represented; and thus to be able to influence the eventual outcomes of such issues in the negotiations.

Nature of the negotiations and expected outcomes

Before attending an intergovernmental meeting, the national delegation needs to know the nature of the negotiation they are preparing to attend, as such knowledge will have an impact on the nature of the national preparations they will need to undertake while still at home. It might be, for instance, that the negotiation is an MEA CoP or MoP; or it might be a meeting of the Subsidiary Bodies/Committees of an MEA; or it might be an Ad Hoc Open-ended Working Group or an Expert Workshop. Furthermore, the national delegation needs to know where the session fits within, for example, the MEA's institutional structure (for instance, the CBD's CoP meets every two years, and its Subsidiary Body on Scientific, Technical and Technological Advice meets twice or thrice between CoPs). To participate effectively in the negotiations and present the national position or proposal optimally, the delegation should have a good understanding of the rules of procedure and be able to use them effectively for its purpose. It needs to understand how the decisions at a particular negotiation are taken in order to be able to lobby and to gauge adequate support for its proposals, or for the proposals of others which it seconds, associates itself with or supports. For instance, decisions might be required to be taken by consensus (as is the case in CBD CoPs), by a two-thirds majority (as in CoPs of the Convention on International Trade in Endangered Species of Wild Fauna and Flora of 1973); by a three-fourths majority (for instance, in the International Whaling Commission, a 75 per cent majority vote is needed in order to amend the Schedule to the International Convention for the Regulation of Whaling (ICRW) of 1946); or by a double majority (for instance, the European Union has introduced a system of voting where both a majority of Member States and a majority of the population of the Union may be required).

National delegations should additionally understand the expected outcomes of the negotiations. For instance, the outcome might be expected to be in the nature of conclusions, or recommendations, or resolutions, or decisions. If the meeting is likely to adopt more than one outcome, then the difference in content of those outcomes needs to be known in advance so as to ensure that interventions and proposals are made that are conducive toward the appropriate outcome. In cases where there are undecided issues or elements from the previous negotiation meeting, the delegation needs to know about these – especially in situations where they had proposals still to be debated upon, and thus need to be ready to follow these to their logical conclusions.

Understanding the role and effect of language used in negotiations

It is important to understand the basic language of negotiations, as a negotiator must choose his/her words carefully in the course of making interventions or participating in various groups, including drafting groups. Negotiators can spend hours arguing about words in a negotiated text. Words such as 'affirms', 'agrees', 'calls', 'considers', 'endeavours', 'endorses', 'guided', 'notes', 'permits', 'prohibits', 'pursuit', 'recalls', 'recognizes', 'recommends', 'requests', 'requires', 'takes note of', and 'urges' have different meanings.

It is important to note that a slight change in a verb or tense can make an enormous difference in the kind of commitment that a country makes. For instance, a word such as 'may' is permissive and discretionary, and creates no obligation for a country to carry out an action. In contrast, use of the word 'must' renders the provision peremptory, with the result that a country is required to take an action. 'Must' is almost always legally binding. 'Shall' means that an action is required, and will be binding, unless used with another word that weakens its strength. For instance, Article 15(2) of the CBD provides that '[e]ach Contracting Party *shall endeavour* to create conditions to facilitate access to genetic resources for environmentally sound uses by other Contracting Parties and not to impose restrictions that run counter to the objectives of [the] Convention' [emphasis added]. 'Should' means that an action is not required, but is advised. For instance, Article II(2) of the 1995 Agreement on the Conservation of African-Eurasian Migratory Waterbirds (AEWA), developed under the framework of the 1979 Convention on Migratory Species, reads: '[i]n implementing the measures prescribed in paragraph 1 above, Parties *should* take into account the precautionary principle' [emphasis added].

It should be understood that there may be considerable overlap between binding and non-binding terms. An obligation such as that in Article 15(2) of the CBD might use the mandatory word 'shall' and constitute a legally binding obligation; but where the obligation created is that Parties shall 'endeavour', then the content of the obligation is watered down. This may be useful to a negotiator, of course, and enable him/her to bring aboard a Party that might otherwise have refused to commit to the text.

The importance of mechanisms for resolving conflict

It should be understood that international environmental law is not a sub-field of international law with a very lengthy history. The earliest multilateral environmental conventions resembling their current form date only from some 130 years ago (see Couzens and Lewis, chapter 8 in this volume: 97–126). In this span of time it is already possible to see that new understandings of international environmental law, and of the diplomacy required to create such effective law, have moved through several phases. For instance, when the 15 original Parties to the ICRW negotiated and adopted the Convention in 1946, they were all apparently of much the same mind as to their reasons for doing so and what they hoped to achieve. As such, they envisaged that any conflict arising *inter se* might easily be resolved, and so did not include in the Convention provision for a means of resolving disputes. Today the Convention is in many ways a byword for conflict, but lacks effective means for resolving such conflict. More modern conventions instead make provisions for both the settlement of disputes and the assessment and facilitation of compliance.

This is merely one example. The modern negotiator needs to understand the importance of including such a mechanism, what different forms such a mechanism might take, and how other negotiators might be persuaded to agree to an effective means of resolving conflict. Beyond that, even, the modern negotiator needs to understand how such a mechanism can be included as part of a broader compliance regime, so that the mechanism will hopefully not need to be employed as Parties falling out of compliance might be brought back into compliance without the need for formal dispute resolution.

General challenges and hindrances to negotiations

Delegation-specific challenges

Insufficient or deficient expertise regarding the substance, process, and institutional dimensions of the issue under negotiation is the main challenge for effective negotiations. Other delegation-specific challenges can include last-minute decisions on the composition of delegations (resulting in inadequate time for preparation and national consultation); unclear negotiating instructions from national capitals; and lack of political support therein. Undue influence by other government delegations and specific national interest groups sometimes introduces additional challenges for negotiators.

Many developing countries receive support to attend major multilateral environmental negotiation meetings and can only afford to send one representative, who cannot divide himself/herself during complex negotiations that are organized in parallel sessions and various breakaway groups. When these small delegations are given an opportunity, for instance, to preside over a session, steer a group, or serve as a Chair of a meeting, they may end up losing the opportunity to participate as effective representatives of their countries.

Procedure-specific challenges

Inability to reach agreement on important rules of procedure, or having long debates regarding procedure, which overwhelm the substantive negotiations, are the main challenges relating to procedures in multilateral environmental negotiations. A negotiator can also be challenged by his/her failure to appreciate the relevant rules of procedure. Most negotiators are technical experts in the field who, although understanding the substantive issues being discussed and articulating their interventions skilfully, may nevertheless lack understanding regarding the rules of procedure. When, in the course of representing his/her country, a negotiator fails to present his/her point in accordance with the rules of procedure (for instance, if a negotiator attempts to make an intervention on an agenda item that has already been decided according to the rules of procedure), this can result in the point being rejected.

Challenges specific to the negotiations bloc

Despite the advantages of negotiating coalitions, there are challenges or disadvantages that are unique to the group dynamic. There are various types of negotiation blocs: some are large (such as the G77 and China, which represents over one hundred countries), while others are small. Negotiation blocs that are too large to ensure meaningful and coherent group positions are the main challenge in this category. These large groups have sub-groups within them, which may have different interests and differing levels of development and thus present a challenge when attempting to filter the positions/views of each country and group into the negotiation bloc's position. Other challenges include a polarized negotiating climate within and between blocs, which can hinder progress in building consensus at the plenary. Undue influence by certain actors, who dominate the discussion at the expense of other negotiators, is another challenge, as is inefficient decision-making machinery within a bloc.

Problems inherent in the plenary/contact process

The main challenge in the plenary or contact group process arises when options are not well articulated so as to assist in brokering compromise and facilitating bargaining. It is also problematic when certain Parties exercise excessive political influence or leverage instead of focusing on the resolution of pending issues. Other factors that may hinder progress during negotiations include the lack of a sense of urgency and deadlines, the lack of political will to settle the tough issues in the eleventh hour, and psychological barriers to final settlement.

Problems with the Secretariat

Secretariats are expected to service the meeting and support the negotiations, without exerting inappropriate political influence by imposing their views on the deliberations or outcome of the meeting. It is the Secretariat's role to ensure that relevant documents are prepared for discussion and decisions by the intergovernmental body; to provide guidance on the format and content of, and political sensitivities regarding, documents; and to monitor their timeliness and ensure their availability and accessibility. The Secretariat is further expected to provide participants with guidance regarding rules of procedure and practices that govern intergovernmental negotiations; to prepare briefing notes and speaking notes (scripts) for the Chair/President; and, where possible, to consult with the Chair/President in advance of the meeting so as to explain matters to watch out for (which may not be reflected in any formal document) and provide a background to any particular negotiation. A Secretariat's failure to prepare adequate groundwork for negotiations or to monitor the process will present a serious hurdle to a conference's success.

Attributes of a good negotiator

Negotiation skill and experience are arguably under-acknowledged as essential components of the world's efforts to build an effective international environmental governance framework. Being a good negotiator is a skill that does not necessarily come from specific training, but is more likely honed over time with practice and experience. A good negotiator is one who is well-prepared, shows patience, listens, and controls his/her emotions. He/she is able to break bigger, more difficult issues down into smaller, more manageable ones, focusing on interest-based decisions while rejecting weak solutions that make it difficult to achieve necessary agreements or compromises. Good language skills and strong analytical skills are needed.

A negotiator needs to have a clear understanding of his/her country's interests and positions and knowledge of prior negotiations and their outcomes. Knowing the positions of other states and coalitions gives a good negotiator an edge across coalition divides and gives him/her an added advantage in negotiating (UNEP, 2007b: 41–43).

The good negotiator needs to be both respectful and diplomatic when presenting positions or when commenting on another delegation's position. He/she will have the ability to build a package as an outcome of the negotiation discussions; which may have been antagonistic, have gone off topic, or have revealed fundamental differences of interpretation or understanding (to mention but a few factors that would make resolution difficult). In other words, the skilled negotiator will be able to define the problem, find implementation options and be flexible in dealing with them during the discussion.

Conclusion

It can be argued that effective international environmental governance is imperative if the world is to achieve the goals of environmental protection, intra- and intergenerational equity, and sustainable development – goals with which few would argue. It can further be stipulated that a realistic foundation for an effective international environmental governance regime is one that rests on a bedrock of solid textual drafting; in other words, treaty texts that have been adopted in a consensual spirit, are inclusive of a wide range of interests, are responsive to all major concerns, are unambiguous (although sometimes the only way of reaching an agreement is to allow for some 'constructive ambiguity', unambiguous text still narrows the scope for confusion), and are widely agreed upon. It can only be conducive to treaty texts as described becoming the norm, rather than being the exception, if negotiation skills worldwide improve.

International environmental diplomacy continues to grow to include features that were not initially anticipated in international diplomacy. In recent years, negotiations at various environment-related conferences and meetings have become increasingly complex, as they include economic, financial, legal, technical and technological-related issues. The growing list of agencies that are designated as financial mechanisms, for example, are bringing relatively new players, including banks, into the negotiation processes. In addition, apart from normal sessions, the work of inter-sessional meetings such as the implementation committees, Open-ended Ad Hoc Working Groups of MEAs, Scientific and Technical bodies and the activities of international organizations have increased the opportunities for governments and related stakeholders to negotiate. All of these meetings call for a multi-disciplinary set of negotiators, with competence in both legal and technical skills, who are conversant with the substantive and procedural issues at hand.

To be effective and confident in negotiations, a negotiator is expected to have the knowledge and skills for negotiations and to be on top of the issues at hand when negotiating in the field of the environment. The information provided in this chapter should enable a negotiator better to appreciate his/her role and to understand the organization of work and formats of meetings that take place in the course of negotiations.

References

Stendahl, K. (2008) 'Enhancing Cooperation and Coordination among the Basel, Rotterdam and Stockholm Conventions' in Kolari, T. and Couzens, E. (eds) *International Environmental Law-making and Diplomacy Review 2007*, UEF-UNEP Course Series 7, University of Eastern Finland, Joensuu, 127–141.

UNEP (2007a), *Compliance Mechanisms under Selected Multilateral Environmental Agreements*, www.unep.org/pdf/delc/Compliance_Mechanism_final.pdf (accessed 24 May 2015).

UNEP (2007b) *Guide for Negotiators of Multilateral Environmental Agreements*, www.unep.org/pdf/delc/Guide_for_MEAs_final.pdf (accessed 24 May 2015).

8 Learning from the past

A reflection on the roles of people and problems in the development of international environmental law

Ed Couzens and Melissa Lewis[1]

International environmental law

It is not easy to pinpoint when and where international environmental law began as a core field of its own. It is possible to look back at historical events – and occasionally curiosities – and label them examples of international environmental law, but they would not at the time have been understood as we understand environmental law today.

Examples of early multilateral environmental agreements can be seen from the late nineteenth century. In 1881 and 1889, for instance, international conventions were agreed concerning measures to be taken against *Phylloxera vastatrix* (Conventions *Phylloxera*, 1881, 1889). This root louse is native to Mississippi in the United States. So small as to be almost impossible to detect, in the twenty years from 1865, the species (which feeds on vine roots and leaves) devastated 70 percent of European vineyards. From such early beginnings, international environmental law today comprises detailed regimes covering a broad range of environmental issues. These regimes develop and emanate from treaties, general principles, judicial decisions and custom.

Multilateral environmental agreements are the source of most international environmental law. This does of course have its own inherent problems. The difficulty of achieving a firm commitment to change from large gatherings of states can be seen in one of the most important Principles in the Stockholm Declaration, in which acknowledgement is made of state sovereignty. Principle 21 states that:

> [s]tates have, in accordance with the Charter of the United Nations and the principles of international law, the sovereign right to exploit their own resources pursuant to their own environmental policies, and the responsibility to ensure that activities within their jurisdiction or control do not cause damage to the environment of other States or of areas beyond the limits of national jurisdiction.
>
> (Stockholm Declaration, 1972)

---

1 Considerable appreciation must be extended to Marko Berglund, Tuula Honkonen and Tuomas Kuokkanen for their advice and valuable comments on this chapter.

While Principle 21 has been repeated verbatim in so many subsequent international instruments that it is generally considered to represent firm customary law, it may have achieved this status more for its non-environmental aspect – in other words, it might be the aspect of entrenching sovereign rights that makes states feel secure enough to accept it. Principle 21 can be seen as an attempt to accommodate the interests of individual states – after the decolonization of many African states in the 1960s, sovereignty was a concept guarded especially jealously by the newly independent states – while at the same time attempting to entrench as binding a commitment to environmental protection as possible. Without 'escape clauses' similar to that which Principle 21 provides, it becomes far more difficult to persuade states to relinquish any sovereignty.

With no easy route to a court akin to a national court, states faced with environmental disputes sometimes have agreed to put matters to arbitration. Although binding only on the states parties to, and in the context of, the respective disputes, certain of these arbitral decisions have come to be recognized as authoritative and influential. An important arbitration, the *Lac Lanoux Arbitration*, took place in 1957 (*Affaire du Lac Lanoux Arbitration*, 1957). France had within its own territory diverted a watercourse, thereby affecting Spain. The arbitral tribunal confirmed as a principle of customary international law that states are required to cooperate with each other in order to mitigate transboundary environmental risks. The tribunal held that France had indeed complied with its obligations – in terms of treaty and customary law – to negotiate with Spain, in good faith, before diverting the watercourse. However, the tribunal noted that France's obligation extended to informing and consulting with Spain in regard to the proposed diversion, and that Spain did not have a right to prevent France from going ahead with the project. Arguably, the *Lac Lanoux* principles have been extended to the management of other transboundary risks. In other words, prior notification and consultation are called for when states perform acts of a hazardous or potentially harmful nature.

Custom is of course an important source of international law. An important attempt at the codification of customary international law came in 1982 with the adoption of the United Nations Convention on the Law of the Sea (UNCLOS). The Convention built upon previous conventions and itself took nearly a decade of negotiation before adoption, eventually entering into force in 1994. The Convention contains comprehensive provisions on the marine environment. A significant step, which arguably even went beyond what was then considered to have been customary international law, is taken, for example, in Article 206 of the Convention, which reads:

> [w]hen States have reasonable grounds for believing that planned activities under their jurisdiction or control may cause substantial pollution of or significant and harmful changes to the marine environment, they shall, as far as practicable, assess the potential effects of such activities on the marine environment and shall communicate reports of the results of such assessments in the manner provided in article 205.
>
> (UNCLOS, 1982)

It is important to note the precautionary element of the phrase: '*may* cause substantial pollution'. The article effectively requires that states undertake assessments before carrying out planned activities, even without substantive proof that the proposed activities *will* cause substantial damage. Interestingly, in 2010, the International Court of Justice (ICJ) held that the practice of undertaking an environmental impact assessment 'where there is a risk that a proposed industrial activity may have a significant adverse impact in a transboundary context, in particular, on a shared resource' has gained so much acceptance among states that it may now be considered a requirement under general international law (*Case Concerning Pulp Mills*, 2010: para. 204). The Court also concluded, however, that general international law fails to specify the scope and content of such assessment (*ibid.*: para. 205), and so there is still work to be done.

In many cases, international environmental law takes the form of statements of intent, declarations, guidelines or principles. In other words so-called 'soft law', which does not impose binding obligations on states. It is important to understand, though, that there is considerable overlap between 'hard' and 'soft' law. Often, a convention will contain a firm obligation (requiring, for instance, that its Parties 'shall' do something), but the action to be taken remains 'soft' in nature – for instance, that 'Parties shall endeavour to...'. The hope of the international environmental lawyer or analyst must be that over time, as principles are repeated in conventions and other international instruments, this soft law will 'harden' and environmental principles come to be seen as hard, binding customary law.

This chapter provides an overview of the history of international environmental law and, in so doing, considers some of the ways in which people working as individuals or in small groups, or playing individual roles in driving governments and international negotiations, and the process of learning from environmental disasters, have had an effect on the development of international environmental law through its various sources. Environmental problems, or even disasters, are obviously not a formal source of international law; but it is noteworthy that often a disaster or the arising of a significant problem seems to be a *sine qua non* before action is taken.

The role of intergovernmental organizations and non-governmental organizations (NGOs)

The period between the two World Wars was not marked by great concern for the environment, but it is important for the founding of a number of bodies that were later to have significant environmental influence. In 1922, for example, the International Committee for Bird Protection was founded in England; it later became the International Council for Bird Preservation. Eventually, in the 1990s, the organization transformed into Birdlife International – a 'global conservation federation with a worldwide network of partner organizations' (www.birdlife.org). In 1929, the Dutch Government funded the establishment of an International Office for Documentation for the Protection of Nature (IOPN). This was subsequently restructured in 1948, under the wing of UNESCO, as the International Union for the Protection of Nature (IUPN). In 1956, the organization became the International Union for Conservation of Nature and Natural Resources: the IUCN. From 1990, the name World Conservation Union has been used, although the organization is still probably better known as the IUCN. The World Conservation Union is, according to its own website, the world's largest and most important conservation network. The Union comprises more than 1,200 member organizations, including over 200 governmental and over 900 non-governmental organizations; and nearly 11,000 voluntary scientists and experts, in about 160 countries in a worldwide partnership (www.iucn.org). The Union's mission is 'to influence, encourage and assist societies throughout the world to conserve the integrity and diversity of nature and to ensure that any use of natural resources is equitable and ecologically sustainable' (*ibid.*). These two entities, Birdlife International and the IUCN, show how individuals responding to perceived problems can create organizations that ultimately become extremely influential in educating, raising awareness and even driving policy directions. More than 60 per cent of the IUCN's funding comes from governments.

In 1945 the United Nations (UN) was established, followed by the Food and Agriculture Organization (FAO) and the United Nations Educational, Scientific and Cultural Organization (UNESCO). The significance of these organizations for the history of international environmental law can obviously not be overstated. It is from the UN that the vast majority of multilateral environmental agreements currently in force derive their authority, and within the ambit of which the future of such agreements is likely to be decided. Despite ongoing problems of authority, legitimacy and credibility, the UN remains the world's leading intergovernmental and norm-determining body. If one chooses to see the Conferences and Meetings of Parties (CoPs and MoPs) to multilateral environmental agreements as examples of the work of *de facto* organizations, then the role of the UN becomes even greater.

An important non-governmental organization was created in 1961: the World Wildlife Fund (WWF), today called the Worldwide Fund for Nature. This organization works closely with the IUCN and is involved in raising money and campaigning for the protection of wildlife in many countries (www.worldwildlife.org). In 1970, a small group of environmental activists (including people like Jim and Marie Bohlen, Paul Cote, Robert Hunter, David McTaggart, Ben and Dorothy Metcalfe, Dorothy and Irving Stowe, Paul Watson, and others) in Canada formed and/or worked with an NGO called Greenpeace International (www.greenpeace.org). In 1971 they began a campaign of courageous but non-violent activism in protest against United States' nuclear testing north of Alaska. In 1973 this was expanded to protest against French nuclear testing in the South Pacific. Greenpeace is today the most visible and well-known of environmental protest groups and provides an important example of how the actions of individuals coordinating themselves into a group can influence environmental change.

Pressure from ornithological groups culminated in 1971 with the adoption of the Ramsar Convention on Wetlands of International Importance especially as Waterfowl Habitat. Non-governmental groups were prominent in the process. The Netherlands and the USSR backed the Convention strongly, as did groups such as the ICBP and the IWRB, now called Wetlands International (www.ramsar.org; Matthews, 2013). Over the years, the Convention's focus has shifted away from waterfowl protection to recognize the numerous other values of wetlands, including their socio-economic importance. As highlighted by Bowman *et al.*, one of the reasons behind this shift was to attract accessions from developing countries (Bowman *et al.*, 2010: 409). This approach appears to have been successful, as the Convention's membership has gradually grown to include 168 Parties from all regions of the world (www.ramsar.org). A strong working relationship has been retained with NGOs such as BirdLife International, Wetlands International, the IUCN and WWF (see, for instance, Ramsar Memorandum 2011–2017), and the Convention thus provides a good example of how MEAs may benefit from the participation of such organizations. The Convention's history also illustrates the need for MEAs to be supported by adequate institutional arrangements. The Ramsar Convention's original text failed to provide for these, and thus required amendment (see Bowman *et al.*, 2010; Bowman, 1995).

The Ramsar Convention was one of a cluster of international conventions, agreements and declarations on the environment that saw the light of day in the early 1970s, and it remains a central international conservation convention. One of the most important early instruments was the Stockholm Declaration agreed at the 1972 United Nations Conference on the Human Environment (UNCHE). The Conference itself was, at the time, the largest ever gathering of heads of state. The Declaration consisted of key environmental principles: the idea that 'man bears a solemn responsibility to protect and improve the environment for present and future generations' can be found in Principle 1. The Conference (chaired by Maurice Strong, who played an active role in international environmental treaties over three decades) also resulted in the founding of the United Nations Environment Programme (UNEP). Non-governmental organizations played an unprecedented role in the creation of UNEP in December 1972.

The early 1970s also saw the Convention concerning the Protection of the World Cultural and Natural Heritage, which was driven by UNESCO (World Heritage Convention, 1972). At the time of writing, 1,007 sites (779 cultural, 197 natural and 31 mixed) have been inscribed on the World Heritage List – there are 161 Parties (whc.unesco.org). Unlike the Ramsar Convention, which requires states Parties to designate their own sites, the World Heritage Convention has a World Heritage Committee, which approves ('inscribes') nominated sites.

Sovereignty and environmental thought

A significant treaty was adopted in 1959 and a regime ultimately created: the Antarctic Treaty and the Antarctic Treaty System. A number of states had made claims to the area based on discovery, contiguity or significance. The treaty froze all these claims, however. The subsequent Protocol on Environmental Protection to the Antarctic Treaty, 1991, designated Antarctica as a natural reserve (Art. 2) and provides (in Art. 7) that '[a]ny activity relating to mineral resources, other than scientific research, shall be prohibited' and (Art. 25) that the operation of the Protocol cannot be reviewed until 50 years after date of entry into force. Although dated – it would be extremely unusual to find a more modern treaty requiring unanimity of states Parties – the Antarctic Treaty shows how states can, if they so desire, form an agreement that benefits the environment and states generally, rather than the individual state itself – and also how a Protocol can be used to shift the objective of a parent treaty toward greater environmental protection.

Academic writers have their part to play. In 1968 an extremely influential article, 'The Tragedy of the Commons', was published by Garrett Hardin in the journal *Science* (Hardin, 1968). Hardin postulated a commons on which tribesmen grazed livestock at no cost to themselves. For each tribesman there would always be an incentive to add animals as they could also graze on the common area. If only one tribesman did this, carrying capacity would not be exceeded. If many did, however, then the commons might collapse as a resource that was able to support all. As a metaphor for unsustainable use of the environment, the article has resonated in much future thinking. In 1972, Christopher Stone published an article entitled 'Should trees have standing?'. In one of the seminal articles in environmental legal thinking, Stone argued that the history and process of law has been the gradual extension of legal rights to entities to whom it was at one time unthinkable that such rights should be granted. These include slaves, children or women, for example. Might it not be, he argued, that at some future time people will look back on today and claim that it was unthinkable that the environment – forests and trees even – should *not* have been given legal rights? Four decades later, Stone's projections do not seem as outlandish as they may have when initially published. Indeed, in 2008, Ecuador became the first country to provide for 'rights of nature' in its Constitution, providing that: 'Nature or Pachamama, where life is reproduced and exists, has the right to exist, persist, maintain and regenerate its vital cycles, structure, functions and its processes in evolution' (Constitution of the Republic of Ecuador, 2008: Chapter 7, Art. 71).

The 1972 Stockholm Conference (UNCHE) saw agreement on the founding of the United Nations Environment Programme (UNEP), the only United Nations programme based in a developing country and the only dedicated environmental programme.

The 1987 release of 'Our Common Future' (WCED, 1987), the Report of the World Commission on Environment and Development, is significant for introducing formally into international environmental discourse the phrase 'sustainable development'. The Report, adopted by the General Assembly in 1987, provided a significant stepping stone for future conventions and laid the foundation for the convening of the 1992 United Nations Conference on Environment and Development. Often known as the 'Brundtland Report', after its Chair Gro Harlem Brundtland who has played a role in many environmental conferences over four decades, the Report suggested that:

> sustainable development, which implies meeting the needs of the present without compromising the ability of future generations to meet their own

> needs, should become a central guiding principle of the United Nations, Governments and private institutions, organizations and enterprises.
>
> (Preamble)

In 1992, the United Nations Conference on Environment and Development (UNCED), or Rio Summit, was held. This was, at the time, the largest ever gathering of world leaders and non-governmental organizations and led to the adoption of a number of important instruments – including three conventions. The Rio Declaration on Environment and Development (Rio Declaration, 1992) and the global blueprint for sustainable development, 'Agenda 21', were adopted; and the Commission on Sustainable Development (CSD) was established (in 2012 it was decided that this would be replaced by a high-level political forum). Despite setbacks, such as the reluctance of the United States to commit to the Convention on Biological Diversity, which is an example of ongoing North–South division in the environmental field, the Conference sought not merely to issue non-binding principles, but to provide world states with a convincing agenda for sustainable development, in order that real progress might be made.

In 1993, a seven-member Chamber of the International Court of Justice (ICJ) with a remit to deal with environmental issues was established. Unfortunately, in the next 13 years no state requested that an environmental matter be heard and, in 2006, the ICJ chose not to elect a Bench for the Chamber – effectively discontinuing it. Although the special chamber was never seized of an environmental matter, a few have been heard by the ICJ. In the *Gabčíkovo-Nagymaros Case (Hungary/Slovakia)*, for example, heard by the 15 judges presiding in plenum (*Gabčíkovo-Nagymaros* case, 1997), the Court found that Hungary had been wrong to withdraw from a joint project but that Slovakia had been wrong in proceeding in any case to complete the project against Hungary's wishes. The ICJ found, in fact, that each state had an obligation to compensate the other. From the environmental point of view, the case is important as the ICJ stated that:

> in the field of environmental protection, vigilance and prevention are required on account of the often irreversible character of damage to the environment and of the limitations inherent in the very mechanism of reparation of this type of damage.
>
> Throughout the ages, mankind has, for economic and other reasons, constantly interfered with nature. In the past, this was often done without consideration of the effects upon the environment. Owing to new scientific insights and to a growing awareness of the risks for mankind – for present and future generations – of pursuit of such interventions at an unconsidered and unabated pace, new norms and standards have been developed, set forth in a great number of instruments during the last two decades. Such new norms have to be taken into consideration, and such new standards given proper weight, not only when States contemplate new activities but also when continuing with activities begun in the past. This need to reconcile economic development with protection of the environment is aptly expressed in the

> concept of sustainable development.
>
> For the purposes of the present case, this means that the Parties together should look afresh at the effects on the environment.
>
> (*ibid.*)

The ICJ then held that it was not its role to dictate the result of such consideration of the effects on the environment. As raised earlier, the ICJ went further, however, in the *Case Concerning Pulp Mills on the River Uruguay Case (Argentina v Uruguay)*, holding that certain environmental practices – such as the undertaking of environmental impact assessments where proposed developments might have significant adverse impacts on environments in a transboundary context – may now be considered requirements under general international law (*Case Concerning Pulp Mills*, 2010: paras 203–19).

In 2010 Australia, later joined by New Zealand, instituted litigation against Japan in the ICJ seeking to have a particular scientific whaling programme of Japan's declared illegal (*Whaling in the Antarctic*, 2014). Australia was successful, the ICJ ruling that the particular programme ('JARPA II') did not constitute genuine scientific research. While the ICJ found that research permit whaling itself was unobjectionable and only the specific programme in question was ruled illegal, and Japan later in 2014 announced that a new programme would begin, the case was not an unmitigated disaster for the successful litigant, Australia. It is significant that the ICJ held that it was entitled to rule on the issue, and that Japan was not therefore entitled to make its own decisions unfettered.

Approaching the ICJ remains a radical step not often taken by states, and only a few matters that are environmental in nature have been adjudicated by the Court. Sands suggests that states are 'hesitant about referring international environmental disputes to international adjudication'; and '[t]o the extent that states want international adjudicatory mechanisms, they do not seem to want those that apply a contentious and conflictual procedure to environmental matters' (Sands, 2008). Nevertheless, the potential remains for the ICJ to become more involved than it has hitherto – and it does appear that when apprised of an environmental matter the ICJ has not shrunk from 'entering the arena' and making rulings with wide-reaching effect.

The early years of the twenty-first century saw a potentially important environmental development, which mirrored the increasing linkage of environment and development. The rise of an anti-globalization protest movement in the area of international trade also incorporated environmental protests. In the so-called 'Battle for Seattle', the best-known protest saw the 1999 World Trade Organization meeting in Seattle unable to continue after disruptions. Similar protests were then seen at the 2000 Amsterdam Conference on Global Warming, the 2001 World Economic Forum held in Davos, the 2000 and 2002 International Monetary Fund (IMF) meetings in Washington DC, the 2001 Free Trade Area of the Americas Agreement (FTAA) meeting in Quebec, the 2001 European Union Leaders' Summit in Gothenburg, and the 2001 G-8 Summit in Genoa, where a protester was killed by police. While similarly violent protests have not been a recent feature, it is noticeable that the involvement of civil society – and business and industry – in the negotiation processes toward international conventions and also in their ongoing meetings has become entrenched.

Ten years after the Rio Summit there were high hopes for the 2002 World Summit on Sustainable Development (WSSD), held in Johannesburg, South Africa, as a major summit at which practical solutions could be found for the world's environmental and developmental problems. It is probably still a little too early to judge the WSSD's place in history, but it certainly did not achieve the immediate results that it might have (its main focus became the improving of implementation of existing instruments). According to a surprisingly candid summary on the dedicated website for the Summit itself:

> [b]y any account, the Johannesburg Summit has laid the groundwork and paved the way for action. Yet among all the targets, timetables and commitments that were agreed upon at Johannesburg, there were no silver bullet solutions to aid the fight against poverty and a continually deteriorating natural environment. In fact, there was no magic and no miracle – only the realization that practical and sustained steps were needed to address many of the world's most pressing problems.
>
> As an implementation-focused Summit, Johannesburg did not produce a particularly dramatic outcome – there were no agreements that will lead to new treaties and many of the agreed targets were derived from a panoply of assorted lower profile meetings. But some important new targets were established, such as: to halve the proportion of people without access to basic sanitation by 2015; to use and produce chemicals by 2020 in ways that do not lead to significant adverse effects on human health and the environment; to maintain or restore depleted fish stocks to levels that can produce the maximum sustainable yield on an urgent basis and where possible by 2015; and to achieve by 2010 a significant reduction in the current rate of loss of biological diversity.
>
> (WSSD, 2002)

What *were* adopted were a Declaration of Principles (the Johannesburg Declaration); and the Plan of Implementation, which included that states should 'continue to promote coherent and coordinated approaches to institutional frameworks for sustainable development at all national levels, including through, as appropriate, the establishment or strengthening of existing authorities and mechanisms necessary for policy-making, coordination and implementation and enforcement of laws' (Johannesburg Plan, 2002: para. 162(a)).

In 2012 there was a follow-up to the Rio Conference of 1992 and the WSSD of 2002. The United Nations Conference on Sustainable Development (UNCSD, the 'Rio+20 Conference') was held in Rio. While a gathering of a high proportion of world leaders (79 heads of state or government were present, and 191 states represented), the Conference was less ambitious than had been the previous two conferences – it ran for less time (three days) and produced only a single instrument: the so-called Outcome Document titled 'The Future We Want'. The Outcome Document was subsequently adopted by the UN General Assembly, without need of a vote. It has been met with mixed responses, with some stakeholders criticizing the Rio+20 Conference for 'either failing to take specific tangible actions on some of the important issues or leaving some issues pending or not addressed' (Mrema, 2014: 43). Gro Harlem Brundtland, for instance, has commented that '[t]he Rio+20 declaration does not do enough to set humanity on a sustainable path, decades after it was agreed that this is essential for both people and the planet' (*ibid.*: 48). On the other hand, the Conference was an important milestone in the history of UNEP, for which the Outcome Document recommended various improvements and upgrades (see Urho and Niinistö, this volume: 201–215). It is uncertain at this stage how important the Outcome Document might turn out to be, but at least it should keep momentum going and understanding growing.

International environmental law and forestry

Lyster suggests that '[f]orestry conservation laws in Babylon date back to 1900 B.C.' and that 'Akhenaten, King of Egypt, set aside land as a nature reserve in 1370 B.C.' (Lyster, 1985: xxi). The Norman Conquest of England in 1066 could, for example, also be seen in this light. Before 1066, and certainly from the time of the Franks and similar tribes in the seventh century, hunting in continental Europe was regarded as being the exclusive right of the king and his nobles; the Franks were the first to introduce the *foresta* system, which reserved areas and animals for the exclusive use of certain classes (Trench, 1967: 16). While William the Conqueror had basically accepted and enforced existing English laws, the forest laws were different; the system imposed on the Saxon English was like none they had seen before (prior to this wild animals had been ownerless property, which could be hunted by anyone, subject only to the laws of trespass). Vast areas of land were designated as royal forests (*foresta regis*) (Young, 1979: 5); to protect these arbitrarily imposed rights William imposed the death penalty for the killing of a royal deer, and all deer were by definition considered royal (Ingram, 1978: 5). This attempt to extend laws across boundaries can arguably be seen as an early attempt to create international law in the forest context. Little attention was given to forestry in international law over the next millennium, however; and it is only in the second half of the twentieth century that we begin to find attention turned once again to forestry (the *Trail Smelter Arbitration*, 1941, for example, concerned damage to forests).

In 1983 the International Tropical Timber Agreement (ITTA) was concluded. The intention behind this agreement was '[t]o provide an effective framework for co-operation and consultation between tropical timber producing and consuming members with regard to all relevant aspects of the tropical timber economy' (Art. 1(a)). The Agreement was significant for its recognition of the different responsibilities held by the timber producing (largely developing) and consuming (largely developed) states, and for its recognition of the need to:

> encourage the development of national policies aimed at sustainable utilization and conservation of tropical forests and their genetic resources, and at maintaining the ecological balance in the regions concerned.
>
> (ITTA, 1983, Art. 1(h))

This latter recognition of the need for sustainability is significant in the face of the obvious utilitarian thrust of the Agreement, which is visible in goals such as:

> [e]ncourag[ing] increased and further processing of tropical timber in producing member countries with a view to promoting their industrialization and thereby increasing their export earnings.
>
> (ITTA, 1983, Art. 1(e))

In 1988, the murder of Chico Mendes in the Amazon rain forest in Brazil highlighted the plight of the world's old growth forests, which are being rapidly logged and cleared with consequent loss of biodiversity and carbon sink capacity. Mendes was a rubber tapper and community activist who was murdered by ranchers, against whose encroachment into the Amazon he was leading a campaign. As a result of the international pressure that followed his murder, the Brazilian government created a number of comparatively large extraction reserves to be restricted from ranching activity (Smith *et al.*, 1995).

The issue of forests was one of the most politically sensitive issues at the 1992 Rio Conference, there being a strong divide between the positions of industrialized and developing countries. It has been suggested that this was due to 'tropical forest' countries having grown 'weary' of criticism and seeking to have all forests considered (Michaelsen/FAO, undated). Although the Conference did not succeed in negotiating a convention on forests, it did ultimately adopt the Rio Forest Principles, which sought to provide a framework in which both conservation and use of forests can be compatible. Although firmly expressed to be non-binding, as a statement of intent – and as recognition of the importance to the world of forests – the Principles are of significance. While it might have been hoped at the time that the adoption of the Principles might have led toward a convention, states have thus far been unable to reach consensus on this issue. In 2007, the UN General Assembly did, however, adopt a 'non-legally binding instrument on all types of forests', which, *inter alia*, builds upon the Rio Forest Principles (UNGA Res. 62/68) and is currently the only global agreement on the sustainable management of all types of forests.

It should be added that although there is no overarching convention, various other MEAs do contribute toward the sustainable management of forests – such as the Convention on Biological Diversity, 1992, which has a thematic programme on forest biodiversity; and the UN Framework Convention on Climate Change, which has its UN-REDD and UN-REDD+ programmes, which encourage preservation of forests by creating financial incentives for storing carbon.

A significant case in a national jurisdiction, with important potential implications for the development of international environmental law, was reported in 1993. In *Juan Antonio Oposa et al. v. Fulgencio S. Factoran, Jr. et al.* (1993), the Philippines Supreme Court was called on to decide on the legality of the Filipino government's decision to issue licences to log timber in land areas greater than were available, potentially leading to the complete destruction of Filipino forests within a decade. The case was brought on behalf of Filipino minors, on the basis of their right to a sound environment for generations to come. The case, said the Court:

> has a special and novel element. Petitioners minors assert that they represent their generation as well as generations yet unborn. We find no difficulty in ruling that they can, for themselves, for others of their generation and for the succeeding generations, file a class suit. Their personality to sue in behalf of the succeeding generations can only be based on the concept of intergenerational responsibility insofar as the right to a balanced and healthful ecology is concerned. Such a right, as hereinafter expounded, considers the 'rhythm and harmony of nature'.
>
> (*ibid.*)

The Court ruled that the minors had *locus standi in judicio*, on the grounds that:

> [n]eedless to say, every generation has a responsibility to the next to preserve that rhythm and harmony for the full enjoyment of a balanced and healthful ecology. Put a little differently, the minors' assertion of their right to a sound environment constitutes, at the same time, the performance of their obligation to ensure the protection of that right for the generations to come.
>
> (*ibid.*)

On the merits, the Court then found in favour of the minors' petition.

Although the case has not been repeated, the idea remains alive. In recent times some attention has been given to the possibility of creating a UN Commissioner for Future Generations (Office of the Commissioner, Australia). This proposal did not meet with favour in Rio in 2012 with, particularly, developing countries' representatives expressing concern that it might detract from current attention to poverty alleviation. Nevertheless, some countries have taken steps (such as Finland, which has a Committee for the Future with the function of advising on technological and other future-related aspects) and momentum may yet build.

In October 2004 the Nobel Peace Prize was awarded to Professor Wangari Maathai, in recognition of 'her contribution to sustainable development, democracy and peace'. A Kenyan, she had founded the Green Belt Movement, which planted more than 30 million trees across Africa. In the face of strong opposition from political and business interests she did much to raise awareness of the importance and the vulnerability of indigenous forests and of the need for the increased planting of trees to sustain people and their livelihoods and to preserve both natural environments and ways of life. The award signals global recognition of this.

In an echo of the murder of Chico Mendes in the Amazon in 1988, in February 2005 a Catholic nun named Dorothy Stang was assassinated in the Amazon. She had worked for years to protect the Amazon rainforests from being opened up to ranching interests. In an ironic parallel to the Mendes case, Brazil's government almost immediately declared that it would take steps to protect some four million hectares of rainforest, by declaring it a conservation area.

Individuals have important roles to play in the development of international environmental protection, and sometimes pay the ultimate sacrifice in making their contributions.

Overfishing and whaling

As early as 1882 it was recognized that the world could have a problem in respect of overfishing. In that year, the United Kingdom, Germany, France, Denmark and Belgium signed the North Sea Fisheries Police Convention and agreed to mutual rights of visit, search, and arrest of the treaty powers' public vessels. This agreement is staggering when looking at the lack of protection that has been given to the oceans by 2015; after more than 130 years little has been done to offer substantive protection to marine species.

Before World War II, concern about overfishing could be seen in the 1937 International Convention for the Regulation of Meshes of Fishing Nets and the Size Limits of Fish. Although the United States and Canada did not become Parties and the Convention never entered into force, fisheries did, however, receive a temporary reprieve. During the six years of World War II there was very little fishing activity worldwide, and fish stocks recovered somewhat. After World War II, although a new fishing treaty was negotiated and entered into force (Convention on Meshes and Sizes, 1946), fishing intensified dramatically worldwide. One can only conjecture as to why, if there was international concern in 1882 and again in 1937 and 1946 in relation to fish stocks, there is not now, in 2015, widespread panic. In fact, there has been startlingly little movement. In 2002, the states represented at the WSSD committed themselves, in the Johannesburg Plan of Implementation, to the following:

> [t]o achieve sustainable fisheries, the following actions are required at all levels: (a) Maintain or restore stocks to levels that can produce the maximum sustainable yield with the aim of achieving these goals for depleted stocks on an urgent basis and where possible not later than 2015.
>
> (Johannesburg Plan, para. 31(a))

What is arguably most terrifying about this commitment, which the Parties must have known at the time was 'pie in the sky', is that in 2012 in the UNCSD Outcome Document this commitment was not scrapped but renewed:

> [w]e commit to intensify our efforts to meet the 2015 target as agreed to in the Johannesburg Plan of Implementation to maintain or restore stocks to levels that can produce maximum sustainable yield on an urgent basis.
>
> (UNGA, 2012, 'The Future We Want': para. 168)

Writing from the perspective of 2015 itself, this is deeply depressing. It seems that global fisheries are an area where states refuse to acknowledge the scope of the problem and make only the most desultory of efforts at meaningful regulation. UNCLOS settled states' exclusive economic zones at 200 nautical miles. This provides an important potential (if not actual, as many governments have responded to the enhancement of their rights by encouraging the development of their fishing industries) protective measure, as the majority of marine living resources are to be found within coastal waters rather than on the high seas. The high seas remain, however, an open-access commons; and so, unfortunately, are the exclusive economic zones of many developing states unable to enforce conservation measures. At Rio+20, delegates committed to address 'on an urgent basis, the issue of the conservation and sustainable use of marine biological diversity beyond national jurisdiction, including by taking a decision on the development of an international instrument under [UNCLOS]' (UNGA, 2012, 'The Future We Want': para. 162). This paragraph was disappointing insofar as it failed to include a commitment actually to *negotiate* a new international instrument. However, an Ad Hoc Open-ended Working Group, which was mandated to provide recommendations on this issue (UNGA Resolution 68/70) recently recommended that the UN General Assembly decide to develop an 'international legally binding instrument under [UNCLOS] on the conservation and sustainable use of marine biological diversity of areas beyond national jurisdiction' and, to this end, establish a preparatory committee to make substantive recommendations on the draft text (UNGA Doc. 69/780).

In 1946 the International Convention for the Regulation of Whaling (ICRW) was adopted. The Convention provides an interesting example of how Parties' views of a multilateral agreement can change over time. The ICRW began as a utilization treaty with 15 contracting governments, all of whom were active whaling nations. The premise was that they would annually decide on quotas, in order to manage whales as a resource, with an annual meeting of an International Whaling Commission (IWC). The quota system was inefficient, however, and whale numbers continued to drop markedly. By the late 1970s and the years immediately afterward, a number of countries had announced that they would cease whaling, showing how consumer perceptions toward use of natural resources had changed in large parts of the world. In 1982, the IWC adopted a moratorium on commercial whaling, to take effect from 1986. This represented a sea change from the utilitarian focus of the initial contracting governments to the ICRW in 1946. In the interim years, a number of the Parties (Australia, South Africa, the United Kingdom, and the United States, for instance) had changed their attitudes to whaling and, there being no stipulations as to membership other than statehood, new Parties (Austria and Switzerland, for instance) without histories of whaling had joined. Those state Parties that wished to continue commercial whaling (Iceland, Japan and Norway, for instance) found themselves outvoted. Subsequent to this, there was something of a 'numbers race' as both sides sought to bring in more and more supporters – today there are 88 contracting governments. With a little less than half of the world's states being Parties, the ICRW is a significant convention – and it is important also for the precedent it provides.

While the ICRW has become a 'byword' for conflict, and the IWC is often seen as a 'dysfunctional' organization, one of the reasons why the infighting is so bitter is because of its precedential value. The conflict over so high profile a species pits against each other core values in respect of the use of natural resources – 'preservation' against 'conservation'; consumptive versus non-consumptive use. It should not be forgotten, however, that while the IWC may be struggling to carry out – even to agree on – its core mandate, it continues to perform important research and other managerial mandates.

Protection of biodiversity

In the context of biodiversity, an important early arbitral ruling was the *Bering Sea Fur Seals Arbitration* (1898). Due to overhunting, the stocks of Bering Sea fur seals were being rapidly depleted. As the seals had their birthing grounds on United States territory, the US government essentially argued that the seals were US property, giving the US the right to protect them. Consequently, the US arrested a number of British (Canadian) vessels on the high seas. The US also argued that it was the trustee of the seals for the benefit of mankind generally. Britain (Canada) argued that it had the right to hunt seals on the high seas as they were property either *res communis* or *res nullius*. The arbitral tribunal found against the US arguments and freedom of the high seas was held to be the prevailing doctrine. Birnie *et al.* comment that:

> [t]he importance of this decision to the development of the law concerning conservation of marine living resources cannot be overstressed. It laid the twin foundations for subsequent developments over the next century. First, it confirmed that the law was based on high seas freedom of fishing and that no distinction was to be made in this respect between fisheries and marine mammals despite the very different characteristics of the latter, which the tribunal had examined; secondly, it recognized the need for conservation to prevent over-exploitation and decline of a hunted species, but because of the former finding, it made this dependant on the express acceptance of regulation by participants in the fishery.
>
> (Birnie *et al.*, 2009: 707)

By way of recommendation, the tribunal also outlined a nine-point plan for conservation, which included

> a prohibited zone; a closed season in a defined area of the high seas, with specific exemptions in favour of indigenous peoples hunting for traditional purposes, using traditional methods; a limitation on the type of vessels used; a licensing system to be operated by the governments concerned; use of a special flag while sealing; the keeping of catch records; exchange of data collected; governmental responsibility for selection of suitable crews; the provisions were to continue for five years or until abandoned by agreement. Moreover, the tribunal went on to recommend that these regulations be enacted into apposite and uniform national laws in both states and that national measures be adopted to ensure their enforcement. Thus, the priority of national measures of enforcement, rather than international means, also was established.
>
> Finally, a three-year ban on all sealing was recommended, laying the foundation of the moratorium approach to conservation of marine mammals.
>
> (*ibid.*: 707–708)

Although contractually binding on the participants, the ruling was not binding on other users of the fur seals, such as Russia and Japan, and in practice it made little difference to the overexploitation of the resource. Birnie *et al.* suggest that:

> although it perpetuated the high seas freedom of fishing and hence made conservation more difficult, especially in relation to enforcement, the *Bering Sea* arbitral tribunal strongly supported the need for restraint in exploitation, clearly indicated the requisite measures, and recognized that freedom was not absolute but had to be regulated to take reasonable account of the interests of other states.
>
> (*ibid.*: 708)

Elsewhere, of importance in understanding the history of conservation of wild animals and birds were two conventions agreed around the turn of the twentieth century: the 1900 Convention for the Preservation of Wild Animals, Birds and Fish in Africa (London Convention); and the 1902 Convention for the Protection of Birds Useful to Agriculture (Paris Convention). Driven by Germany, the London Convention suggested that all colonial powers in Africa should introduce game regulations. Although the Convention never entered into force, as Mackenzie puts it the Germans and British ratified 'enthusiastically' (Mackenzie, 1988: 205). Many of the provisions suggested in the London Convention echoed the *Bering Sea Fur Seals* Arbitration. A closed season was introduced, the hunting of male animals was only permitted during certain periods and restrictions were placed on weapons that were allowed to be used for hunting. Of relevance for the history of international environmental law is the separation of animals into species worthy of protection and those not so worthy or even those considered noxious and which should be actively exterminated. The latter group contained many species which today are seen as being most worthy of protection: the predators, such as lions and, amongst birds, the raptors and vultures. The Paris Convention similarly drew a distinction between species considered to be useful to humans and noxious species, which were excluded from protection. The species targeted for significant reduction under both of these instruments were amongst the most valuable for their ecosystems. Had these instruments been successful in their original aims, ecosystem collapse may well have been the result in the areas of application.

Wildlife-related conventions continued to take a species-based approach as the twentieth century progressed, while becoming more aware of the complexities of species interaction. The 1973 Convention on International Trade in Endangered Species of Wild Fauna and Flora (CITES) was another Convention in the early-1970s cluster. Although arguably promoting trade in wild animal species through attempting to regulate such trade, the Convention probably provides the most visible and significant international protection for wild animal species today. Again, protection of state sovereignty is emphasized in the Convention; the mandate of the Convention does not extend to jurisdiction within national boundaries. Furthermore, the Convention continues to categorize wild animal species; CITES affords different degrees of protection from trade to species depending on their listing in the three appendices of the Convention.

The Convention on the Conservation of Migratory Species of Wild Animals (CMS) and the Bern Convention on the Conservation of European Wildlife and Natural Habitats, which were both adopted in 1979, heralded a new approach to the conservation of species. There is recognition in both that habitat conservation is as important as the conservation of individual species. This recognition can perhaps already be seen in the 1971 Ramsar Convention and in some regional conventions, but arguably not in the core text of CITES. The 1980 Convention for the Conservation of Antarctic Marine Living Resources (CCAMLR) further emphasized an ecosystem approach. According to Article I of the Convention:

> 2. Antarctic marine living resources means the populations of fin fish, molluscs, crustaceans and all other species of living organisms, including birds, found south of the Antarctic convergence (Art. I.2).
>
> 3. The Antarctic marine ecosystem means the complex of relationships of Antarctic marine living resources with each other and with their physical environment (Art. I.3).

In 1980 the 'World Conservation Strategy' was launched by the IUCN, UNEP and the WWF. This influential document was arguably the first to recognize that long-term efforts were required to solve environmental problems, and that this could not be done unless environment and development objectives were integrated (IUCN *et al.*, 1980). The World Conservation Strategy was followed in 1982 by the adoption of the United Nations World Charter for Nature (UNGA, 2012, 'World Charter for Nature'). This Resolution of the United Nations General Assembly 'recalled' that it had 'recognized the need for appropriate measures at the national and international levels to protect nature and promote international cooperation in that field …' (Preamble); and then set out general principles, including that '[n]ature shall be respected and its essential processes shall not be impaired' (Principle 1). While being aspirational soft law in nature, rather than binding hard law, the Charter did require that '[t]he principles set forth in the present Charter shall be reflected in the law and practice of each State, as well as at the international level' (Principle 14).

The Convention on Biological Diversity (CBD), adopted at UNCED in 1992, goes beyond the species-based approach of earlier conventions and provides for states to commit to the preservation of habitats and ecosystems within their own boundaries. This holistic and ecosystem-based approach surely reflects new understanding of the way in which biodiversity functions and the ways in which it must be protected. While the CBD's provisions are mostly 'soft' in their effect, with its Parties committing themselves to obligations like 'endeavouring' to conserve, it represents an important step forward and will hopefully operate as a 'central hub' for biodiversity-related conventions. The CBD's Strategic Plan for the period 2011–2020 is intended to provide 'an overarching framework on biodiversity, not only for the biodiversity-related conventions, but for the entire United Nations system and all other partners engaged in biodiversity management and policy development' (CBD, undated, Strategic Plan).

A recent initiative provides further hope of greater coordination in this area. In April 2012 a new 'platform' was established by an intergovernmental and multi-stakeholder meeting – the 'Intergovernmental Platform on Biodiversity and Ecosystem Services' (IPBES) (see UNEP, 2010, 'Busan Outcome'). This is an independent intergovernmental body open to all UN member states – as at time of writing there were 124 members. The members are 'committed to building IPBES as the leading intergovernmental body for assessing the state of the planet's biodiversity, its ecosystems and the essential services they provide to society' (www.ipbes.net). It is probably too difficult at this stage of the development of biodiversity-related international law to envisage the creation of a new, coverall convention; and so the fostering of greater cooperation and information-sharing between existing conventions is a sensible alternative.

Pollution

Pollution of the atmosphere

The years 1935–1941 saw the deliberations of an important arbitral tribunal. The *Trail Smelter* Arbitration concluded that:

> no state has the right to use or permit the use of its territory in such a manner as to cause injury by fumes in or to the territory of another or the properties or persons therein, when the case is of serious consequence and the injury is established by clear and convincing evidence.
>
> (*Trail Smelter* Arbitration, 1941)

The case concerned pollution damage caused to forests and crops in the United States by pollutants from a smelter in the town of Trail, Canada. Trail had a lead and zinc smelting factory complex with 400-foot high chimneys. As astounding as it might seem today, the question in dispute was whether Canada was liable for the damage caused by the smelter, and whether it had any duty to prevent further damage from occurring. The tribunal decided that Canada did indeed have to take responsibility for past and future damage; the reason that the question would surprise us so much today is in part due to the effect of the arbitral tribunal's decision on subsequent legal discourse. The tribunal, however, took a narrow view to damages, compensating for injury to persons and property, but appeared to exclude wider environmental interests such as wildlife, aesthetic considerations or the unity and diversity of ecosystems. Although Canada was held to have no right to cause damage within the United States, its right to continue to operate the smelter was affirmed.

Birnie and Boyle comment that:

> [d]espite criticism of the tribunal for the limited range of national and international sources on which it relied in determining rules of international law, there is no reason to doubt that states remain responsible in international law for harm caused in breach of obligation by transboundary air pollution.
>
> (Birnie and Boyle, 2002: 504–505)

A more difficult question, however, was how to address transboundary air pollutants (such as sulphur dioxide), which travel long distances, making it impossible to link the harm suffered to specific sources. This issue came to the fore during the 1970s, and was one of the factors underlying Sweden's decision to host the 1972 Stockholm Conference. In 1979, the Convention on Long-range Transboundary Air Pollutants was adopted to provide a framework for addressing such pollution in Europe.

Ozone is a gas which, at upper levels in the atmosphere, acts as a barrier to dangerous ultraviolet light. In the mid-1970s scientists like Frank Rowland and Mario Molina, and then in the early 1980s scientists including Shigeru Chubachi, indicated grave concern over ozone depletion in the Antarctic, which depletion was strongly suspected to be caused by the anthropogenic emission of chlorofluorocarbons. This then led to the international community showing itself capable of acting swiftly and in concert, and of adopting a precautionary approach. The 1985 Vienna Convention on Protection of the Ozone Layer was adopted without firm data that ozone depletion was occurring or scientific consensus regarding its causes (see Tolba and Rummel-Bulska, 1998: 55–88). However, virtually contemporaneously, evidence was released (particularly by scientists Joseph Farman, Brian Gardiner and John Shanklin, writing in May 1985) indicating that there was a large, and growing, hole in the ozone layer above Antarctica; that the ozone layer had been depleting since at least 1970; and that this was due largely to increased use of chlorofluorocarbons worldwide.

The Vienna Convention was followed two years later in 1987 by the Montreal Protocol on Protection of the Ozone Layer, which committed states Parties to meeting targets for reductions and the eventual phasing out of ozone-depleting substances. At time of writing, 197 states (or 'states', such as the Holy See) had ratified the Montreal Protocol. Although an apparent example of speedy and determined action, the early commitments made by states Parties in fact allowed limited increases in production of chlorofluorocarbons before eventually reducing these – in order to persuade developing countries to ratify, a special exemption period was granted (Art. 5(1); and see, generally, Gribbin, 1988). This was therefore an example of early application of the principle of 'common but differentiated responsibilities' (see Honkonen, chapter 11 in this volume: 160–183). However, Parties to the Protocol have, over the years, shown a remarkable willingness to tighten restrictions in response to improved scientific knowledge, and the ozone regime is generally considered to have been very successful in achieving its object. In addition to its precautionary approach, flexibility to evolve over time, and universal membership, noteworthy aspects of this regime include its creation of a Multilateral Fund to assist developing countries and its development of an innovative compliance mechanism, which has provided a model for similar mechanisms in other regimes.

The 1992 United Nations Framework Convention on Climate Change (UNFCCC), has its Parties 'reaffirming the principle of sovereignty of States in international co-operation to address climate change' and 'acknowledg[ing] that change in the Earth's climate and its adverse effects are a common concern of humankind' (Preamble). Although a lukewarm commitment and protective once again of the jealously guarded idea of sovereignty, the UNFCCC set the stage for concrete emissions-control targets to be agreed to in further Protocols. When the states Parties to UNFCCC negotiated the text, they were well aware that – in itself – the Convention would be hopelessly inadequate to meet the challenges of climate change. The 1997 Kyoto Protocol to the Convention was intended to remedy this. The Protocol significantly strengthens the Convention 'by committing Annex I [industrialized] Parties to individual, legally-binding targets to limit or reduce their greenhouse gas emissions'. The Protocol received sufficient ratifications to come into force only in February 2005, after 55 UNFCCC Parties, including Annex I states accounting for at least 55 percent of the total 1990 carbon dioxide emissions from that determined group, had ratified. That the Protocol came into force can be seen as testament to a welcome determination by the global community to deal with the problem of global warming, even in the face of the refusal by the largest emitter of greenhouse gases, the United States, to ratify. Unfortunately, the efforts made to reduce emissions have not matched the commitment – and the first seven-year commitment period under the Kyoto Protocol expired without significant progress having been made. At time of writing, a second commitment period has been entered into; and the Parties are due to meet the commitment made in 2011 (at the UNFCCC CoP 17) to:

> develop a protocol, another legal instrument or an agreed outcome with legal force under the Convention applicable to all Parties, which is to be completed

> no later than 2015 in order for it to be adopted at the twenty-first session of the Conference of the Parties (COP) and for it to come into effect and be implemented from 2020.
>
> (Ad Hoc Working Group, UNFCCC, 2014)

Progress has been slow, all of the efforts made since 1992 have not apparently been successful at slowing the rate of global warming, and the reality is that the impacts of human-induced climate change are such that an average rise of more than 2 degrees Celsius (above pre-industrial levels) cannot now be prevented and the international community needs to concentrate more on adapting to living with this. Nevertheless, a case can probably be made that significant progress *has* been made, the fundamentals of an effective regime are in place, and that given the cross-cutting nature and wide scope of the issue-area, that is as much as we could reasonably have expected by this time.

Marine pollution

In 1954 the International Convention for the Prevention of Pollution of the Sea by Oil (OILPOL), a precursor of later marine pollution conventions that would also deal with pollutants other than oil, was signed. The main concern of the 1954 Convention was operational discharge; the world was not yet overly concerned with major oil spills. Marine pollution received further attention in 1958, with the Convention on the Law of the Sea signed in Geneva. However, protection of the marine environment generally was given little attention and the Convention focused – as the 1954 OILPOL Convention had done – on operational discharge. The Conventions seemed to suggest, as Birnie and Boyle put it, that states 'enjoyed substantial freedom to pollute the oceans, moderated only by the principle that high seas freedoms must be exercised with reasonable regard for the rights of others' (Birnie and Boyle, 2002: 351).

The realities of large marine oil spills first came to global attention in 1967, with the grounding – caused by human error – off the English coast of the tanker *Torrey Canyon*, which spilled some 120,000 tonnes of oil. Marine pollution control was at the time in its infancy and the United Kingdom was unprepared to deal with the disaster. The incident led to a number of marine pollution conventions being signed in 1969 (Intervention Convention, 1969; Convention on Civil Liability, 1969) and in the early-mid 1970s. In 1973, the 1954 OILPOL Convention was replaced by the International Convention for the Prevention of Pollution from Ships (MARPOL). The MARPOL Convention did not come into force on its own, but in 1978 was subsumed into a Protocol that has come into force). The MARPOL Convention covers pollution from ships at sea by oil and also substances other than oil. In a set of six annexes, the Convention deals respectively with oil, noxious liquid substances carried in bulk, harmful substances carried in packaged form, sewage, garbage generated on vessels, and atmospheric pollution from ships. States Parties are required to adopt Annexes 1 and 2, and may adopt the others.

Another major oil spill from a tanker in 1989 occurred when the *Exxon Valdez* ran aground in Prince William Sound, Alaska. The impact on the psyche of the American people was significant, with the images of a pristine environment spoiled reverberating to this day. Ironic comment on the disaster has been made, however, by Al Gore, former Vice-President of the United States:

> [w]hen expenditures are required to clean up [...] pollution, they are usually included in the national accounts as another positive entry on the ledger. In other words, the more pollution we create, the more productive contributions we can make to national output. The *Exxon Valdez* oil spill in Prince William Sound, and efforts to clean it up, to take one example, actually increased our GNP.
>
> (Gore, 1992: 187)

It may not be a good thing that attention has been shifted by the impact of large-scale tanker spills away from operational discharge. Daily discharges continue virtually unabated, and large-scale spills continue to happen.

That sea-changes are possible in international environmental law is well demonstrated by a development in this area – the transition from the London Dumping Convention of 1972 to its 1996 Protocol. The original Convention provided that states Party could dump any materials, bar those subject to restrictions; the Protocol, which is in the process of replacing the Convention, provides a list of relatively harmless substances that *may* be dumped, and all others may not. There are currently 87 Parties to the Convention and 47 to the Protocol.

Pollution from chemicals and wastes

In 1956, the Minamata (or Minamoto) disaster in Japan occurred, where it became apparent that contamination from mercury waste was causing illnesses and birth defects. This drew the world's attention to the dangers of uncontrolled industrialization. It was not, however, until 1968 that the Japanese government finally acknowledged the source of the pollution and chemical dumping finally ceased.

The Minamata disaster shows both how the courage of individuals can lead to change – the contamination caused Japanese fishermen to riot at a factory in 1959 and bring a number of court actions against the large corporations responsible – and also how slow governments can be to act.

The disaster did lead, however, to the most recent global-scale multilateral environmental agreement – the Minamata Convention on Mercury, adopted in January 2013. The aim of the Convention is to protect both human health and the environment from the damaging effects of mercury. It is not yet in force. At time of writing the Convention had received 12 ratifications[2] – 50 are required for entry into force.

2 Djibouti, Gabon, Guinea, Guyana, Lesotho, Madagascar, Monaco, Nicaragua, the Seychelles, the United Arab Emirates, the United States, and Uruguay.

The early 1960s saw increasing awareness of the scale of environmental problems facing the international community. As part of this new awareness 1962 saw the publication of a book that might arguably be described as the 'bible' of environmental literature. After World War II, a 'miracle' pesticide – dichlorodiphenyltrichloroethane (DDT) – was much used. The pesticide was not directly harmful to humans. In 1962, however, scientist Rachel Carson published *Silent Spring*, which documented how DDT works its way through the food chain, ultimately having devastating environmental effects (Carson, 1962). This did much to increase understanding of ecological linkages. Pilloried by the chemical industry, Carson died from cancer in 1964 without ever knowing that her work eventually had the influence she would have wanted it to have. It was not long before *Silent Spring* was recognized to be accurate, and it was not long before environmental concern became an essential part of the 1960s zeitgeist.

In 1978, a national incident in the United States – the 'Love Canal' disaster – in which it was realized that industrial chemicals buried secretly in a town had, for years, been causing inordinately high rates of cancer and children to be born with congenital defects focused attention worldwide on the health problems of dumping of hazardous chemicals (Beck, 1979). It was thanks to the activism of individual residents – particularly a local mother named Lois Gibbs – that the problem was discovered, the causes identified, and the area eventually abandoned.

A pollution tragedy occurred in 1984, when there was a chemical leak from the Union Carbide factory in Bhopal, India. Some 2,000 people died almost immediately and some 15,000 later; 150,000–600,000 were injured. The disaster showed how, in a globalized world, a disaster within national borders could be blamed on the actions of foreign states or private companies. Union Carbide, an American company, was apparently taking advantage of less stringent environmental standards in the developing world. In a 1992 settlement agreement, Union Carbide agreed to pay US$ 470 million to the victims, a figure almost certainly substantially less than would have been ordered had judgment been granted within the United States.

Several incidents during the 1980s also drew international attention to problems surrounding the transboundary shipment of hazardous waste. For instance, from 1987–1988, five ship-loads of Italian hazardous waste were stored on a farm in Koko, Nigeria, where they polluted a local water source (see, generally, Allen, 1992).

While there is no overarching framework convention to regulate chemicals and hazardous wastes, three important global conventions are the 1989 Convention on Transboundary Movement of Hazardous Wastes and their Disposal (Basel Convention), the 1998 Convention on the Prior Informed Consent Procedure for Certain Hazardous Chemicals and Pesticides in International Trade (Rotterdam Convention) and the 2001 Convention on Persistent Organic Pollutants (Stockholm Convention). These conventions have provided something of a testing ground for the establishment of formal synergies between MEAs, having experimented with simultaneous meetings of their Conferences of the Parties and merged secretariat services under a Joint Executive Secretary. Should these institutional changes prove to be a success, and it is probably a little too early to be conclusive on this, they could potentially provide a model to be used within other thematic clusters of MEAs.

As regards the transportation of hazardous waste, an important regional instrument is a convention agreed by the Organization of African Unity (now the African Union), the 1991 Convention on the Ban of the Import into Africa and the Control of Transboundary Movements and Management of Hazardous Wastes within Africa (Bamako Convention). This Convention contains stronger provisions than its global counterpart (the Basel Convention), such as the general obligation that:

> [a]ll Parties shall take appropriate legal, administrative and other measures within the area under their jurisdiction to prohibit the import of all hazardous wastes, for any reason, into Africa from non-Contracting Parties. Such import shall be deemed illegal and a criminal act.
>
> (Bamako Convention, 1991, Art. 4(1))

This is not surprising, since it is often easier to achieve more stringent provisions in a regional instrument (negotiated between countries that share similar interests/perspectives) than in an instrument of global scope. Progress under the Convention has, however, been slow – it took until 1998 to enter into force; there are currently only 25 Parties; and the first meeting of its CoP took place only in June 2013. The jury therefore remains out on its effectiveness, despite the stringency of its provisions. At its first CoP it was decided, though, that UNEP will carry out its Secretariat functions, and that the Secretariat will be encouraged to strengthen collaboration with the Secretariat of the Basel, Rotterdam and Stockholm – and other relevant – Conventions. This bodes well for the future.

It is further significant that, although attempts by African states to include a ban on the transboundary movement of hazardous waste in the Basel Convention itself were initially unsuccessful, in 1995 the Convention's CoP adopted an amendment, which requires Annex VII countries (these being members of the OECD, Member States of the European Union, and Liechtenstein) to prohibit the transboundary movement of hazardous wastes to non-Annex VII countries for final disposal, reuse, recycling and recovery (Decision III/1). This 'Ban Amendment', while an extremely important milestone in the history of the Basel Convention, which demonstrated the regime's flexibility, has yet to enter into force. For years, Parties differed in their interpretation of the number of ratifications required for the amendment to enter into force. Per Article 17(5) of the Convention text, amendments enter into force on the 90th day following ratification by at least three-fourths 'of the Parties who accepted them'. The dispute was over whether this required ratification by three-fourths of the states that were Parties *at the time of the Ban Amendment's adoption*; or three-fourths of the *current* Parties. Ultimately, in 2011, Parties agreed upon the former interpretation (Decision 10/3).

This example illustrates the importance of careful legal drafting during the negotiations towards a treaty's adoption. More recently adopted instruments appear to have learned from the Basel experience. For instance, Article 26(5) of the Minamata Convention explicitly provides that amendments to the Convention shall enter into force 90 days following ratification by 'at least three-fourths of the Parties that were Parties at the time at which the amendment was adopted'.

Radioactive pollution

The International Atomic Energy Agency (IAEA) was created in 1956 – the dangers of nuclear proliferation being a particular concern following World War II. A number of international conventions on nuclear energy were to follow in the 1960s. Following the 1986 Chernobyl nuclear disaster in Ukraine, the two 1986 IAEA Conventions: the Convention on Early Notification of a Nuclear Accident and the Convention on Assistance in the case of a Nuclear Accident or Radiological Emergency were adopted. Once again, the world community showed that it could respond quickly to environmental problems, but that it will often take an international disaster to prompt it to do so – no matter how apparent the potential for disaster might be beforehand.

In 1985, France was preparing to conduct nuclear weapon testing in the South Pacific. In protest, the environmental organization Greenpeace was preparing to sail its ship, *Rainbow Warrior*, into the path of the proposed test fallout. While at anchor in Auckland harbour, New Zealand, the *Rainbow Warrior* was sunk by a bomb placed on the boat. A crewman, Fernando Pereira, was killed. France initially denied involvement; but finally conceded responsibility after several members of its armed forces were arrested and put on trial in New Zealand. Arbitration followed and in 1986 United Nations Secretary-General Javier Perez de Cuellar ruled that France was to make a formal apology and to pay US$ 7 million to New Zealand (UN Case *Rainbow Warrior*, 1986) – in a later adjunct arbitration France was ordered to pay a further US$ 2 million; Greenpeace, in a separate arbitration led by Dr Claude Reymond in 1987, was awarded approximately US$ 7 million; and France also paid reparations to the family of Fernando Pereira, by agreement. The significance of the case for the involvement of civil society in international environmental law can hardly be overstated. A state, one of the five permanent members of the United Nations Security Council, had apparently 'gone to war' with an NGO environmental protest group, and had then submitted to international arbitration and been required to pay reparations.

Learning from the course of international environmental law

It is difficult to know which of the many significant individuals and organizations who have contributed to the development of international environmental law – nor which environmental disasters – should best be included in so short a chapter. As such, what has been presented here is necessarily a precise account of the overall rise of international environmental concern and the development of international environmental law.

The point being made is that it should never be forgotten that, while the majority of the efforts of individuals go unrecorded in the grand sweep of history, they had and will continue to have roles to play. From the people who bravely stand up to protect their own environments from harm; through the people who form non-governmental organizations to represent other people or the environment itself; through the administrators of national environmental laws; through the diplomats representing states who bring their efforts and skills to often difficult, even seemingly impossible, negotiations; to the leaders who respond, drive and persuade; to a large extent, the rise of international environmental law has been driven and directed by the courage of individual people and by the zeitgeist of the times they represent.

International environmental law has been inevitably shaped too by the occurrence of environmental disasters, for which the world has never seemed properly prepared. At the beginning of the twenty-first century we have many new legal tools with which to tackle environmental problems, yet many familiar problems. The International Court of Justice has shown itself receptive to hearing environmental disputes and to developing environmental jurisprudence through them. There are international agreements and firm commitments to them by their states Parties. There are coherent guidelines for sustainable development practice. There are environmental principles recognized by states as approaching the status of fundamental rights, although these tend still to be seen as non-binding soft law.

Although it is impossible to know how much worse off the environment would be today had these developments not occurred, it is clear that progress towards meeting the objectives of many of the instruments discussed in this chapter has been very limited. Many specific problems have yet to be addressed, such as the growing problem of plastic debris accumulating in the world's oceans. The clash between the proponents of sustainable consumptive use and preservation in the area of wildlife trade is yet to be resolved. Environmental disasters are ongoing, and the world still seems woefully unprepared to meet them. Despite the various conventions agreed to in the area of marine pollution, there are still single-hulled tankers of dubious seaworthiness carrying large quantities of oil through dangerous seas. The difficulties caused by the importance given to the doctrine of state sovereignty are still a hindrance to effective international environmental protection, despite the efforts by the drafters of international instruments like the Convention on Biological Diversity and the UN Framework Convention on Climate Change. International environmental diplomacy continues to struggle to accommodate the divergent perspectives of developed and developing countries, with the result that concrete legal rules have yet to be adopted on such issues as sustainable forest management.

Negotiators, and the scientists who inform them, are still struggling to understand the complicated relationships that comprise the natural world and in some situations the taking of a species-based approach to wildlife conservation might remain a hindrance to effective protection, despite the holistic approaches taken in more recent international instruments like the Convention on Biological

Diversity, the Convention on the Conservation of Migratory Species of Wild Animals and the Convention for the Conservation of Antarctic Marine Living Resources. Balance is difficult to achieve, but it needs to be found between the more detailed and legally rigorous commitments often present in single-issue treaties and the 'softer', more widely embracing approaches taken in wider-issue treaties.

Overfishing of the world's oceans is today a greater problem than it has ever been. The efforts of the drafters of conventions aimed at the protection of fisheries, such as CCAMLR, have not kept pace with the technological expertise of fishermen, nor have the various marine pollution conventions proved effective in combating pollution of the seas, either by way of dramatic oil spills or the continual hazard of operational discharge from the countless vessels plying the seas daily.

In the face of continued environmental degradation, some treaty regimes have introduced innovative approaches aimed at improving implementation, such as compliance mechanisms to facilitate (or even compel) adherence to international commitments, and synergies between instruments with a similar focus. Attempts have also been made to strengthen international environmental governance in general by, for instance, upgrading UNEP. For most such approaches it is probably still too early to judge success or failure.

Negotiations are proving particularly difficult within the context of the climate change regime, but this is probably because it is so broad and cross-cutting an issue-area that it will inevitably take longer to understand and to reach agreement on the way forward. Its importance, nevertheless, lies within this overarching relevance and it is crucial that the legalities of so important a regime be crafted with great care and be informed by all lessons that can be learned from previous regimes.

Despite all of these difficulties, it should never be forgotten that multilateral environmental agreements, in the form in which we currently understand them, date only from approximately 130 years ago – this is a very short span of time and our understanding of the operation of legal instruments for the protection of the environment has developed rapidly within this period. The progress which we have already made since, for instance, the creation of a list of 'noxious' predator species in the Paris Convention of 1902 has been objectively amazing.

Much remains for individuals, whether acting on their own, in groups, or playing their parts as administrators, diplomats or negotiators for governments, still to do, and it is important that an understanding of the past informs the future. In this way, the mistakes of the past can be avoided and the diplomatic skills needed to craft effective future multilateral environmental agreements enhanced.

References

Ad Hoc Working Group on the Durban Platform for Enhanced Action (ADP) (2014), United Nations Framework Convention on Climate Change, www.unfccc.int/bodies/body/6645/php/view/documents.php (accessed 24 April 2015).

Affaire du Lac Lanoux, XII *United Nations Reports of International Arbitral Awards* 285–317, Lake Lanoux Arbitration (English Translation) 1957), 24 *International Law Reports* 101.

Agenda 21 (1992) UN Conference on Environment and Development, Rio de Janeiro, 13 June 1992, UN Doc. A/CONF.151/26/Rev.1.

Allen, R. (1992) *Waste Not Want Not: The Production and Dumping of Toxic Waste*, Earthscan, London.

'Amendment to the Basel Convention', Basel Convention Decision III/1 (1995).

Beck, E.C. (1979) 'The Love Canal Tragedy', *Environmental Protection Agency Journal* 1–5.

Bering Sea Fur Seals Arbitration, (Great Britain v USA), Moore's International Arbitration Awards (1898) 755.

Birnie, P. and Boyle, A.E. (2002) *International Law and the Environment* (2nd ed.), Oxford University Press, Oxford.

Birnie, P., Boyle, A.E. and Redgwell, C. (2009) *International Law and the Environment* (3rd ed.), Oxford University Press, Oxford.

Bowman, M.J. (1995) 'The Multilateral Treaty Amendment Process – A Case Study', *International and Comparative Law Quarterly*, 44: 540–559.

Bowman, M.J., Davies P. and Redgwell, C. (2010) *Lyster's International Wildlife Law* (2nd ed.), Cambridge University Press, Cambridge.

Carson, R. (1962) *Silent Spring*, Hamish Hamilton, London.

Case Concerning Pulp Mills on the River Uruguay (Argentina v. Uruguay), ICJ judgment of 20 April 2010.

CBD (Undated), Strategic Plan 2011–2020, www.cbd.int/sp/ (accessed 24 May 2015).

Committee for the Future, Finland (Undated), web.eduskunta.fi/Resource.phx/parliament/committees/future.htx?lng=en (accessed 9 April 2015).

Constitution of the Republic of Ecuador (2008), www.ramsar.org/sites/default/files/documents/pdf/moc/MoC_5IOPs_19-5-11_SIGNED.pdf (accessed 9 April 2015).

Declaration of the United Nations Conference on the Human Environment, Stockholm, 16 June 1972, 11 *International Legal Materials* (1972) 1416.

Gabčíkovo-Nagymaros Project (Hungary/Slovakia), ICJ judgment of 25 September 1997.

Gore, A. (1992) *Earth in the Balance: Forging a New Common Purpose*, Earthscan, London.

Gribbin, J. (1988) *The Hole in the Sky*, Corgi, London.

Hardin, G. (1968) 'The Tragedy of the Commons', *Science*, 162: 1243–1248.

'Indonesian-Swiss country-led initiative to improve the effectiveness of the Basel Convention', Basel Convention Decision 10/3, (2011).

Ingram, A. (1978) *Trapping and Poaching*, Shire Album 34, Shire Publications, Princes Risbourough.

IUCN with the assistance of UNEP and WWF (1980) *The World Conservation Strategy: Living Resource Conservation for Sustainable Development*.

Johannesburg Summit, 'The Johannesburg Summit Test: What will Change?', www.johannesburgsummit.org/html/whats_new/feature_story41.html (accessed 9 April 2015).

Juan Antonio Oposa et al. v. The Honorable Fulgencio S. Factoran, Jr., in his capacity as the Secretary of the Department of Environment and Natural Resources, and the Honorable Eriberto U. Rosario, Presiding Judge of the RTC, Makati, Branch 66, respondents [G.R. No. 101083. 30 July, 1993].

Lyster, S. (1985) *International Wildlife Law*, Grotius Publications, Cambridge.

Mackenzie, J.M. (1988) *The Empire of Nature*, Manchester University Press, Manchester.

Matthews, G.V.T. (2013) *The Ramsar Convention on Wetlands: its History and Development*, Ramsar Convention Bureau, Gland.

Memorandum of Cooperation between the Secretariat of the Convention on Wetlands (Ramsar, Iran, 1971) and the Ramsar Convention's International Organisation Partners (IOPs) 2011–2017, www.ramsar.org/sites/default/files/documents/pdf/moc/MoC_5IOPs_19-5-11_SIGNED.pdf (accessed 6 April 2015).

Michaelsen, T. (Undated) 'The Intergovernmental Forest Policy Dialogue: From Rio to UNFF', FAO, 'FAO and Industry Activities in Forestry', www.fao.org/docrep/003/y1720e/y1720e04.htm (visited 23 April 2015).

Mrema, E.M. (2014) 'Reactions to the Rio+20 Outcome Document "The Future We Want", in Honkonen', T., Lewis, M. and Couzens, E. (eds), *International Environmental Law-making and Diplomacy Review 2013*, UEF-UNEP Course Series 13, University of Eastern Finland, Joensuu.

Non-legally Binding Authoritative Statement of Principles for a Global Consensus on the Management, Conservation and Sustainable Development of all Types of Forests, Rio de Janeiro, 3–14 June 1992, UN Doc. A/CONF.151/26 (Vol. III).

Office of the Commissioner for Sustainability and the Environment (Undated), 'About the Commissioner', www.environmentcommissioner.act.gov.au/ (accessed 24 May 2015).

Plan of Implementation of the World Summit on Sustainable Development, UN Doc. A/CONF.199/20 (2002).

Programme of Action of the United Nations International Conference on Population and Development, Cairo, 13 September 1994, UN Doc. A/CONF.171/13 1994.

Rio Declaration on Environment and Development, Rio de Janeiro, 14 June 1992, UN Doc. A/CONF.151/5/Rev.1 (1992), 31 *International Legal Materials* (1992) 876.

Sands, P. (2008) 'Litigating Environmental Disputes: Courts, Tribunals and the Progressive Development of International Environmental Law', *Proceedings of the OECD Global Forum on International Investment*, 27–28 March 2008.

Smith, N.J.H. *et al.* (1995) 'Extractive Resources' in *Amazonia: Resiliency and Dynamism of the Land and its People* , United Nations University, Tokyo, www.unu.edu/unupress/unupbooks/80906e/80906E00.htm#Contents (accessed 9 April 2015).

Stone, C.D. (1972/1996) 'Should Trees Have Standing? Towards Legal Rights for Natural Objects', in Stone, C.D. *Should Trees Have Standing: And Other Essays on Law, Morals and the Environment* (25th Anniversary ed.), Oceana Publications, New York.

Tolba, M.K. and Rummel-Bulska, I. (1998) *Global Environmental Diplomacy: Negotiating Environmental Agreements for the World, 1973–1992*, MIT Press, Cambridge, MA.

Trail Smelter Arbitration (USA v Canada) (1941), *American Journal of International Law*, 35: 684.

Transnational Environment Law, 'Case No. 6: "The Rainbow Warrior"', www.jura.uni-muenchen.de/einrichtungen/ls/simma/tel/case6.htm (accessed 9 April 2015).

Trench, C.C. (1967) *The Poacher and the Squire: A history of poaching and game preservation in England*, Longmans, London.

UN Case *Rainbow Warrior* (1986) Case concerning the differences between New Zealand and France arising from the *Rainbow Warrior* affair, Ruling of 6 July 1986 by the Secretary-General of the United Nations, *Reports of International Arbitral Awards* Vol. XIX: 199–221.

UNEP (2010), 'Busan Outcome', www.unep.org/pdf/SMT_Agenda_Item_5-Busan_Outcome.pdf (accessed 24 May 2015).

UNGA (1982) 'World Charter for Nature', UNGA Res. 37/7, 28 October 1982.

UNGA (2012) 'The Future We Want' Outcome Document, UNGA Res. 66/288, 27 July 2012.
Young, C.R. (1979) *The Royal Forests of Medieval England*, University of Pennsylvania Press, Philadelphia.
Whaling in the Antarctic (Australia v. *Japan, New Zealand* intervening), ICJ judgment of 31 March 2014.
World Commission on Environment and Development (WCED) 1987, *Our Common Future*, Oxford University Press, Oxford.

9 The development of the concept of sustainable development and the birth of UNEP

Donald W. Kaniaru

Introductory remarks

The concept of sustainable development and its translation into concrete actions is of concern to all countries, whether developed or developing. There can be no debate about whether it should be more of a concern to one group of countries rather than any other. This concern, however, must still be perceived in historical terms. Developed countries reached their current level of development at a considerable cost, having not always been sensitive to the rate at which natural resources within their reach were used. Resources, both renewable and non-renewable, were used voraciously so that these countries' industrial development arguably used up more than their fair share of the global common resources. Indeed, that pattern of development may also have produced more than its fair share of wastes, dumping these in so-called global common sinks. In this light, it is in order to ask the following questions: when, by whom and how was the risk of global warming created? How did we deplete the global ozone layer that protects us all from damaging ultra violet rays? The purpose of raising such questions and concerns is not to point an accusing finger, far from it. This would, in fact, clearly be counter-productive.

The present author does not argue that developing countries should now pursue development patterns similar to those of the past, ignoring the grave consequences that would surely result for all of us. Mahatma Gandhi has been quoted as asking: '[i]f it took Britain half the resources of the globe to be what it is today, how many globes would India need?' (Tolba and Rummel-Bulska, 1998: 1).[1] What this chapter suggests, therefore, is that the concept of sustainable development is now able to provide a common agenda for both developed and developing countries. Indeed, it provides the only feasible basis for assured common development. This pattern has been concisely encapsulated in the international debate on development by the phrase: 'common agenda with differentiated responsibilities'. The alternative, i.e. the patterns of development of traditional industrialized societies, could, if followed and emulated now by developing countries, only result in mutually assured under-development, perhaps even mutual destruction.

1 Original attribution of quote doubtful. The earliest reference found appears in the journal of the South Place Ethical Society, London: (1983) *The Ethical Record* 88:2 at 12.

Sustainable development and international law have created a symbiosis. In the United Nations Environment Programme (UNEP), prior to the full development of the concept of sustainable development, the international environmental law programme was embryonic. With the consolidation of the concept of sustainable development, it has grown and is still growing to new levels of importance. The present chapter will first address the period leading up to the 1972 Stockholm Conference and look at the process leading to the birth of UNEP. Thereafter, the chapter focuses on the concept of sustainable development in more detail and shows how it is being applied in practice, as well as how it has been promoted by UNEP.

The significance of the Stockholm Conference and the story of the birth of UNEP

The lead-up to and outcomes of the Conference

The mid-1960s witnessed many important issues being raised and many decisions being taken at the global level in such diverse fields as social, economic and industrial development, oceans, and the future direction of the environment. In the industrial development sector, this culminated in 1965 in the establishment by the United Nations General Assembly of the United Nations Industrial Development Organization (UNIDO), its location being competitively settled in Vienna with Nairobi having lost to Vienna in the final vote (which vote was taken by secret ballot).

In other sectors, policy efforts were also being made at the international level. In 1967, the Maltese Ambassador to the UN, Arvid Pardo, called on the international community to regulate the resources and wealth of the oceans beyond the limits of national jurisdiction as the common heritage of mankind. This opened the process of intense global negotiations in the Third Conference on the Law of the Sea, resulting in the adoption of the United Nations Convention on the Law of the Sea (UNCLOS) in 1982. In addition, a series of expert discussions elaborating on relationships between the environment and development culminated in the Founex Report, released in 1971, which sought to reconcile environment and development (Founex Report on Development and Environment, 1971).

At about the same time as Arvid Pardo's policy opening, in 1968, concern about emerging environmental degradation as a result of human activities led Sweden to call on the global community to address issues relating to the human environment. Initially, the matter was raised in the UN Economic and Social Council (ECO SOC), which recommended to the General Assembly that a UN Conference on the Human Environment (UNCHE) be held in Stockholm in June 1972, and that its preparatory process be set in motion. The General Assembly approved the Council's recommendations.

The focus by Sweden on the environment, and thus the impetus for addressing environmental issues at the global level, resulted from pollution concerns arising from human activities that were degrading the environment. It is notable that

Sweden, in raising this matter globally, had also taken steps at the national level by instituting an environmental statute in 1968. Other countries, led by Japan and the United States, in 1969 and 1970 respectively, followed suit.

The preparations for the Stockholm Conference were brisk, and took place between 1968 and 1972.[2] During the preparatory meetings[3] and consultations, several key concerns of different regional and political groupings emerged. For developing countries, it became clear that the focus of the Conference, perceived as being on pollution, was too narrow and that it might constrain their industrial development, something on which they were not prepared to compromise. Equally, developing countries had to be assured of additional financial resources and technical assistance before they would attend the conference. These were serious concerns and the Secretary-General of the Conference moved to address them so as to secure the attendance of developing countries. Major efforts were made to clarify the relationship between environment and development, the best known of which was at the 1971 experts meeting in Founex, Switzerland. The Founex Report's acknowledgement that many of the world's environmental problems result from underdevelopment and poverty was apparently a factor that helped to persuade many developing countries to attend the Stockholm Conference (IISD, 1997).

Developing countries were not the only ones with specific concerns. Eastern European countries, led by the then Soviet Union, had their political concerns as well. Participation by the German Democratic Republic needed to be guaranteed to avoid the bloc as a whole boycotting the Conference. This issue was resolved and, as developing country matters had also been addressed, the Conference successfully took place.

The Stockholm Conference was held from 5–16 June, 1972. It produced a clear outcome presented in a three-chapter UN report. First, 26 principles were agreed in the Declaration of the United Nations Conference on the Human Environment (Stockholm Declaration, 1972). Second, the Action Plan for the Human Environment was agreed. Its 109 recommendations broadly embrace three types of action or functions: environmental assessment, environmental management and supporting measures (Action Plan for the Human Environment, 1972).

Although the Stockholm Declaration did not expressly mention the term 'sustainable development', in a visionary way at least one third of its 26 principles anticipated or implied the concept, thus generally promoting future action on the subject. In value and vision, it can even be argued that the Stockholm Declaration was more advanced even than the later Rio Declaration, 1992.

---

2 See Problems of the Human Environment, GA Res. 2398 (XXIII), 3 December 1968; ECOSOC Res. 1448 (XLVII); United Nations Conference on the Human Environment, GA Res. 2581 (XXIV), 15 December 1969; Development and Environment, GA Res. 2849 (XXVI), 20 December 1971; Institutional and Financial Arrangements for International Environmental Co-operation, GA Res. 2997 (XXVII), 15 December 1972.

3 First session, New York, 10–20 March 1970; second session, Geneva, 8–19 February 1971; third session, New York, 13–24 September 1971; and fourth session, New York, 6–17 March 1972.

The process of establishing UNEP

This framework established by the outcome of the Stockholm Conference provided the basis for establishing the United Nations Environment Programme (UNEP) (on the establishment, see generally Kimani, 2004; Mwaura, 2004; and Ivanova, 2007) and the substantive basis for cooperation within, and to some extent outside, the UN system. The Conference had produced a Resolution on Institutional and Financial Arrangements where the structure of the 'international cooperative programme in the environment field' was agreed to consist of a governing council for environmental programmes; an environment secretariat headed by an executive director; an environment fund; and an environmental coordination board.

Regarding the programmatic side of the new programme, the overall thrust of the Conference was sufficiently clarified and consensus was reached in Stockholm. In the period leading up to the 27th Session of the UN General Assembly, a few months after the Stockholm Conference, these programmatic issues were by and large uncontroversial, particularly as it became clear to specialized agencies that governments were determined to set up a mechanism within the UN rather than to have one of the existing agencies, such as the Food and Agriculture Organization (FAO) or the UN Educational, Scientific and Cultural Organization (UNESCO), carry out the new tasks.

It is important here to underline an issue raised but not resolved during the Stockholm Conference: the location of the aforementioned environment secretariat. The Report of the Conference gave any state wishing to offer to host the secretariat the opportunity to do so (Report of the Stockholm Conference, 1972: paras 54 and 292). Many offers came forward, becoming the subject of intense negotiations both in New York and in the capitals of the competing countries. The location of the secretariat is an issue which is always highly political and contentious. Having lost its bid for Nairobi to host UNIDO, the decision proved to be a catalyst for intensified Kenyan diplomatic efforts to become the home of a future UN agency or organization. Various developed countries, apparently sensing that the location might be different from what they had hoped, mooted the idea that the decision be postponed until the next session of the UNGA, the 28th, in 1973. Developing countries strongly opposed such a postponement.

There were, however, certain problems related to taking a decision in the 27th Session. First, not all of the offers had been presented with the necessary level of detail. The financial implications, which were, of course, necessary before the General Assembly could reach any decision, were only available with respect to locating the secretariat in New York, Geneva or another established UN headquarters. Second, with numerous offers, it was uncertain whether a clear direction on the preferred location would emerge before the end of the session. (Some developed countries inclined towards co-locating the new secretariat either with the UN Secretariat in New York or with, or in the vicinity of, the UN offices in Geneva or Vienna. Other offers by developed countries included London, Madrid, Monaco and Valletta. Developing countries, on the other hand, put forward Kampala, Kinshasa, Lagos, Mexico City, Nairobi and New Delhi as possible locations.) It should also be noted that while the Geneva-based secretariat that prepared for the Stockholm Conference should have been neutral, it seemed to lean towards Geneva or New York in its report. Given this scenario, it was not an easy task for the Kenyan delegation, of which the present author was a member, to convince the General Assembly that Nairobi should become the location of the new secretariat.

As noted above, in 1965 Nairobi had lost to Vienna in its bid to host UNIDO. This occurred despite the issue of industrial development being very important to developing countries. However, when the location of UNIDO was determined, Kenya had only been independent for two years. By the 27th Session of the General Assembly, Kenya had been independent for nine years, and had already played a pivotal role in international affairs in Africa, amongst developing countries and within non-aligned countries. It had also played a pivotal role in key issues within the UN. Notably, in 1972 it was elected a member of the Security Council, effective from 1973. It had also played a crucial role in the law of the sea negotiations, in outer space issues and in questions related to apartheid as well as to Southern Rhodesia. Efforts in these areas brought votes for Nairobi from states outside the developing world. In addition, it will be recalled that the 1965 vote on UNIDO's location was by secret ballot. This perceived obstacle was overcome by the Kenyan delegation by insisting, with the support of the other African delegations, that a vote first be taken on whether or not to vote through secret ballot. Voting by secret ballot was rejected this time around.

Outside Europe and the United States, Africa had the largest number of countries expressing an interest to host what is now the UNEP Secretariat. It was important, therefore, for Kenya to obtain the support of other African countries before negotiating with delegations from other regions. In 1972, however, it was not common for the then Organization for African Unity (OAU; now the African Union (AU)) to take from the start a unified position on the basis of which negotiations would proceed with other countries or groupings. A common position was nevertheless reached and an early draft resolution was sponsored by the African Group, signalling that African states were moving together. Considering that at the time all global UN headquarters were located either in Western Europe or North America, and that a good argument could be made that such bodies ought to be geographically equitably located, this draft resolution proposed that the operative paragraph read: 'Decides to locate the environment secretariat in a developing country' (Draft Res., 1972: para. 1). As this wording would not hurt the candidatures of New Delhi or Mexico City, Asian and Latin American countries could also support it. Backing was also obtained from other Group of 77 countries, such as Albania and Yugoslavia, as well as from China. With sponsors from such a geographical spread, Kenya was able successfully to introduce the draft resolution in the UN General Assembly's Second Committee.

This, however, left the Western European and Others Group (WEOG) uneasy. It was argued that the UN Secretariat had no basis for calculating the financial implications of selecting Nairobi. It was also felt that as the organization or secretariat that was to be established would be small and would mainly coordinate the environmental aspects within the UN system, the best location for it would be within or near the other UN agencies, i.e. in Geneva, New York or Vienna. It was feared that an alternative in a 'remote' place like Nairobi or New Delhi might be very expensive (see Ivanova, 2005). Developing countries did not share this fear. Moreover, if such arguments were relied on, no UN body would ever be located in a developing country. To guarantee that a decision would not be postponed, Kenya introduced a second operative paragraph into the draft resolution, calling for the matter to be settled during the 27th Session of the General Assembly (Draft Res., 1972: para. 2). By then, Mexico City had withdrawn, leaving Nairobi and New Delhi as the only developing country contenders to host the secretariat.

As noted above, one of the key issues to be addressed related to financial implications of the draft resolution. It was important, therefore, to obtain an accurate estimate of what the costs of locating to Nairobi might be. A two-person UN team visited Nairobi to assess whether Nairobi met the necessary criteria; for example, the number of diplomatic missions there, transport connections, etc. Their overall report was favourable.

Having thus successfully addressed the financial aspects, Kenya needed to address New Delhi's rival candidature. Through negotiations both at UN headquarters in New York, and between the Indian and Kenyan capitals, it became apparent that India would eventually concede to Kenya. Due to good relations between the two countries, their respective leaders (Indira Gandhi and Jomo Kenyatta) settled the issue: India withdrew in favour of Kenya. A draft resolution (Draft Res., 1972) was presented before the Second Committee. With the financial aspects prepared and India having withdrawn in favour of Kenya, the matter proceeded to a vote in the Second Committee and later, on 15 December 1972, the General Assembly unanimously selected Nairobi as the location of the future UNEP Secretariat (UNGA, 1972, Res. 3004 (XXVII)).

There were numerous practical challenges involved in setting up the Secretariat in Nairobi. The 1st session of the UNEP Governing Council (GC) had to be held in Geneva, which already had the best-suited facilities and where the staff that had prepared for the Stockholm Conference was located. Subsequent regular sessions of the GC, starting with the 2nd Session in 1974 and including the first United Nations Environment Assembly (UNEA), in June 2014, were held in Nairobi at the new Secretariat headquarters.

After the decision was made to locate the UNEP Secretariat in Nairobi, the negotiations still had to be finalized. An interim agreement was quickly agreed according UN officials the privileges availed to diplomats in Kenya. With regard to a permanent agreement, some difficulties did arise but these were few and quickly dealt with, and the agreement was signed between the United Nations and the Government of Kenya in less than two years, on 26 March 1975. There were immediate gains from the Headquarters Agreement. The Agreement applies, *mutatis mutandis*, to any global organization that may be located in Kenya (Headquarters Agreement, 1975: Art. 16 s 45). Consequently, Nairobi presently hosts, besides UNEP, the UN-Habitat (this being the UN programme for human settlements) and the United Nations office at Nairobi (UNON). Before the Headquarters Agreement was concluded, Kenya made a concession to allow its internationally recruited nationals to enjoy equivalent privileges to other internationally recruited staff. Other agreements with intergovernmental and non-governmental organizations in Kenya do not enjoy such status. Kenya's commitment from the highest echelons of government to support the UN in Nairobi was unequivocal.

Having become one of the four UN headquarters after Geneva, New York and Vienna, Kenya was obliged to allow all officials coming to the UN in Nairobi to enter the country. Several points related to this made Kenya anxious at times. The question of apartheid South Africa, which at the time was not yet suspended as a UN member state, was a case in point, as were countries with which Kenya had no diplomatic relations, such as North Korea. Both of these countries were, however, expected to attend UN meetings in Nairobi, and Kenya had no choice but to allow these countries' delegates into the country.

The birth of UNEP may be regarded as having initially resulted from the Stockholm process, but the discussions and negotiations took many turns before the issue was settled. Skilful diplomacy was and is required to settle many issues before the core work of an international organization can even begin.

The definition of the concept of sustainable development in 1987

The concept of sustainable development offers different connotations depending on the expertise of the speaker: whether it is ecology, economics, law, politics, sociology, and so on. Many commentators have given it attention in the form of philosophical analysis and criticism. A common starting point for presentations is the definition offered in the book *Our Common Future*. Released in 1987, this is the final report of the World Commission on Environment and Development, the so-called 'Brundtland Commission' named after its chairperson Gro Harlem Brundtland. The Commission was established by a UN General Assembly Resolution (UNGA, 1983, Res. 38/161), following a resolution by the UNEP Governing Council (GC Res. A/37/25, II), which recommended to the General Assembly to establish a voluntarily financed special commission to propose environmental strategies to the year 2000 and beyond. The report provided the popular coinage of sustainable development, defining it as 'development that meets the needs of the present without compromising the ability of future generations to meet their own needs' (*Our Common Future* – WCED, 1987: 43).

This broad understanding of sustainable development denotes development, equity, fairness, and growth in a world of so many poor across the globe. Estimates of people living in poverty range from between one-quarter and one-third of the global population of seven billion, the worst affected regions being in the developing world. In 2012, at the UN Conference on Sustainable Development, the signatories to the Outcome Document 'The Future We Want' indicated that '[w]e are deeply concerned that one in five people on this planet, or over 1 billion people, still live in extreme poverty, and that one in seven or 14 per cent is undernourished' (UNGA, 2012, 'The Future We Want': para. 21). In such a situation it is quite a challenge to realize sustainable development at the local, national, regional and global levels. However, the phrase still underlines all the right words and intentions. The Brundtland Commission further acknowledged that:

> [i]n essence, sustainable development, addressed in its broadest context of social, economic and environmental spheres, is a process of change in which the exploitation of resources, the direction of investments, the orientation of technological development and institutional change are all in harmony and enhance both current and future potential to meet human needs and aspirations.
>
> (WCED, 1987: 46)

It has been pointed out by Hunter *et al.* that even if the Brundtland Commission did not invent the term sustainable development, it popularized the term and placed it squarely in the centre of international policy-making (Hunter *et al.*, 2011: 148). Hunter *et al.* add that partly because of its 'brilliant ambiguity', the concept has received nearly universal acceptance among every sector of international society (*ibid.*, 2011: 148).

Interestingly, in the same year that the Brundtland Commission report was released, Mostafa Tolba, the Executive Director of UNEP from 1975 to 1992, contemplated the emerging interlinkage of 'environment and development', 'environmentally sound development' and 'sustainable development' in his book *Sustainable Development: Constraints and Opportunities* (Tolba, 1987). He stated that long-term development can only be achieved through sound environmental management, that is, sustainable development (Tolba, 1987: vii). Commenting on the relationship between the environment and development since the 1960s, he noted that past practices and beliefs had changed dramatically:

> [i]t is now clear that without environmental protection, it is not possible to have sustained development, and without development, it is not possible to have a high quality of our environment and an improved quality of life for all the world's citizens. Thus, what we need is sustainable development, that is, development that can be sustainable over the long-term by explicitly considering the various environmental factors on which the very process of development is based.
>
> (*ibid.*)

The statement reflects the interconnectivity between different elements of (sustainable) development. The perception of the environment–development nexus was as actual then as it is now.

The 1992 UNCED: Reaffirming sustainable development

The concept of sustainable development itself and the principles arising from it were endorsed by heads of state and government during the United Nations

Conference on Environment and Development (UNCED) in Rio de Janeiro in 1992. The significance of the UNCED within this context is that it gave the concept political legitimacy (Dowdeswell, 1995: x) and unrivalled momentum through all of the Rio Declaration, with no less than ten of the Declaration's 27 Principles expressly mentioning sustainable development; Agenda 21, the Declaration's companion blueprint document; the Forest Principles; the Convention on Biological Diversity (CBD); and the United Nations Framework Convention on Climate Change (UNFCCC).

After Rio, sustainable development has been included in all major global and regional parleys and the concept has become a rallying point for all who address environment and development issues. In this connection, efforts to integrate sustainable development into decision-making, planning, development and management processes have abounded at all levels. It can be said with confidence that, since the UNCED, global policy and law have shaped not only global and regional conventions and instruments, but national environmental law and policy as well.

Conferences on sustainable development since 1992

Several global and regional conferences on the theme of sustainable development – both within and outside of the United Nations system – have taken place since 1992. These include the 1994 Global Conference on the Sustainable Development of Small Island Developing States in Barbados; the 1994 United Nations International Conference on Population and Development in Cairo; and the 1995 World Summit on Social Development in Copenhagen. Also noteworthy are the regular reviews of the UNCED: the five-year review by the 19th UN General Assembly Special Session in 1997; the ten-year review by the World Summit on Sustainable Development (WSSD) in 2002; and the twenty-year review by the UN Conference on Sustainable Development (UNCSD), or 'Rio+20', held in Rio in 2012, respectively. In these reviews of Agenda 21 and other sustainable development policies, concern over the lack of progress in the implementation of the Rio blueprint has been conspicuous. Indeed, at WSSD new emphasis was predictably placed on implementation. In the Rio+20 Conference, sustainable development was treated in a holistic manner, emphasizing its equitable and far-sighted implementation, for instance through applying 'green economy' models.

The role of the judiciary in defining sustainable development

It should be noted that earlier global and regional conferences and efforts mostly involved only the executive branches of governments; and to some extent parliaments that were involved in voting resources for global and regional parleys, in ratifying conventions and being involved in the governing bodies of intergovernmental organizations. It was not until late 1996 that the judiciary at the regional and global levels became deliberately sensitized to environmental matters – primarily through UNEP-related initiatives (which are discussed below). Since then, much national judicial activity has taken place in many countries and in all regions, followed by the extensive sharing of law reports and guidelines for use by the judiciary and legal practitioners at the national level. For example, at Rio+20 in 2012, over 250 of the world's Chief Justices, Attorneys General and Auditors General seized a generational opportunity to contribute to the debates on the environment at the World Congress on Justice, Governance and Law for Environmental Sustainability organized by UNEP and follow-up in conjunction with UNEP's first session of the UNEA in Nairobi.

HE Judge Christopher Weeramantry, the former Vice-President of the International Court of Justice (ICJ) has emphasized that sustainable development is not a new concept. This was made clear in the Separate Opinion that Judge Weeramantry attached to the judgment of the ICJ in the *Gabčíkovo-Nagymaros* case in 1997. The Judge stated that

> sustainable development is thus not merely a principle of modern international law. It is one of the most ancient of ideas in human heritage. Fortified by the rich insights that can be gained from millennia of human experience, it has an important part to play in the service of international law.
>
> (Separate Opinion, 1997: 107)

The Judge reviewed various dimensions of the appreciation of the concept from thousands of years ago in Africa, in Australia among the Aborigines, in Asia and Sri Lanka, as well as among North American Indians. He has subsequently observed, quite rightly, that:

> the human family has learnt to live in harmony with the environment for thousands of years and has achieved this in a very successful manner. If we fail to look at the past for its traditional wisdom in facing our environmental problems, we may be depriving ourselves of this very important source of wisdom.
>
> (Weeramantry, 2004: 439)

The often cited Separate Opinion of Judge Weeramantry has provided some legal clarification, or at least it elaborated the contents, of the principle of sustainable development. It could be said that in the *Gabčíkovo-Nagymaros* case, the ICJ as a whole missed out on an opportunity to elaborate on and apply the principle of sustainable development; instead only mentioning the matter in paragraph 140 of the Judgment. However, obiter minority judgments can sometimes be as, or more, influential as majority judgments and the Separate Opinion could be described as likely to open new avenues and horizons for regional and national jurisdictions to expound the principle judicially. Regional courts have played a role in applying the principle of sustainable development. Discernible judicial efforts have also been seen at the national level in all regions in countries such as Australia, Canada, India, Italy, Malawi, New Zealand, Pakistan, the Philippines, South Africa, Uganda, and so on.

Right before and after the ICJ Judgment in the *Gabčíkovo-Nagymaros* case, UNEP organized (and later organizations have carried them out independently) judicial symposia where judges have committed to taking up the challenge of applying the set of sustainable development principles. This has led to a number of promising initiatives, such as the creation of regional judicial networks through which members of the judiciaries of various countries can locate information and gain support. An example is the Asian Judges Network on Environment – an 'information and experience sharing arrangement' involving senior judges from the Association of Southeast Asian Nations (ASEAN) (Asian Judges Network on Environment, 2015). It should be remembered that sustainable development, indeed environmental law itself, remains a relatively recent development and many members of national judiciaries will have received their formal legal training before the development of cohesive concepts in the field.

Sustainable development in practice under international environmental law

The levels of discussion and negotiation of the concept of sustainable development have been myriad. The concept has been addressed globally in academic circles, by diplomats at conferences and other intergovernmental fora and within global and regional non-governmental organizations (NGOs); at the national level it has been addressed in integrating decision-making, in institutional review and restructuring and in law-making and application. The high watermark, however, was the overwhelming global endorsement of the sustainable development agenda at UNCED in 1992 by over 100 heads of state and government, and its subsequent reinforcement in various fora and instruments, both binding and non-binding. These are summarized below.

Sustainable development principles find expression in the preamble(s) and in the operative articles of numerous global, regional and sub-regional conventions, treaties and protocols. In some instruments, reference is made in the preamble to the entire Rio Declaration without specifying a particular aspect of the Declaration. For example, Recital 2 of the Preamble to the 1998 Convention on the Prior Informed Consent Procedure for Certain Hazardous Chemicals and Pesticides in International Trade recalls 'the pertinent provisions of the Rio Declaration' (Rotterdam Convention). In other treaties, sustainable development principles are not only recognized in preambles but in one or more articles. Examples of this may be found in Articles 2 and 3 of the UNFCCC; in the Preamble and Articles 1 and 10 of the CBD; and in the Preamble and Article 9(1) of the 1994 United Nations Convention to Combat Desertification.

As mentioned above, no less than ten of the Rio Principles are themselves integral to sustainable development, and these find, individually or severally, express reference and/or endorsement in many treaties. These include the polluter pays principle; the precautionary principle or approach; international cooperation; intergenerational equity, etc., all of which add to due recognition and endorsement of the broader principle of sustainable development.

The Rio Principles are also applied in legally binding regional instruments including in the Preamble of the North American Free Trade Agreement, 1992; in Article 2 of the Treaty on European Union, 2002; and in the African Union's 2003 African Convention on the Conservation of Nature and Natural Resources, which updated the 1968 Algiers Convention on the same subject, making the revised Convention the most comprehensive regional biodiversity convention. The 2003 Convention is not yet in force, however.

Specific instruments have also been elaborated based on specific Rio Principles. For example, Principle 10 suggests that environmental issues are best handled with the participation of all concerned citizens at relevant levels; that individuals should have appropriate access to information concerning the environment held by public authorities; that individuals should be given the opportunity to participate in decision-making processes; that information should be made widely available by states to encourage public awareness and participation; and that effective access to administrative and judicial proceedings, including redress and remedy, should be provided. Principle 10 has been developed in the 1998 Convention on Access to Information, Public Participation in Decision-Making and Access to Justice in Environmental Matters (Aarhus Convention). Although this instrument is essentially designed for the United Nations Economic Commission for Europe (UNECE) region, per Article 19(3), it is also open to states from outside this region. However, this offer has not been taken, most likely because states from other regions were not part of the process to negotiate the instrument.

Rio Principle 10 is widely applied across all regions through strategy and policy documents and through legally binding regional and sub-regional conventions. Upon adoption, the Aarhus Convention was shared with regional commissions by the Executive Secretary of UNECE as well as by the Executive Director of UNEP, whose unit, Infoterra, was fully involved in the discussions leading to the Convention as well as during its negotiation. In fact, in 1999 the Executive Director brought the Convention to the attention of the Governing Council, which was not enthusiastic about moving in the direction of a global convention on Principle 10. It did, however, encourage UNEP to review the practice of different countries and regions. This led to a report to the Council in 2001. In Africa, the Southern African Development Community (SADC), with financing from Ireland, studied the Aarhus approach during the Aarhus negotiations themselves, and thereafter in Gaborone in 1998. At the national level, the majority of the more than 50 African states have incorporated Principle 10 in national statutes or constitutional provisions.[4]

Policy instruments on sustainable development are widespread and include national Agenda 21 documents, derived from the UNCED Agenda 21, and National Action Plans and Sustainable Development strategies. Policy dialogue

---

4 See UNEP-PADELIA, *Compendium of Environmental Laws of African Countries*, www.unep.org/padelia/publications/laws.html; and UNEP-PADELIA, *Compendium of Environmental Provisions in African Constitutions* (forthcoming).

vis-à-vis policy action, or inaction, is often taken up by the media and NGOs to put pressure on governments to take action to ratify or accede to conventions, or to institute administrative and legal measures on sustainable development, for instance. Institutional reviews and restructuring also take place as a means of implementing law and policy.

Many national constitutions, such as those in Kenya (2010, s.42) and South Africa (1996, s.24), include legal provisions surrounding sustainable development principles. Specific principles are also often found embedded in framework legislation in developing countries. Examples include the Environmental Management and Co-ordination Act of Kenya (No. 8 of 1999); the National Environment Management Act of South Africa (No. 107 of 1998); and the National Environment Act of Uganda (No. 4 of 2000). In the case of Kenya, Section 3 of the Act pools together several principles into one sustainable development principle. The six relevant principles are:

a) the principle of public participation in the development of policies, plans and processes for the management of the environment;
b) the cultural and social principles traditionally applied by any community in Kenya for the management of the environment or natural resources in so far as the same are relevant and are not repugnant to justice and morality or inconsistent with any written law;
c) the principle of international cooperation in the management of environmental resources shared by two or more states;
d) the principles of intergenerational and intragenerational equity;
e) the polluter pays principle; and
f) the precautionary principle (section 3(5)).

The goals of sustainable development have been accepted and championed in the programmes and efforts of both UN and non-UN organizations within their respective global, regional and national mandates, where they are primary players. Within the UN family these include the UN itself and organs such as the United Nations Development Programme (UNDP), UNEP, UNIDO, the United Nations Conference on Trade and Development (UNCTAD), etc. UN specialized agencies that have taken up this challenge include FAO, UNESCO and the UN Regional Economic and Social Commissions. Non-UN organizations that have taken up this challenge include the World Bank Group, regional development banks, the International Union for Conservation of Nature (IUCN), and regional organizations like the European Union and the African Union.

UNEP as a promoter of sustainable development

Sustainable development has given rise to a new pattern of internationalism. This pattern in turn gave rise to new impetus in the field of international environmental law. The two, sustainable development and international environmental law, have created a symbiosis. In the United Nations Environment Programme, prior to the full development of the concept of sustainable development, the international environmental law programme was embryonic. With the consolidation of the sustainable development concept, it has grown and is still growing to new levels of importance.

After the 1972 Stockholm Conference, the effort to clarify further the relationship between environment and development continued. UNEP spearheaded this effort in attempting to influence the UN system, especially through the UN Economic Commissions and through governments. UNEP tried to demonstrate that environment and development were compatible: that they were in fact 'two sides of the same coin'. A series of seminars on alternative patterns of development and lifestyles (see UNEP, 1980) were prepared with the regional commissions, and a final interregional seminar was held pooling the results. As a result, the debate on environment and development became increasingly relegated to the background, despite a UNEP programme on Environment and Development, which continued to clarify the relationship over the first decade of UNEP's existence. Later, UNEP continued to address the challenges of sustainable development. One could, for instance, mention UNEP's participation in policy-making and numerous publications on the theme (for instance, Dowdeswell, 1995; and the Global Environment Outlook (GEO) reports).

In the 1974 Declaration of Cocoyoc, UNEP and UNCTAD focused on poverty alleviation and held a series of regional meetings on consumption patterns. However, it is to be noted that the Cocoyoc outcomes were not followed up; a fate that has tended to befall many recommendations made by global and regional fora. Unfortunately, despite the good intentions evident in many initiatives, numerous factors then militate against effective implementation – including factors related to cost, education, expertise, industrial and political opposition, knowledge, and understanding of long-term consequences.

UNEP has worked as a programme for over four decades and has helped to midwife the birth of several mechanisms under the overall guidance of respective Conferences of the Parties (CoPs). These include (to name but a few) the Vienna Convention on the Protection of the Ozone Layer, 1985 and its 1987 Montreal Protocol; the Convention on Transboundary Movement of Hazardous Wastes, 1989 (Basel Convention); the CBD; the regional seas conventions (www.unep.org/regionalseas); and the 1995 Global Programme for the Protection of the Marine Environment (www.gpa.unep.org).

The modality of work from UNEP's inception has been that of partnership with the UN system, and specifically with UNDP, the regional commissions and key specialized agencies including UNESCO, FAO, the World Health Organization (WHO) and the International Maritime Organization (IMO). The main focus of UNEP's partnerships was with these institutions. Close cooperation has also taken place with governments and NGOs, particularly the IUCN, as well as with the scientific community.

Concluding remarks

The content and definition of sustainable development is not closed and will not close within the foreseeable future. The principle and concept can be said to be vague, even 'brilliantly vague' (per Hunter *et al.*, 2011: 148). This permits the definition and application of sustainable development to be tailored to specific situations and circumstances. At the local level, the state of knowledge, experience and resources will always be key, and local cultural and social values should be integrated into sustainable development legislation. Further insight can be gained from local experience of centuries of sustainable living in tough desert environments, for instance. Vagueness in interpretation will therefore remain a positive attribute of the concept, giving it life in different situations and circumstances over time.

One could argue, perhaps, that this reflects also the caution with which states approach the creation of international environmental law. Many conventions in the field have needed to work through an initial stage characterized by a wide, 'framework' convention before moving to firmer obligations through protocols or other subsequent instruments. Perhaps what was needed with sustainable development was an initial wide concept to give a backdrop for the creation of more specific obligations, and as stated earlier, subject to situations and circumstances over time.

The concept has been widely embraced and championed worldwide and its application or implementation should be monitored and experiences should be shared. Despite their best endeavours, no country can yet claim to be a role model and to provide ideal examples of sustainable development in practice. None can claim total harmony in the integration and application of sustainable development into development, planning and decision-making. In fact, no society has yet reached its apex in its understanding and application of the concept, despite the fact that aspirations to concretize the concept abound and are held by many. In this regard, all have a contribution to make to translate these sentiments into action.

In essence, sustainable development, addressed in its broadest context of social, economic and environmental spheres, is a process of change in which the exploitation of resources, the direction of investments, the orientation of technological development and institutional change are all in harmony and enhance both current and future potential to meet human needs and aspirations.

Regarding the birth and operation of UNEP, it can be argued that Kenya, which enjoyed the overwhelming support of other developing countries, has hosted the organization in a sort of 'trust' for all developing countries. As the fourth UN centre after Geneva, New York and Vienna, Nairobi is a symbol of global integration and the universal presence of the United Nations system is vindicated. It is, therefore, not insignificant that UNEP has its seat in the developing world. While impossible to quantify, this probably influences UNEP and helps to give it legitimacy and drive its efforts.

The history of the creation of UNEP as a global 'organizing', educating and knowledge-disseminating, and promoting force, is fascinating. The organization was not easily 'won' and its history is well worth close study – as an example of the diplomacy required for, and the legal considerations toward creating, a global organization in the environmental field. Environmental issues are inevitably cross-cutting issues, across most fields of human interest, and this is where the true importance of the field lies.

The unfurling history of the concept of sustainable development is – likewise – crucial. Our understanding of the present needs always to be informed by awareness of what went before so that we can avoid repeating mistakes and build on past steps taken, as sustainable development unfolds in the future. Africa, and the developing world as a whole, has fought hard to gain recognition within the international community of its sustainable development needs and UNEP has played an important role within that battle. As Kenya was once seen as 'far from anywhere', so were environmental considerations seen as far from mainstream. Both views have changed!

References

Action Plan for the Human Environment, 16 June 1972, UN Doc. A/CONF.48/14/Rev.1 (1973).

Agenda 21 (1992) UN Conference on Environment and Development, Rio de Janeiro, 13 June 1992, UN Doc. A/CONF.151/26/Rev.1 (1992).

Asian Judges Network on Environment, www.asianjudges.org/ and www.asianjudges.org/about-ajne/ (accessed 13 April 2015).

Declaration of Cocoyoc, the UNEP/UNCTAD Symposium on Patterns of Resource Use, Environment and Development Strategies, Cocoyoc, Mexico, 8–12 October 1974.

Declaration of the United Nations Conference on the Human Environment, Stockholm (1972) UN Doc. A/CONF.48/14/Rev.1, 16 June 1972, *International Legal Materials*, 11: 1416.

Dowdeswell, E. (1995) 'Preface', in *UNEP's New Way Forward: Environmental Law and Sustainable Development* (Nairobi: UNEP) IX–XII.

Draft Resolution A/C.2/L1246/Rev.1 'Location of the Environment Secretariat' (1972).

Environmental Management and Co-ordination Act of Kenya, No 8 of 1999.

Founex Report on Development and Environment, Founex, Switzerland, 4–12 June 1971, www.stakeholderforum.org/fileadmin/files/Earth%20Summit%202012new/Publications%20and%20Reports/founex%20report%201972.pdf (accessed 24 May 2015).

Headquarters Agreement between the United Nations Environment Programme and the Government of Kenya, 26 March 1975, in Report of the UNEP GC on the work on its third session, 17 April–2 May 1975.

Hunter D., Salzman, J. and Zaelke, D. (2011) *International Environmental Law and Policy* (4th ed.), Foundation Press, New York.

IISD (1997) 'Sustainable Development Timeline', www.iisd.org/rio+5/timeline/sdtimeline.htm (accessed 9 April 2015).

Ivanova, M. (2005) 'Can the Anchor Hold? Rethinking the United Nations Environment Programme for the 21st Century', Yale Center for Environmental Law and Policy, Report No. 7 (New Haven: Yale School of Forestry and Environmental Studies), www.yale.edu/gegdialogue/Ivanova-FESReport7.pdf (accessed 1 April 2015).

Ivanova, M. (2007) 'Designing the United Nations Environment Programme: A Story of Compromise and Confrontation', *International Environmental Agreements: Politics, Law and Economics*, 7: 337–361.

Kimani, N. (2004) 'From Stockholm to Nairobi', *Environmental Policy and Law*, 34: 231–241.

Mwaura, P. (2004) 'United Nations Information Centre', *Sunday Nation* (Nairobi), 19 December 2004.

National Environment Act of Uganda, No. 4 of 2000.

National Environmental Management Act of South Africa, No. 107 of 1998.

Non-legally Binding Authoritative Statement of Principles for a Global Consensus on the Management, Conservation and Sustainable Development of all Types of Forests, Rio de Janeiro, 3–14 June 1992, UN Doc. A/CONF.151/26 (Vol. III).

Report of the United Nations Conference on Human Environment, UN Doc. A/CONF.48/14/Rev.1 (1973).

Resolution on Institutional and Financial Arrangements, 16 June 1972, UN Doc. A/CONF.48/14/Rev.1 (1973).

Separate Opinion of Vice-President Weeramantry, ICJ *Gabčíkovo-Nagymaros Project (Hungary/Slovakia)*, Judgment of 25 September 1997.

Tolba, M. (1987) *Sustainable Development: Constraints and Opportunities*, Butterworth-Heinemann, Guildford.

United Nations Declaration on Environment and Development, Rio de Janeiro (1992) UN Doc. A/CONF.151/5/Rev.1, 14 June 1992, *International Legal Materials*, 31: 876.

UNEP GC Res. A/37/25, II (1982).

UNEP (1980) *Choosing the Options: Alternative Lifestyles and Development Patterns*, UNEP, Nairobi.

UNEP, (n.d.) 'Regional Seas Programme', www.unep.org/regionalseas/.

UNGA (1972) Res. 3004 (XXVII), 'Location of the Environment Secretariat', 15 December 1972.

UNGA (1983) 'Process of Preparation of the Environmental Perspective to the Year 2000 and Beyond', UNGA Res. 38/161, 19 December 1983.

UNGA (2012) 'The Future We Want' Outcome Document, UNGA Res. 66/288, 27 July 2012.

Weeramantry, C.G. (2004) *Universalising International Law*, Martinus Nijhoff Publishers, Leiden.

World Commission on Environment and Development (WCED) (1987) *Our Common Future*, Oxford University Press, Oxford.

10 An overview of milestones in international environmental diplomacy and suggestions for improved environmental governance

Shafqat Kakakhel

Introduction

Environmental diplomacy can be defined, narrowly, as comprising negotiations among government representatives with the aim of concluding legally binding agreements, conventions or treaties, or non-binding instruments (such as plans of action or guidelines) for addressing environmental issues, requiring action both within national boundaries and across frontiers, by either a group of countries or all countries concerned with those issues. A broader definition would refer to all relevant factors and actors, such as socio-economic drivers, science and technology, or civil society and the media, where these affect the relationship between human actions and the ability of our planet to sustain life.

Environmental diplomacy is a relatively new field, diplomacy having historically focused on military and peace-making efforts. This changed as industry developed and led to the increased destruction of flora and fauna and the generation of waste and pollution, threatening the health of both humans and the natural world.

During the past two centuries, industrialization has been seen as the indispensable prerequisite of – indeed synonymous with – progress. The Industrial Revolution spawned, and is sustained by, a culture of materialism and consumerism viewed as being essential for human well-being. However, since the second half of the 20th century, growing numbers of individuals, groups, governments, and lately, industry, have begun to reduce the negative effects of industrial civilization through cleaner and more resource-efficient production processes. There is increasing recognition that durable solutions to environmental problems, especially those of a transboundary nature, require not only actions within national boundaries but also cooperative efforts between states.

The 1950s and 1960s saw the emergence of domestic action and international cooperation in addressing local, transboundary, and global environmental issues. In the United States (US) and Western Europe, campaigns by concerned citizens led to the enactment of laws and regulations aimed at avoiding or mitigating health hazards from many different forms of pollution. Domestic successes encouraged the revival and strengthening of pre-war efforts to negotiate agreements on international cooperation to deal with environmental threats that could only be countered through joint efforts by several or most countries. The 1960s and the 1970s saw a rapid increase in the number of regional and global environmental agreements, which were focused for the most part on the protection of wildlife and migratory species and the prevention and control of marine pollution. The 1972 UN Conference on the Human Environment (UNCHE) in Stockholm was truly a watershed event with regard to the evolution of the global environmental agenda.

Milestones in international environmental diplomacy

The UNCHE (1972)

The UNCHE in 1972 highlighted the international community's recognition that protection and improvement of the human environment was a global objective, whose realization would require action within countries as well as international cooperation. The Conference initiated a high-level debate process among government representatives, non-governmental organizations (NGOs) and other non-state actors, over the negative ecological impacts of human actions and population growth, and how the international community could act in concert to avoid and mitigate these. Stockholm brought to the fore points on which global consensus could be achieved, but also areas where rich and poor countries sharply disagreed on the genesis of the problems and the best methods for addressing them.

In June 1971, Maurice Strong, the Conference's Secretary-General, convened a discussion in Founex near Geneva between economists and senior officials from both developed and developing countries, whose meetings helped to clarify the issues to be addressed at the Conference (Strong, 2000: 124–125; Tolba and Rummel-Bulska, 1998: 2.6). Participants agreed that most serious environmental problems in poor countries resulted from extreme poverty and lack of economic development; and that developed countries must provide financial and technical resources to enable developing countries to achieve the linked objectives of socio-economic development and environmental protection.

Representatives of 113 countries, as well as scores of intergovernmental and non-governmental organizations attended the UNCHE, many apparently with different agendas. Developed countries paid lip service to the protection of the global environment but appeared unenthusiastic about providing financial support to developing countries. Developing countries conceded the importance of environmental protection but insisted that rich nations should lead, both with regard to domestic action and in assisting them to achieve economic development. The environmental organizations assembled in Stockholm carried out a spirited campaign demanding serious efforts within, and cooperation between, states to counteract environmental threats.

Eventually, two compromise texts were produced: a short, eight-page paper comprising a proclamation and a set of 26 principles known as the Stockholm

Declaration (Stockholm Declaration, 1972), and a longer Action Plan containing 109 recommendations on addressing environmental challenges (Action Plan for the Human Environment, 1972). The Stockholm Declaration proclaimed that 'protection and improvement of the human environment is a major issue which affects the well-being of peoples and economic development throughout the world' (Stockholm Declaration, 1972: Principle 2). It stressed the links between environment and development and called for the narrowing of gaps between rich and poor countries. The Action Plan addressed major environmental issues and suggested action by governments and the United Nations system to deal with them.

The UN General Assembly considered the outcomes of the Stockholm Conference in December 1972. It adopted a resolution establishing the United Nations Environment Programme (UNEP) with a mandate to promote international cooperation in the field of the environment, review world environmental threats in order to facilitate their intergovernmental consideration, and promote the acquisition, assessment and exchange of environmental knowledge and information, as well as facilitate and coordinate the implementation of environmental activities of the UN system (UNGA, 1972, Res. 2997, 'Institutional and financial arrangements').

The post-Stockholm years witnessed the establishment of environmental ministries and agencies – as well as increasing budgets for these – in most developed countries and in a growing number of developing ones; the enactment of environmental laws, especially in industrialized countries; a proliferation of global and regional environmental treaties; the strengthening of existing academic and scientific research and policy centres dealing with environmental and developmental issues, and the establishment of new ones. New processes and networks were also set up for the comprehensive assessment of global environmental issues such as climate change, the ozone layer, effects of atomic radiation, biodiversity, solid and hazardous waste, marine and inland water pollution caused by shipping as well as land-based activities, conservation of wildlife, prohibition of trade in endangered species of flora and fauna, and so forth.

At the end of the 1970s and the beginning of the 1980s, environmental movements in the US and Europe grew both in size and impact. The emergence of Green Parties in many countries lent a new legitimacy and authority to environmental activism and served to highlight the mismatch between ecological deterioration and the local and global efforts to arrest and reverse it.

Stockholm+10 (1982)

In May 1982, a special session of the UNEP Governing Council was held to mark the 10th anniversary of the Stockholm Conference, to review the developments since 1972 and to identify emerging challenges. This session, held immediately after the Stockholm+10 meeting, adopted the Montevideo Programme for the Development and Periodic Review of Environmental Law to serve as strategic guidance for UNEP in catalysing the development of international treaties and other agreements in the field of the environment (Montevideo Programme, 1982).

The Brundtland Commission

In 1983, the UN Secretary-General requested Gro Harlem Brundtland to head a commission to review environmental and developmental issues. The Commission undertook an exhaustive examination of critical environmental and developmental issues, such as growth in the world economy, technology, globalization and interdependence, and the impacts of economic growth in terms of resource depletion and pollution and degradation. It also reviewed the number, quality and impact of international efforts in addressing these issues and considered measures for enhanced cooperation.

In 1987, the Brundtland Commission's report, published as *Our Common Future*, referred to a clear demonstration of the widespread feeling of frustration and inadequacy in the international community about our own inability to address vital global issues and deal effectively with them. It declared that 'a new development path was required, one that sustained human progress not just in a few places for a few years but for the entire planet into the distant future' (WCED, 1987: 4) and used the term 'sustainable development', which was defined as 'development that meets the needs of the present without compromising the ability of future generations to meet their own needs' (*ibid.*: 43–48) The report called for renewed and greater efforts to eliminate widespread poverty, which it asserted was 'no longer inevitable' (*ibid.*: 8) and referred to the need for 'not only a new era of economic growth for nations in which the majority are poor, but an assurance that those poor get their fair share of the resources required to sustain that growth' (*ibid.*).

Our Common Future contains a thorough review of the correlation between population, energy, industry, food security, agriculture and forestry, human settlements, international economic relations and decision support systems, and environment and development, as well as of the quality and quantum of international cooperation. It offers recommendations for addressing environmental protection gaps and developmental needs, as well as a set of principles to inspire and shape action by the international community. The report emphasized the importance of international cooperation, urging 'new dimensions of multilateralism' to achieve sustainable human progress. In response, in December 1989, the UN General Assembly decided to convene the UN Conference on Environment and Development (UNCED), in order 'to elaborate strategies and measures to halt and reverse the effects of environmental degradation in the context of increased national and international efforts to promote environmentally sound development in all countries' (UNGA, 1989, Res. 44/228, 'UN Conference on Environment and Development').

The Earth Summit (1992)

UNCED, also known as the Earth Summit, was held in Rio de Janeiro in June 1992, in the optimistic atmosphere accompanying the end of the Cold War. It was preceded by a worldwide official and scientific preparatory process during which virtually every environment and development issue was comprehensively analysed by experts and negotiated by representatives of governments and other stakeholders. Attended by over 10,000 delegates, including 116 heads of state and 1,400 NGOs, and covered by 9,000 journalists, UNCED was at the time the largest meeting in the history of the UN.

The UNCED preparatory process and the negotiations during the Summit were marked by North–South polarization. While the former called for greater efforts by developing countries to address environmental threats, the latter placed a higher priority on development than environment, insisting that developed countries agree to provide new and additional financial resources and technology transfer as a condition for developing countries' acceptance of environmental commitments. Notwithstanding the protracted and often acrimonious negotiations of the Rio Summit, consensus was eventually reached by the Rio negotiators on the Rio Declaration, a short document comprising 27 principles (Rio Declaration, 1992), and on Agenda 21, a 279-page Action Plan (Agenda 21, 1992). The Summit also witnessed the signing of the UN Framework Convention on Climate Change (UNFCCC) and the Convention on Biological Diversity (CBD), and the approval of a statement of principles for the sustainable management of forests (Rio Forest Principles). A recommendation made at UNCED led also (in 1994) to the signing of the UN Convention to Combat Desertification in those Countries Experiencing Serious Drought and/or Desertification, Particularly in Africa (UNCCD).

The Rio Declaration affirmed states' responsibility to 'ensure that activities within their jurisdiction or control do not cause damage to the environment of other states or areas beyond the limits of national jurisdiction' (Principle 2); stressed that 'environmental protection shall constitute an integral part of the development process' (Principle 4); and emphasized the importance of cooperation (Principle 5) and the 'special needs of developing countries' (Principle 6). The Declaration also called for 'a global partnership to conserve, protect and restore the health and integrity of the Earth's ecosystems', adding that states have 'common but differentiated responsibilities' (Principle 7), and recommended 'the reduction and elimination of unsustainable patterns of consumption and production' (Principle 8). It supported the participation of citizens in environmental decision-making as well as access to relevant information and justice (Principle 10) and recommended the application of the precautionary approach for environmental protection (Principle 15).

Agenda 21 addressed all major sectoral and cross-sectoral environmental and developmental challenges. Its 40 chapters are divided into four sections entitled Social and Economic Dimension, Conservation and Management of Resources for Development, Strengthening the Role of Major Groups, and Means of Implementation. The environmental issues addressed included: agriculture; atmosphere; biodiversity; biotechnology; chemicals; de-forestation; fragile ecosystems; fresh water; hazardous, solid, and radioactive wastes; land resources; and seas and coasts. Agenda 21 called for action to be taken by all stakeholders within and across national boundaries to address environmental threats in the framework of sustainable development, embracing sustained economic development based on equity, enhancement of the social well-being of people, and protection of the environment. It called for integrated policies and action in all these interdependent and mutually reinforcing areas. Agenda 21 spelt out the mandates, roles and responsibilities of UN agencies and bodies, including the United Nations Development Programme (UNDP) and UNEP. It also recommended the establishment of the Commission on Sustainable Development (CSD) as a high-level forum for discussing, monitoring and expediting the implementation of Agenda 21 through dialogue that would synthesize economic, social and environmental imperatives while promoting enhanced international cooperation and improved decision-making.

The Nairobi Declaration (1997)

The biennial meetings of the UNEP Governing Council began to attract participation of ever-growing numbers of ministers of environment, who discussed global environmental matters and how UNEP could respond to these. The 19th Session of the Governing Council, held in Nairobi in February 1997, four months prior to the special session of the UN General Assembly to mark the 5th anniversary of the Earth Summit, considered and adopted the Nairobi Declaration on the Role and Mandate of the United Nations Environment Programme (1997, UNEP/GC.19/1). The Declaration sought to convey the participating governments' conviction that 'a strong, effective and revitalized UNEP is essential to assist the international community in its efforts to reverse environmentally unsustainable trends' through a new statement on the role and mandate of UNEP.

Rio+5 (1997)

In 1997, the UN General Assembly organized a special session in New York, popularly known as Rio+5, to review progress in implementation of proposals made at Rio, and to agree on measures to overcome obstacles impeding full implementation. The Commission on Sustainable Development's session during the same year served as a preparatory meeting for Rio+5. The Special Session's outcome is contained in a document entitled 'Programme of Action for the Further Implementation of Agenda 21' (UNGA, 1997, Res. S/19-2).

The meeting's deliberations were characterized by widening of the North–South divide. Developing countries castigated developed countries for the continued, in fact accelerated, degradation of the global environment. They also accused developed countries of not fulfilling their Rio commitments, either in terms of facilitating the creation of a global context enabling the improvement of developing countries' developmental prospects through resolution of the problems of aid, debt, trade and technological transfers, or by providing new and additional financial resources for supporting the efforts of developing countries to deal with global environmental issues. Perhaps more seriously, there was little enthusiasm among either developed or developing countries to propose any significant new initiatives or drastic solutions in response to the deteriorating trends, nor was there the spirit of compromise without which diplomacy cannot work.

The Millennium Summit (2000)

In September 2000, the General Assembly held the Millennium Summit to address the serious issues facing humankind in the new millennium. The six fundamental values identified, in the UN Millennium Declaration which resulted (UNGA, 2000, Res. 55/2), as being 'essential to international relations in the twenty first century' included 'respect for nature' (*ibid*: Art. 6). The Declaration called for the prudent management of all living species and natural resources in a sustainable manner, and for change in unsustainable patterns of consumption and production.

Section IV of the Declaration, entitled 'Protecting Our Common Environment', laid down several goals and targets, which have since been called the Millennium Development Goals (MDGs). Goal 7 ('Ensure Environmental Sustainability'), calls for the integration of the principles of sustainable development into national policies and programmes and for reversal of loss of environmental resources. The specific targets set by the Summit include reducing by half the proportion of people without access to safe drinking water by 2015 and achieving significant improvement in the lives of at least 100 million slum dwellers by 2020.

Malmö Declaration (2000)

A Special Session of the UNEP Governing Council was held in Malmö in May 2000. After prolonged negotiations it adopted a statement known as the Malmö Ministerial Declaration as input on the environmental perspective of sustainable development challenges, to be considered by the World Summit on Sustainable Development (WSSD) to be held in 2002. Bringing these significant points to the fore, the Declaration stated that there is an 'urgent need for reinvigorated international co-operation based on common concerns and a spirit of international partnership and solidarity' (Art. 1); called for 'mobilization of domestic and international resources, including development assistance, far beyond current levels' (Art. 2); emphasized 'the central importance of environmental compliance, enforcement and liability … the precautionary approach … as well as capacity-building' (Art. 3); and identified threats resulting from climate change, depletion of biological resources, drought and desertification, de-forestation, environmental emergencies and health hazards posed by chemicals and pollution, the freshwater crisis, and urbanization and development of mega cities, as issues that need to be addressed (Art. 5).

The Declaration took cognizance of the pressures exerted by globalization but also of the potentially positive roles that business and civil society can play. Moreover, one of the most significant recommendations of the Malmö conference was its call for the WSSD to 'review the requirements for a greatly strengthened institutional structure for international environmental governance based on an assessment of future needs for an institutional architecture that has the capacity to effectively address wide-ranging environmental threats in a globalizing world' (Art. 24). Heeding this call, in 2001 the Governing Council of UNEP set up a high-level group to address issues of international environmental governance. The Working Group negotiated a set of proposals, which were subsequently endorsed by the WSSD.

The World Summit on Sustainable Development (2002)

The WSSD, held in Johannesburg in August–September 2002, aimed to review implementation of the outcomes of the UNCED with a view to reinvigorating, at the highest political level, the global commitment to sustainable development. However, the WSSD, also called Rio+10, Earth Summit+10 or the Johannesburg Summit, was held in a global context far less optimistic than that of UNCED. The signs observed during Rio+5 that the post-Cold War euphoria had begun to subside were replaced by evidence of what Martin Khor, a leading spokesman for the developing world, called 'a crisis atmosphere'. Secretary-General Kofi Annan's special personal efforts to energize and focus the preparatory process, including his so-called WEHAB initiative proposing that the Summit give priority attention to the problems of 'Water, Energy, Health and Agriculture, and Biodiversity', alongside a series of regional preparatory meetings, helped in arresting widespread scepticism in the developing countries towards the Summit. Eventually over 30,000 representatives of state and non-state sectors attended, making the WSSD to that point the largest UN meeting in history.

Negotiations during the preparatory process of the WSSD and the Summit itself were tortuous. The Conference's proceedings once again highlighted the differences between developed and developing countries, as well as the fissures within the Organization for Economic Cooperation and Development (OECD). Developing countries recalled the North–South deal forged in Rio: developing countries had agreed to integrate the objective of environmental sustainability in their overall developmental process in return for substantial new and additional transfers of financial resources, technology, scientific and technical know-how and a more equitable global context resulting from the resolution of problems of debt repayment, development assistance and better access for their products into the rich countries' markets. They lamented the failure of the North to respect the Rio compact. Spokesmen from developing countries also underlined gaps in the Rio outcomes in respect of the actions of transnational corporations and implementation mechanisms, which had resulted in the accelerated deterioration and degradation of the global environment and the increase in absolute poverty. Furthermore, developing country governments and NGOs called for structural change in the global economic agenda based on the environment–development nexus, the revival of North–South dialogue, and a strengthened North–South partnership based on just and durable solutions relating to the debt owed by the South and issues, such as inequitable agricultural subsidies in rich countries, impeding exports from developing countries.

Notwithstanding positive developments since Rio, the Johannesburg delegates acknowledged that all environmental and socio-economic indicators had registered several-fold deterioration. Nearly all the developed countries also accepted not having kept the Rio promises and made assurances that they would try harder in the future to comply with their commitments.

The outcomes of the intergovernmental negotiations in Johannesburg are recorded in a short four-and-a-half-page political declaration (Johannesburg Declaration, 2002) and a 70-page Plan of Implementation (Johannesburg Plan of Implementation, 2002). The Declaration contains a renewed commitment to poverty eradication, changing consumption and production patterns and protecting and managing the natural resource base for economic and social development, and identifies these as 'overarching objectives' that are 'essential prerequisites' of sustainable development. The Declaration refers to the rich–poor divide within countries and the ever-increasing gap between developed and developing countries. It also mentions the continued degradation of the global environment and specifically notes loss of biodiversity, depletion of fish stocks, accelerated desertification, adverse effects of climate change, more frequent and destructive natural disasters and air, water and marine pollution. The Declaration reaffirms the commitment to multilateralism and the role of the UN in strengthening it. The Plan of Implementation reiterates Agenda 21 and in places supplements it. The most significant feature is the time-bound targets for achieving a set of goals, some of which had been agreed at the Millennium Summit. These include reducing by half the proportion of people living without water and sanitation by 2015; restoring fisheries to their maximum sustainable yields by 2015; reducing biodiversity losses by 2010; and ensuring that, by 2020, chemicals are used and produced in ways that do not harm health. Furthermore, all countries declared that they would have strategies in place for integrated water resource management by 2005.

A significant, and initially controversial, departure from UNCED was that the WSSD served as 'midwife' for roughly 280 partnership initiatives, providing for collaboration among governments of developed and developing countries, multilateral organizations within and outside the UN, and civil society, including the business sector, with the aim of jointly addressing sustainable development issues such as cleaner fuels and vehicles, fresh water, and renewable energy.

The 2005 World Summit

The high-level plenary meeting of the 60th Session of the UN General Assembly, also known as the 2005 World Summit, was held in New York in September 2005. It was attended by more than 180 heads of state and governments and addressed a host of important and urgent global issues including, *inter alia*, the subject of global environmental governance. The Outcome Document adopted by the General Assembly contains not only important paragraphs on managing and protecting our common environment but also paragraphs on international environmental governance. In Paragraph 169, the General Assembly supports stronger system-wide coherence by implementing the following measures in the area of environmental activities:

> Recognizing the need for more efficient environmental activities in the United Nations system, with enhanced coordination, improved policy advice and guidance, strengthened scientific knowledge, assessment and cooperation, better treaty compliance, while respecting the legal autonomy of the treaties, and better integration of environmental activities in the broader sustainable development framework at the operational level, including through capacity-building, we agree to explore the possibility of a more coherent institutional framework to address this need, including a more integrated structure, building on existing institutions and internationally agreed instruments, as well as the treaty bodies and the specialized agencies.
>
> (UNGA, 2005, '2005 World Summit Outcome', Res. 60/1)

This commitment aims to initiate a process, rather than outline a more or less fixed structure, and suggests that the international community will be dealing with the subject of an appropriate architecture for global environmental governance for quite some time to come. However, placing international environmental governance at the heart of the global agenda represents a new milestone in the evolution of the international community's consensus on the continued degradation of the global environment and the need for reversing it.

Rio+20 (2012)

In June 2012, forty years after the UNCHE and twenty years following the Rio Earth Summit, the UN Conference on Sustainable Development (UNCSD) was held in Rio de Janeiro. The Conference was mandated by the General Assembly (UNGA, 2009, Res. 64/236) and brought together 50,000 representatives of more than 190 states and other stakeholders. The two main themes of the conference were green economy and the institutional arrangements for sustainable development. The marathon negotiations on both themes revealed wide differences among countries along the familiar North–South divide, with developing countries reminding the developed countries of their earlier commitments on assistance, and these reminders being stubbornly declined by the developed countries led by the US. Developing countries also voiced reservations about the concept of 'green economy', and insistence on sustainable development as the essential goal and framework for actions.

In regard to the institutional arrangements, the divergence of views cut across the North–South divide, as underlined by the opposition of the US and Japan to the transformation of UNEP into a specialized agency, as favoured by the European Union. The G77 was divided on this issue. The Conference adopted an Outcome Document titled 'The Future We Want', which had been agreed after prolonged negotiations prior to the conference. In Section I, headed 'Our Common Vision', the heads of state and government and high-level representatives 'acknowledge that democracy, good governance and the rule of law, at the national and international levels, as well as an enabling environment, are essential for sustainable development' (UNGA, 2012b, 'The Future We Want': para. 10), and 'reaffirm that, to achieve our sustainable development goals, we need institutions at all levels that are effective, transparent, accountable and democratic' (*ibid.*). In Section II, headed 'Renewing Political Commitment', states 'reaffirm' their commitment to implement fully various instruments and programmes, of which some 19 were listed – including the Rio Declaration, Agenda 21 and the Johannesburg Declaration. Section V contains a 'Framework for action and follow-up', which identifies a wide range of actions (divided into several thematic areas and cross-sectoral issues) aimed at addressing both the prevailing gaps in the implementation of previous commitments, and new and emerging challenges. Notably, the Outcome Document does not suggest any specific institutional follow-up on green economy.

The Rio+20 Outcome Document, which was endorsed by the UN General Assembly in July 2012, led to the establishment of an intergovernmental process to develop a set of 'sustainable development goals' (SDGs), which will be integrated into the UN development agenda beyond 2015 (when the Millennium Development Goals expire), 'thus contributing to the achievement of sustainable development and serving as a driver for implementation and mainstreaming of sustainable development in the United Nations system as a whole' (*ibid.*: paras 246–250). An Open-ended Inter-governmental Working Group has formulated a set of 17 proposed SDGs and 169 targets, which will be negotiated and adopted by a summit of UN member states from 25–27 September 2015, during the 70th session of the UNGA. During 2015, an important global summit was held on financing for development (in Addis Ababa in July) and another will be held on climate change (in November–December in Paris).

Several parts of the Rio+20 Outcome Document are aimed at strengthening the institutional framework for sustainable development. For instance, it was decided that a 'universal, intergovernmental, high-level political forum' would be established to replace the Commission on Sustainable Development, and the UN General Assembly was invited to take various measures to strengthen and upgrade UNEP (*ibid.*: paras 84–86 and 88). In the wake of Rio+20, the UN General Assembly has adopted resolutions on both the High-level Political Forum on sustainable development (the inaugural meeting of which was held in September 2014) and the strengthening of UNEP (UNGA, 2012a, Res. 67/213; UNGA, 2013, Res. 67/290). These developments represent a significant milestone in the evolution of the institutional mechanisms for achieving sustainable development.

It is still too early for a measured assessment of the UNCSD, but it can probably be said that the Outcome Document does represent a modest achievement in building on previous efforts, while not articulating as strong a commitment to change as was sought by the global civil society, which held several demonstrations expressing disappointment over the outcome of the conference.

Current environmental challenges and responses

More than four decades after the UNCHE, how do we see the environmental challenges facing us and threatening the next generation? An objective review of the development, over the last six decades, relevant to the evolution of the global environmental agenda and diplomacy, reveals a mixed picture of significant successes and disappointing failures. Positive signals can be seen, but only in the face of overall degradation of the environment.

Universal recognition of the importance of the environment is indicated by a greater appreciation of the need for operationalizing the acknowledged nexus between environment and development. The definition of environment is no longer confined to the biosphere but also encompasses socio-economic driving forces. Sustainable development is recognized as the overarching goal, comprising economic growth, social justice and environmental protection. To some extent, it can perhaps be argued that Rio took us down an environmental path, the WSSD over-corrected in terms of prioritizing development and poverty alleviation over environmental protection, and Rio+20 has hopefully set us back on a *via media* between these.

Ministries and Departments of Environment and/or Environmental Protection Agencies have been established in virtually every country. UNCED and WSSD stimulated the preparation or revision of national environmental protection and sustainable development strategies and plans. Environmental legislation in response to local concerns as well as in pursuance of commitments under multilateral agreements has witnessed unprecedented development. Schools, universities and scientific institutions teach environmental courses and are greening the activities and syllabuses of professional studies. There is greater recognition of the responsibilities of the legislature and the judiciary as well as the roles of industry, the scientific community, civil society at large and the media in promoting environmental protection and sustainable development.

Our knowledge of environmental threats and the socio-economic forces driving them has grown enormously and at present we have reasonably reliable and comprehensive assessments of the scale and magnitude of all relevant aspects relating to issues of air and land pollution, biodiversity and ecosystems, chemicals, climate change, freshwater and oceans, hazardous wastes, etc. Science and technology have made unprecedented strides in enhancing the efficiency of fossil fuels and other raw materials, thereby reducing the threats linked to the depletion of resources, adverse climate impacts and deadly waste and pollution. Significant successes have been achieved in developing renewable clean energy and in finding answers to various issues of the urban agenda.

The importance of regional cooperation in achieving environmental and sustainable development objectives is evidenced by the proliferation, in all regions, of political, institutional, financial and legal arrangements, for safeguarding and improving shared assets and countering common, transboundary challenges. At the global level, the need for cooperation and partnerships is accepted, as is the especially serious nature and scale of environmental threats in the developing world. Governments have negotiated over 1,500 multilateral environmental agreements (MEAs) at global and regional levels, plans of action or guidelines and have initiated processes for evolving strategic approaches to address all major issues, ranging from climate stability, the protection of the ozone layer, the preservation and sustainable utilization of biodiversity and chemicals, to the protection of animal and plant species, wetlands and wildernesses. It is now widely acknowledged that neither governments nor any other stakeholders acting alone can ensure the protection of the environment or achieve sustainable development, and that only effective and concerted action by all stakeholders will reduce the growing threats to the health of our planet.

The number of transnational corporations claiming commitment to sustainable development or engagement in pro-environment activities or agreeing to report on the environmental effects of their activities is growing by the day. All media organs have increased their coverage of environmental issues and improved its quality. However, the litany of negative environmental trends exacerbated by failures on the part of nearly all stakeholders in the international community to take positive action is far longer.

As noted by the fifth Global Environment Report of UNEP (UNEP, 2012), issued just prior to the Rio+20 Summit, with the exception of the success of efforts to protect the ozone layer, each and every global environmental threat has grown in scale and magnitude, including climate change, de-forestation and forest degradation, poor land-use practices causing land erosion and soil degradation, decrease in the availability and deterioration in the quality of freshwater resources, degradation and eutrophication of oceans, threats faced by coral reefs, and unsustainable management of chemicals and waste, including hazardous waste. Despite growing and incontrovertible scientific corroboration of the threats posed by climate change resulting mainly from emissions of greenhouse gases, the escalating loss of biodiversity and the vulnerability of all ecosystems, especially oceans and forests, and the adverse impacts of agricultural, industrial and household chemicals for human health, there has been negligible progress in effectively dealing with these issues.

While issues on the domestic agenda of developed countries, such as air and water quality, have been dealt with quite well, the trends in most developing countries in respect of the same set of problems show rapid deterioration. Developing countries lack either the policy framework, governance structures or human, financial, technical and technological resources to translate their oft-reiterated commitment to sustainable development into tangible actions. The only redeeming features are the increasingly vocal and effective civil society structures.

Regional cooperation structures are also far more successful in developed countries than in the developing world. The same is the case in regard to the effectiveness of multilateral environmental agreements or plans of action. In terms of global cooperation, the gap between the Rio commitments and promises and the situation on the ground is becoming wider and wider. The Rio compact or deal exists largely only on paper. The Global Environment Facility, the Multilateral Fund for the phasing out of ozone-depleting substances, and the funds established under some MEAs are the only dedicated sources of funding available for meeting the incremental costs incurred by developing countries in implementing MEAs. In any case, most MEAs lack effective mechanisms for compliance and enforcement. Moreover, the favourable global economic order considered necessary for enabling developing countries to eradicate poverty and protect the environment is nowhere in sight.

The global environmental governance architecture continues to be plagued by insufficient political will manifested by the lack of authority, effective coordination and adequate resources that would enable UNEP, UNDP and other multilateral agencies to respond to environmental challenges. The MEA secretariats are geographically dispersed and lack resources to implement the global agreements.

Recommendations

First, the two principal and intertwined challenges that will have to be addressed are what Maurice Strong often describes as a recession in political will to achieve sustainable development, and the lack of trust between developing and developed countries and, consequently, a genuine, functioning partnership in the face of growing threats to our biosphere. The lack of political will is evidenced by the inability of politicians everywhere to place long-term sustainability above short-term electoral exigencies. It is also reflected in inadequate assistance to developing countries through environmentally integrated development cooperation, comprising the transfer of financial and technological resources as well as the removal of trade-distorting subsidies and other tariff and non-tariff measures. Efforts are, therefore, needed to arrest and reverse the recession in political commitment.

Second, efforts to revitalize the environmental governance structure of the UN through better functioning governing bodies, interagency coherence, and provision of sufficient authority and resources need to be redoubled. The Bretton Woods institutions as well as other lending institutions need to make greater efforts to gear their activities towards the achievement of sustainable development.

Third, the private sector should invest more in research and development activities for developing cleaner production processes, renewable energy sources, energy efficient transport and pollution abatement systems, as well as agree to more transparent reporting and the independent evaluation and monitoring of their activities. Governments in both developing and developed countries need to step up efforts to promote sustainable development through necessary policy changes, efficient, transparent and accountable institutions, and the full participation of industry and civil society.

Fourth, the underlying causes of environmental degradation, such as population growth, poverty and underdevelopment, inadequate technologies and market failures due to prices that do not take into account environmental impacts, will have to be addressed.

Fifth, concerted efforts need to be made to achieve a rapid and sustained transition to sustainable patterns of consumption, through green labelling and enlisting the support of consumers with the help of rigorous public awareness campaigns.

Sixth, as noted by Gus Speth, there is a need for the most fundamental transition of all – a transition in culture and consciousness and an environmental revolution for achieving the creation of a world society that is environmentally sustainable, economically equitable and peaceful. Speth has spoken of the imperative of effecting a deeper change, a different way of seeing ourselves in relation to the planet on which we live. For this, he adds aptly, we would need an international movement of citizens and scientists, one capable of dramatically advancing the political and personal changes needed (Speth, 2004).

Conclusion

Clearly, the equilibrium between humans and nature has come under relentless pressure since the Industrial Revolution. The vision of a global solidarity to restore that balance, which was articulated in Stockholm and has been refined in the decades since that landmark event, has become an urgent imperative. Humankind has acquired knowledge and technology, as well as developed resources and policy choices and options, for a fundamental re-ordering of lifestyles that would ensure the ability of our planet to continue to support and sustain peaceful and prosperous human life, if we can summon the political will individually and collectively to read the writing on the wall and act accordingly.

References

Action Plan for the Human Environment, UN Conference on the Human Environment, Stockholm, 16 June 1972, A/CONF.48/14/Rev.1.

Agenda 21 (1992) UN Conference on Environment and Development, Rio de Janeiro, 13–14 June 1992, A/CONF.151/26/Rev.1.

Declaration of the United Nations Conference on Environment and Development, Rio de Janeiro, 3–14 June 1992, A/CONF.151/26 (Vol. I).

Declaration of the United Nations Conference on the Human Environment, Stockholm (1972) 16 June 1972, *International Legal Materials*, 11: 1416.

Johannesburg Declaration on Sustainable Development (2002) World Summit on Sustainable Development, 4 September 2002.

Malmö Ministerial Declaration, 31 May 2000.

Montevideo Programme for the Development and Periodic Review of Environmental Law (1982) UNEP/GC.10/21, 31 May 1982.

Nairobi Declaration on the Role and Mandate of the United Nations Environment Programme (1997) 7 February 1997, UNEP/GC.19/1.

Non-legally Binding Authoritative Statement of Principles for a Global Consensus on the Management, Conservation and Sustainable Development of all Types of Forests (1992) UN Conference on Environment and Development, Rio de Janeiro, 13–14 June 1992, A/CONF.151/26 (Vol. III).

Plan of Implementation of the World Summit on Sustainable Development (2002) A/CONF.199/20.

Speth, G. (2004) *Red Sky at Morning: America and the Crisis of the Global Environment*, Yale University Press, New Haven.

Strong, M. (2000) *Where on Earth Are We Going?*, Alfred Knopf, Toronto.

Tolba M.K. and Rummel-Bulska, I. (1998), *Global Environmental Diplomacy*, MIT Press, Cambridge, MA.

UNEP (2012) *Global Environmental Outlook 5: Environment for the Future We Want*, www.unep.org/geo/geo5.asp.

UNGA (1972) 'Institutional and Financial Arrangements for International Environmental Co-operation', UNGA Res. 2997 (XXVII), 15 December 1972.
UNGA (1989) 'UN Conference on Environment and Development', UNGA Res. 44/228, 22 December 1989.
UNGA (1997) 'Programme for the Further Implementation of Agenda 21', UNGA Res. S/19-2, 28 June 1997.
UNGA (2000) 'United Nations Millennium Declaration', UNGA Res. 55/2, 8 September 2000.
UNGA (2005) '2005 World Summit Outcome', UNGA Res. 60/1, 15 September 2005.
UNGA (2009) 'Implementation of Agenda 21, the Programme for the Further Implementation of Agenda 21 and the outcomes of the World Summit on Sustainable Development', UNGA Res. 64/236, 24 December 2009.
UNGA (2012a) 'Report of the Governing Council of the United Nations Environment Programme on its Twelfth Special Session and on the Implementation of Section IV.C, entitled "Environmental Pillar in the Context of Sustainable Development", of the Outcome Document of the United Nations Conference on Sustainable Development', UNGA Res. 67/213, 21 December 2012.
UNGA (2012b) 'The Future We Want' Outcome Document, UNGA Res. A/RES/66/288, 27 July 2012.
UNGA (2013) 'Format and Organizational Aspects of the High-Level Political Forum on Sustainable Development', UNGA Res. 67/290, 9 July 2013.
World Commission on Environment and Development (WCED) 1987, *Our Common Future*, Oxford University Press, Oxford.

11 The development of the principle of common but differentiated responsibilities and its place in international environmental regimes

Tuula Honkonen

Introduction to common but differentiated responsibilities

In general, relations and cooperation between states are based on the principle of sovereign or judicial equality. This includes, *inter alia*, the principle of reciprocity and similar rights and obligations for states (UNGA, 1970, Res. 2625). Furthermore, the Charter of the United Nations (UN Charter, 1945) prescribes that '[t]he Organization is based on the principle of the sovereign equality of all its Members' (*ibid.*, Art. 2(1)). Increasingly, however, this is perceived as overlooking the situation of the more disadvantaged states, sometimes leading to substantively unjust outcomes. Differentiation of rights and obligations takes into account extra-legal differences amongst states. It makes room for substantive equity in international environmental regimes; compromising over requirements of reciprocity, but achieving other values that count for treaty Parties.

The principle of common but differentiated responsibilities (CBDR) as applied to multilateral environmental agreements (MEAs) has two elements: first, it entitles, or possibly even requires, all concerned states to participate in international response measures aimed at addressing environmental problems. Second, it leads to the adoption and implementation of different commitments for states; taking into account their diverse situations, their circumstances and capacities, their historical contributions to a problem, and their future development needs.

The first dimension of the principle of CBDR is that it lays down a requirement for all members in the international society to participate, and to do their share, in the efforts to ameliorate global environmental problems. From this, corresponding common responsibility arises as an integral part of the CBDR principle. The second dimension of the principle involves a direct response to differences between countries regarding the anticipated effects of environmental degradation and the capacity to take action at the national level. Young has summarized the central thrust of the principle of common but differentiated responsibility: it is 'to couple an acknowledgement that everyone bears some responsibility for coping with large-scale environmental problems with a recognition of the fact that some members of international society are much better situated than others to provide the resources needed to address these problems' (Young, 2001: 169). Common and differentiated responsibilities must be thought of in unison, not as one element without the other.

Differential treatment applies mechanisms and allows for deviations from general state obligations to favour least advantaged countries; usually, but not exclusively, these are developing countries. Perhaps simplistically, this chapter uses the division between developed (or industrial) and developing countries. The author recognizes that this division is over-generalized, but uses it for lack of a better way to discuss the current issue on a general level; moreover, the North–South divide is quite visible and is frequently referred to in multilateral negotiations between states, especially in the environmental and developmental fields. In practice, CBDR is realized by giving states different obligations and/or assistance in the implementation of an MEA. Therefore, differentiation can have two dimensions: allocation of rights or obligations and redistribution of resources. Differentiated obligations mean that treaty commitments may be formulated as being less demanding for a certain group of Parties (or even excluding them completely from binding obligations to take action). Other possible implications are that states might be granted longer periods within which to implement their commitments; exceptions and reservations may be used; or a treaty may create specific mechanisms to account for the different national situations in the participating countries. In other words, state burdens are differentiated according to certain criteria.

Redistribution of resources is another way of differentiating within MEAs, and involves providing assistance to less developed, or especially vulnerable, states. Resource redistribution is primarily realized by allocation of financial and technical assistance and by transfer of technology.

The CBDR principle represents an effort to respond to concerns regarding the legitimacy, equity and effectiveness of international environmental regimes. It attempts to reconcile tension between, on the one hand, the need for universalism in taking action to combat global environmental problems; and, on the other, the need to be sensitive to individual countries' special and relevant circumstances.

This chapter provides an overview on the development, contents and application of the principle of common but differentiated responsibilities under multilateral environmental agreements. First, the history of the approach is discussed. The chapter then proceeds to review the operationalization of CBDR in different MEAs and to consider the implications that the concept has had or may have in the future for international environmental cooperation among states. These implications include, *inter alia*, promotion of fairness and equity, promotion of sustainable development and contribution to better international regulation. Next, the chapter considers different aspects in the negotiation of CBDR under MEAs. Finally, the concluding remarks recognize the principle of CBDR as being of utmost importance for both the political and the environmental effectiveness of international environmental regimes.

History and development of the CBDR principle

The principle of common but differentiated responsibilities is nowadays frequently invoked in the negotiation and application of international environmental treaties. However, the history of this principle can be thought to have begun even before the rise of modern global environmentalism, within the movement for the New International Economic Order (NIEO) of the 1960s and 1970s. During this period, developing countries campaigned for more equitable sharing of resources and wealth. The NIEO process failed to result in a new world order, but seeds were nevertheless planted for the future. The demands and arguments presented by both the developed and developing countries in the contexts of both the NIEO and CBDR have remarkable similarities. There are, however, several differences between the current situation and that of the 1970s. Namely, the developing world now possesses stronger bargaining power, its demands are of a less radical nature, the consequences of no action are generally more severe, and perhaps there has also been a slight softening in the attitudes of at least some industrial countries in this regard.

Within the United Nations, the 1972 Conference on the Human Environment (UNCHE) made a cautious reference to countries' development needs and the issue of differentiated commitments. The Conference's final Declaration underlined the need to consider 'the applicability of standards which are valid for the most advanced countries but which may be inappropriate and of unwarranted social cost for the developing countries' (Stockholm Declaration, 1972: Principle 23).

The principle of common but differentiated responsibility was most prominently defined and brought to the fore at the international level in the documents adopted at the 1992 UN Conference on Environment and Development (UNCED), including the Rio Declaration (UN Declaration on Environment and Development, 1992). The Declaration stated, in its Principle 6, that:

> [t]he special situation and needs of developing countries, particularly the least developed and those most environmentally vulnerable, shall be given special priority. International actions in the field of environment and development should also address the interests and needs of all countries.

Principle 7 went on to declare that:

> States shall cooperate in a spirit of global partnership to conserve, protect and restore the health and integrity of the Earth's ecosystem. In view of the different contributions to global environmental degradation, States have common but differentiated responsibilities. The developed countries acknowledge the responsibility that they bear in the international pursuit of sustainable development in view of the pressures their societies place on the global environment and of the technologies and financial resources they command.

This principle of the Rio Declaration, with its manifestation of CBDR, has been considered to be a major contribution to the development of international environmental law. It affirmed, as a relevant concept for the future development of international environmental law, the idea that developing countries should receive preferential treatment (French, 2000: 38, 52; Birnie and Boyle, 2002: 103). The principle of CBDR was also recognized in Agenda 21, the 'blueprint' adopted at the Rio Conference as an Action Programme for Sustainable Development, which urged states to 'take into account the different situations and capabilities of countries' when devising international standards (Agenda 21, 1992: para. 39.3(d)).

The principle of common but differentiated responsibilities was reaffirmed at the 2002 World Summit on Sustainable Development (WSSD). Although the emphasis of the Summit was manifestly on sustainable development and poverty alleviation, leaving environment to play a supporting role, the principle of CBDR was elevated in the discussions and strongly linked to the programme for the promotion of sustainable development. Importantly, the Plan of Implementation of the Summit (2002) mentioned differentiation as a guiding principle to be used in efforts relating to the enhancement of international cooperation on sustainable development (Chapter I.2 para. 39). In many ways, the WSSD Plan of Implementation repeated what the UNCED documents had already said; nevertheless, the CBDR has been argued to have emerged strengthened, broadened and invigorated by the WSSD (Cordonier Segger *et al.*, 2003: 58; see also, for instance, Statement on Behalf of the Group of G77 and China, 2004). In any case, the Conference sought to include the principle in wider international, both environmental and developmental, cooperation.

In 2012, the UN Conference on Sustainable Development (UNCSD, or the 'Rio+20 Conference') marked the 20th anniversary of the UNCED of 1992. The UNCSD focused on measures to reduce poverty, advance social equity and ensure environmental protection. The major achievement of the Conference was an Outcome Document, 'The Future We Want', which reaffirmed all the principles of the Rio Declaration, specifically mentioning the principle of common but differentiated responsibilities, as set out in Principle 7 of the Rio Declaration (para. 15 of the preamble). There was, however, debate concerning the applicability of the CBDR principle not only in environmental but also developmental matters. Some signatories to the Document also argued, in negotiation, that the principle should not be singled out from the rest of the Rio Principles (see, for example, Third World Network, 2012). In the end, the CBDR principle is specifically mentioned in the context of the international pursuit of sustainable development.

Operationalization of CBDR in MEAs: overview

Montreal Ozone Protocol

Under the international ozone regime, it was recognized early on that the particular situation of developing countries should be given special consideration (see, for example, Draft Res. CFCs 1985). Consequently, the 1987 Montreal Protocol on Substances that Deplete the Ozone Layer came to include a number of applications of the principle of common but different responsibility; and, as a whole, may be regarded as quite an advanced MEA, given that it was created even before the 1992 UNCED.

Under the Montreal Protocol, developing countries were temporarily excluded from binding obligations to phase out ozone-depleting substances (Art. 5). Further, flexibility was introduced to the ozone regime by allowing developed countries to exceed most production restrictions and prohibitions in order to satisfy their 'basic domestic needs', or for the purposes of 'industrial rationalization between Parties' (Art. 2A(1)). In addition to this exemption, many of the Montreal Protocol's phase-out regulations allow for the continued production and consumption of the controlled substances for certain 'essential' uses (Art. 2A(4)). Finally, the Montreal Protocol Multilateral Fund can be seen as a pioneer mechanism for monetary transfers within international environmental regimes.

The climate change regime

The global climate change regime is explicitly based on the principle of common but differentiated responsibility, and differentiation in state commitments has been one of the key elements of the regime. The 1992 United Nations Framework Convention on Climate Change (UNFCCC) calls on its Parties to protect the climate system 'for the benefit of present and future generations of humankind, on the basis of equity and in accordance with their common but differentiated responsibilities and respective capabilities' (Art. 3(1)).

The CBDR principle is operationalized through the subsequent 1997 Kyoto Protocol to the UNFCCC, in terms of both differential commitments and assistance and enabling measures. The Kyoto Protocol explicitly reaffirmed the CBDR principle (Art. 10) and the principle is reflected in the instrument's operational provisions. With regard to the adopted emissions reduction targets, the Protocol made a distinction between industrial and developing countries, the former have binding emissions reduction obligations, the latter do not. A further division was made between different Annex I countries, which have been given different commitments in Annex B of the Protocol. In addition, countries undergoing the process of transition to a market economy were granted extra flexibility to meet their emission reduction targets.

Resource redistribution is exercised under the climate regime through several mechanisms for financial and technical assistance and technology transfer. The Kyoto mechanisms, Joint Implementation (Art. 6 – this being a mechanism whereby Annex I countries can carry out emissions reduction projects in other Annex I countries and transfer the thereby generated 'emission reduction units' (ERUs) towards their own limitation target), Clean Development Mechanism (Art. 12 – this being a mechanism that allows Annex I Parties to use the certified emission reductions (CERs) that have been generated by their sustainable development projects in developing countries) and Emissions Trading (Art. 17 – this allowing Parties listed in Annex B to sell or buy emission reductions in an emissions trading market), can also in a way be regarded as fitting into the sphere of differential treatment. All the Kyoto flexible mechanisms are based on state cooperation and partnership and on the idea of participants sharing the gained benefits. The CDM also has as its formal purpose the promotion of sustainable development in developing countries (Art. 12).

The CBDR principle has been the cornerstone under the global climate change regime. However, even though this principle enabled important agreements in the 1990s, it has also contributed to later climate negotiation deadlocks. The difficulties induced by the use of the principle culminated at the 2009 Copenhagen Conference of the Parties (CoP). The Conference failed to produce a legally binding Outcome Document since the developed countries that were most important for the success of the meeting required emissions reduction targets also for the largest developing countries – which the latter could not accept. Since then, new ways have been sought to open the deadlocks but progress has been slow and the outcomes have left much to be desired after the Durban (2011), Doha (2012), Warsaw (2013) and Lima (2014) negotiations.

It even appears that CBDR is no longer at the forefront of negotiations, but has given way to a number of other issues (such as continuation of the Protocol or adaptation). The most recent CoP decisions regarding the future design of the climate regime contain fewer specific mentions of CBDR than did earlier decisions, and are instead characterized by more general or contextual expressions of differentiated treatment of Parties – such as references to national circumstances, priorities and needs. Indeed, CBDR has become CBDRRC (CBDR and respective capabilities) under the negotiations on a post-2020 international climate regime. Recourse to national circumstances, priorities and needs has become the dominating discourse within the negotiations in recent years. The term, as explicitly included in Art. 3(1) of the UNFCCC, essentially puts responsibilities and capabilities on an equal footing. At the same time, it would go beyond the simple distinction between developed and developing countries (Brunnée and Streck, 2013: 599). By putting emphasis on 'capabilities' rather than 'responsibilities', developed countries have preferred to emphasize the capacity countries now have to address climate change (*ibid.*: 593).

Parties continue to be bound by the provision of common but differentiated responsibilities in Art. 3(1) of the UNFCCC, but they perhaps want to avoid explicit CBDR language, since this could provoke more conflict than cooperation. It seems clear that the obligations of the future regime will be differentiated, and that the principle of CBDR will form the basis of that design, even if the principle is not explicitly acknowledged. It is generally envisaged that, in the forthcoming (November–December 2015) Paris CoP, developing countries will also take mitigation commitments.

Other international environmental regimes

In addition to the ozone and climate regimes briefly discussed above, differentiation of state obligations has over the years been adopted on a slightly smaller scale in numerous other MEAs. The regime created under the framework of the Convention on Long-Range Transboundary Air Pollution (LRTAP), 1979 is a good example of international environmental regulation that has effectively and in small steps introduced differentiation into state commitments, though only among developed countries. The LRTAP regime has, over the years, adopted a number of different mechanisms that differentiate states' obligations: flexibility in selecting base-years for emissions reductions (Volatile Organic Compounds Protocol of 1991, Art. 2(b)(i)) and sets of obligations (*ibid.* Art. 2(2)); a longer implementation period (second Sulphur Protocol, 1994, Art. 2(5)(c)); and country-specific emissions reduction targets (*ibid.* Annex II; Gothenburg Protocol, 1999, Annex II). The primary rationale for the latter has arguably been cost-effectiveness (see, for example, *ibid.*: Preamble) but an additional basis for differentiating between the Parties is that those whose emissions have the most severe environmental or health impacts will be required to make the largest reductions (Sands, 2003: 335). This element also reflects considerations of fairness.

In addition to MEAs that have introduced concrete differentiation of state obligations, of which examples have been given above, many more apply the principle of common but differentiated responsibility in a more subtle way. These treaties make mention of (different) country capacities and make promises of preferential treatment for developing countries and other country groups, but differentiated obligations per se have not been adopted in this respect (for instance, in the Convention on the Law of the Sea (UNCLOS), 1982, Arts 194(1), 207(4), 203; and in the Convention on Desertification (UNCCD), 1992, Art. 3(d)).

As to the second component of the application of CBDR in MEAs, assistance and enabling measures are commonly realized in concrete treaty arrangements. Funding and technology transfer mechanisms of varying legal and practical strength and details have been made available under numerous multilateral environmental agreements. For instance, the Montreal Protocol Multilateral Fund has been active since 1990 and it has effectively assisted developing countries in phasing-out ozone-depleting substances. The global climate change regime has grown to have a number of financing mechanisms. In addition to the Global Environment Facility (GEF), more specific funds and mechanisms designed under the international climate change regime have gained a more prominent place in recent years. Today, financial assistance under the UNFCCC framework is available through the Adaptation Fund, the Special Climate Change Fund, the Least Developed Countries Fund and the Green Climate Fund. In addition, there are arrangements for other, smaller-scale financing activities.

Reservations

Differentiated state obligations also follow from reservations to treaties. These may originally be meant to remain fairly small in scope, but can potentially at some point turn into rather large gaps.

Many international agreements allow for the use of reservations or contain so-called escape clauses. General limits for treaty reservations are provided in the Vienna Convention on the Law of Treaties, 1969; reservations being permissible as long as they are not incompatible with the object and purpose of the particular treaty, or unless the treaty prohibits reservations or allows only specific kinds of reservations (Art. 19). These provide leeway for Parties to remain outside an arrangement established by the treaty; or not to commit to a particular treaty obligation or a set of obligations. Limited deviations from treaty obligations are important for common but differentiated responsibilities, as they allow Parties to proceed towards a common objective yet at a different pace. Nevertheless, they can also undermine, possibly seriously, the effectiveness and perceived legitimacy of the cooperative arrangements.

It is notable that several remarkable MEAs, such as the Montreal and Kyoto Protocols, specifically prohibit the making of reservations. Generally, it appears that the trend has been in more recent MEAs against allowing reservations. It is possible that wider application of the principle of common but differentiated responsibilities is to some extent diminishing the need for reservations. The allowance of reservations is also a more open-ended type of possibility to apply differentiation of state commitments under MEAs. States perhaps nowadays prefer to have better control of differentiation through predetermined treaty provisions rather than via a possibility of reservations, the practical effects of which are more difficult to predict.

Implications of CBDR for MEAs

Promotion of fairness and equity

State inequity and responsibility for environmental problems

State inequity is a real issue for multilateral environmental cooperation. The prevailing inequality between states may be political, economic or ecological in character, and in all cases it leads to some degree of marginalization. It can be said that developing countries are in need of differentiation and assistance in their international environmental commitments because of both historical and current inequities, their fewer available resources, and because they are often in more vulnerable positions with regard to the effects of global environmental problems. Common but differentiated obligations in international environmental agreements are probably most often seen as being intended to make treaty arrangements fairer and as removing imbalances and inequities that would otherwise remain large between the participating states.

The 'historical responsibility of the North', as well as developed countries' better capabilities to take mitigating actions, are frequently used arguments in international environmental treaty bargaining. One of the most commonly relied upon justifications for differentiated commitments is the polluter pays principle (PPP), emphasizing the responsibility aspect of CBDR and the need for the North to take leadership. The PPP attaches the responsibility to take remedial action or to bear the costs of preventive and abatement efforts on the party that has caused the problem. At first glance, the principle appears to be a promising solution to bring justice, real responsibility and even efficiency to environmental regulation and burden-sharing. However, the practical realization of the principle is far from straightforward, especially in an international context.

It can be argued that the principle of common but differentiated responsibilities is not fundamentally different from the polluter pays principle, although the former is of course much broader in scope. It has been argued that the principle of CBDR seeks to bring a new dimension to the PPP by emphasizing both past contributions to causing, and future capacities to solving, given problems (Cullet, 1999: 168-179; Drumbl, 2002: 911). It would seem that the developed countries have the responsibility to take environmental protection action and to repair the harm they have caused in the past in line with the traditional polluter pays principle. In addition, however, the developed world should respect developing countries' right to industrialization. Consequently, simply put, the developed world should pay for the needed adjustments, so that the economic development of the South can indeed occur without excessively burdening the environment.

Ethical approaches

A rights-based allocation of burdens in international environmental agreements has gained support mostly because of the relatively strong respect it secures for state sovereignty; which respect is often seen to be somewhat lacking from the applications of common but differentiated responsibilities. The rights-based allocation scheme is also sometimes called the 'sovereignty principle of equity' with regard to common but differentiated responsibilities. Accordingly, the current level of environmental harm caused can be regarded as reflecting the specific circumstances of particular countries, and differentiation is thus being realized in an acceptable manner (Metz, 2000: 113). A severe downside of a rights-based allocation is that once the idea that Parties have inherent rights has been adopted, the actors might be slow to agree to any meaningful limitations to these rights.

The various ethical approaches to burden-sharing in international environmental cooperation ultimately come down to the interesting question of the role of fairness in international law. In this regard, it needs to be asked whether the rules of international law are tools for realizing fairness in inter-state relations. Irrespective of the answer, it is clear that justice is not an omnipotent force in international law, despite frequent efforts toward its promotion.

Fair burden-sharing

Designing international burden-sharing schemes in multilateral environmental agreements is a delicate issue: a balance should be found that will take into account states' different contributions to the environmental problem, their different capacities to take action and their development needs, while at the same time the arrangement should work towards decreasing the level of environmental degradation. It is clear that there are almost unlimited numbers of possible methods and criteria that could be suggested as a basis for realizing burden-sharing under international environmental regimes. Many of the criteria remain rather narrow in scope and focus on only one element of the complex question, yet there are also models that have potential for wider application.

Even though there exists no commonly accepted definition of equity and fairness, nor is there consensus on how these should be applied in the design of the burden-sharing rules of international environmental treaties, some general guidelines or more widely accepted norms can be distinguished. Responsibility is one important aspect. It can refer to both responsibility for historical behaviour; and also to more ethical kinds of responsibility to assist less well-equipped states in their obligations to reduce emissions or to take other required environmental actions. Other central aspects are ability, on one hand; and willingness to assume responsibility and to take action, on the other.

Ultimately, the aim of differentiation and burden-sharing is an acceptable distribution of mitigation costs, be they monetary or other, across countries and over time. A feasible formula must be based on conceptions of fairness that are widely enough shared in the international society. It is also important not to ignore the broader distributional impacts of an agreed-upon burden-sharing scheme: regressive measures can cause problems because environmental degradation and poverty are closely connected, and the relationship is not one-way (Chichilnisky, 2000: 274). Moreover, an interesting question is whether we should help those that would need it most or those that we can help most. One could imagine a hypothetical example of this where there may be a low-lying middle-income developing country that would suffer massive damages as a result of climate change. That country would need most help, but helping it would become relatively costly, compared to helping a least developed country that has not yet taken any precaution against the detrimental effects of climate change, since the country in question would have already taken the least expensive protective measures. In resolving these kinds of questions, truthful and accurate information on countries' circumstances and capacities is crucial. Finally, it is important to consider whether the purpose of CBDR is to remedy current inequalities; or to rectify past injustices.

Promotion of sustainable development

It can be said that CBDR assists all states to proceed toward the goal of achieving all three aspects of sustainable development; in other words, economic, social and environmental sustainability. First, general economic sustainability is promoted by cost-effective strategies for environmental protection that are based on non-universal commitments. Furthermore, economic sustainability is enhanced at the country level; as the application of CBDR should ensure that the economic development prospects of (developing) countries are not destroyed by, for instance, sudden strict emissions reduction obligations. On the other hand, it is important to recognize the bases on which obligations are differentiated. Not all solutions promote economic sustainability; and it should be remembered that the cost-effectiveness or economic sustainability of a state is not the sole goal of the CBDR principle.

Second, the principle of common but differentiated responsibilities is compatible with, or may actually promote, the social dimension of sustainable development. In taking into account states' different situations and circumstances, CBDR supports justice and equity (or a sense of it) in the burden-sharing of international environmental and developmental cooperation. Developing countries are adamant in arguing that environmental concerns should not override such issues as the efforts for poverty eradication or the realization of the right to development.

Finally, environmental sustainability is enhanced by the common responsibility element of CBDR, which is meant eventually to bring all states under an obligation to restrict their environmentally destructive behaviour. The gradual strengthening of the commitments and participation of developing countries in multilateral environmental agreements will often promote environmental effectiveness and sustainability; especially when compared to a situation where no inducement or allowance is provided for less developed countries.

The principle of common but differentiated responsibilities may also ensure that no element of sustainable development is given dominant weight. However, the criteria for burden-sharing and participation in MEAs are crucial (see Kolari, 2008: 260, 264). Interestingly, this issue received attention at the 2002 World Summit on Sustainable Development. Within this context, developing countries wanted to see a shift in emphasis in the sustainable development dialogue from environmental protection to social and economic development. This trend was to be complemented by making Rio Principle 7, manifesting the CBDR principle, the basis for international action with respect to all three pillars of sustainable development. Developed countries had a mixed attitude toward this issue. In short, it was felt that the scope of the common but differentiated responsibilities should be narrower than that of sustainable development (Rajamani, 2006: 69).

It has been argued that this outcome of the WSSD, with regard to sustainable development and the principle of common but differentiated responsibilities, means that the principle of CBDR is not only applicable when international environmental problems are addressed, as is explicitly done today. Rather, the door has been left open also to the application of the principle in decision-making on social and economic issues, such as under the human rights, labour and trade regimes, at least when sustainable development concerns arise (Cordonier Segger *et al.*, 2003: 60). The principle of CBDR was reaffirmed in the Outcome Document of the 2012 UN Conference on Sustainable Development. The document states that:

> [w]e further recognize the importance and utility of a set of sustainable development goals (SDGs), which are based on Agenda 21 and Johannesburg Plan of Implementation, fully respect all Rio Principles, taking into account different national circumstances, capacities and priorities, are consistent with

> international law, build upon commitments already made, and contribute to the full implementation of the outcomes of all major Summits in the economic, social and environmental fields, including this Outcome Document.
>
> (UNGA, 2012, 'The Future We Want': para. 246)

The statement gives recognition to CBDR in the whole field of sustainable development goals, though by using a paraphrase.

As a whole, the principle of common but differentiated responsibilities is doing its best in trying to accommodate the sentiments of both developed and developing countries to a balanced view of global sustainable development.

Better international regulation

State heterogeneity accounted for in obligations

When states come to the negotiating table to create an international environmental agreement, they might have very different starting points for the process, differing national circumstances and preferences for the negotiated outcome. This heterogeneity of states and their positions sets many challenges for the successful conclusion of international environmental agreements.

In essence, differentiation has the function of trying to reconcile the tension between the need for universal obligations in ameliorating serious environmental problems, and the need to be sensitive to individual countries' circumstances. Consequently, the CBDR principle has been argued to combine 'a universal ethical standard with a pragmatic acceptance of marked differences in the material circumstances of individual members of international society' (Young, 2001: 169). Finding an acceptable balance for all Parties is, understandably, not an easy task.

Promotion of compliance

The success of differentiation is determined by the manner in which the various commitments are upheld and fulfilled in practice. It is important that all Parties comply with the obligations they have accepted. The principle of common but differentiated responsibilities in general has a positive impact on states' compliance with their obligations under MEAs. This is because differentiation, both in the form of lessened obligations and in the form of granted assistance, makes the commitments easier for countries to comply with.

Developing country compliance with MEAs is sometimes even made dependent on the financial aid provided and on transfer of technology. Several MEAs also indicate that the compliance of developing countries with their treaty obligations is linked to, if not dependent on, the effective implementation of the CBDR principle, most often in form of provided assistance, by developed countries. Naturally many developed countries are opposed to the recognition of this kind of legal linkage of the obligations.

By way of an example of the idea of conditional reciprocity under MEAs, one could take the Montreal Protocol where it is provided that developing the capacity to fulfil the obligations of the developing country Parties to implement and comply with the control measures set out in the Protocol 'will depend upon the effective implementation of the financial co-operation as provided by Article 10 and the transfer of technology as provided by Article 10A' (Art. 5(5) under the title 'Special situation of developing countries'). It is to be noted that the Protocol does not use the formulation 'shall depend' but only a more statement-like 'will depend' which is of course not quite equally strong language. However, even the chosen formulation sends quite a solid message on what the idea of the provision is.

The financial mechanism of the Protocol is available to 'Parties operating under paragraph 1 of Article 5 of this Protocol to enable their compliance with the control measures' set out in the specified Articles (Art. 10(1)). The treaty text speaks about enabling developing country compliance by meeting all agreed incremental costs that such Parties face with the control measures. The impression given is that developing countries would not be able to comply with the controls without the prescribed assistance transferred to them. This could, in theory, be further interpreted that these countries would not even have to comply without the needed assistance. On the other hand, the transfers are limited to 'all agreed incremental costs', which in principle gives the funders power to finally determine what particular costs will be met by the financing mechanism.

Interestingly, Iran used insufficient financial assistance as a partial reason for its alleged non-compliance with the Montreal Protocol in 2004 (see UNEP/OzL. Pro.16/17, 2004: para. 157).

Generally, it can be thought, for instance, that, if industrial countries do not pay, as promised, all of the incremental costs the developing nations face in reducing their polluting activities, developing countries need not comply with the treaty requirements for that part. This would imply a kind of conditional reciprocity of commitments. As a consequence, no non-compliance procedures could be invoked against a Party that appeals to this fact for its failure to comply with the agreement. This would act as a strong counter-balance to the implicit power of the developed countries.

Effectiveness: environmental, economic, normative and political

The principle of common but differentiated responsibilities is often said to improve the effectiveness of international environmental regimes. In this section, this claim is briefly examined in the light of three important aspects of regime effectiveness.

The environmental effectiveness of the CBDR principle is a multi-dimensional issue. In general, it can be estimated that common but differentiated responsibilities promotes global environmental protection and contributes towards making international environmental agreements effective from the problem-solving point of view. This occurs through the incentive effects that differentiated obligations have on states.

However, differentiation may also threaten the environmental effectiveness of an MEA. When a group of states is given lower obligations than others, the state of the global environment is naturally improved less than in a situation of strong and effective uniform efforts. Exceptions and lower obligations run directly against the environmental objectives of treaties and undermine their environmental effectiveness, and possibly indirectly their political effectiveness as well. A *caveat* to the above theory is the realpolitik possibility that a treaty without differentiation might lead to less overall compliance with the obligations.

Of the actual international environmental regimes, environmental effectiveness has been seen as a concern – especially in the ozone and climate change contexts. Commentators were concerned about the risk that the differentiation under the Montreal Protocol produces serious environmental harm (Papasavva and Moomaw, 1997: 222). As an overall picture, this scenario was not realized. Instead, the Protocol is today considered the most successful MEA so far in terms of factors such as numerical membership, compliance, and the achievement of its stated goal (naturally there are also other contributing factors to this achievement than the application of CBDR).

Application of the principle of CBDR makes the implementation of an agreement more sensitive to local circumstances and needs. It is not only a fairness aspect but also one of economic effectiveness, as the opportunities and marginal costs of taking action to alleviate an environmental problem are taken into account. However, instead of the criteria of cost-effectiveness, the applications of CBDR would seem currently to be mainly based on political bargaining, willingness to pay, or ethical approaches.

Economic effectiveness is also promoted by the fact that a system that is seen as fair induces cooperation and encourages more states to join the regime. The 'grace period' has been a significant incentive for developing countries to sign the Montreal Protocol. The Kyoto Protocol's flexible mechanisms have been a key element of the global climate change regime – also from a limited efficiency point of view. In fact, the mechanisms were largely developed in order to respond to negotiating parties' concerns over the economic effectiveness of the whole international regulatory arrangement.

Normative effectiveness is here understood as referring in particular to justice and fairness considerations in the design and realization of regulation. This chapter has emphasized how the principle of CBDR generally promotes a sense of fairness in multilateral environmental cooperation.

The political effectiveness of an MEA and, directly or indirectly, of the application of the principle of CBDR, can be judged most importantly from the level of state participation in the regime.

In general, differentiation of state obligations in international environmental regimes should be seen as beneficial for all Parties and thus as promoting effectiveness in many sectors. For developed countries, the CBDR principle fosters greater participation in MEAs and more effective implementation of their obligations; bringing benefits as a result of the environmental, economic and political effectiveness of treaties. Common but differentiated responsibilities reduces implementation and compliance costs of MEAs for developing countries; and enables them to be part of important international cooperative efforts and, thereby, 'respectable' members of the international community. For all Parties, equity and justice are being promoted. Of course, sometimes demands for differentiation provoke different arguments that can stall a negotiation process or even lead to a deadlock.

Negotiating CBDR

The North–South divide in the international community

Negotiations concerning the application of the principle of common but differentiated responsibilities contain challenges. Problems often come down to the North–South ('developed–developing state') divide that is regularly perceived to exist in international cooperative efforts, including in the environmental field (see, for instance, Kaniaru, Chapter 9 in this volume; Egziabher, Chapter 12 in this volume). It can even be argued that the history of international environmental dialogue is a history of conflict between developing and industrial countries (Rajamani, 2006: 8). Fundamentally, the divergence between the North and the South encompasses the framework, nature, and agenda of international environmental law, but is essentially focused on who should take responsibility, in what measure, and under what conditions to contain global environmental degradation (*ibid*). The ultimate tension is concerned with the development needs of the developing countries.

It is important to note that the principle of CBDR does not imply additional obligations for developed states *ad infinitum*. It is evident that situations and circumstances of states change over time, and this should be reflected in their international commitments. Regimes should never remain static. This issue has received much attention over the years as the North–South debate has prevailed within the international community. States dispute which states should be entitled to differentiated commitments, why, how, and for how long. There are no easy answers to these dilemmas, and a case-by-case approach appears the only viable route to be taken.

Within the context of current negotiations on a post-2020 climate agreement, one of the main issues is whether CBDRRC is to be a static or dynamic concept therein. It is generally envisaged that developing countries will also be taking mitigation commitments under the new agreement. The Ad Hoc Working Group on the Durban Platform for Enhanced Action (ADP) is to 'develop a protocol, another legal instrument or an agreed outcome with legal force under the Convention applicable to all Parties' and to 'launch a workplan on enhancing mitigation ambition to identify and to explore options for a range of actions that can close the ambition gap with a view to ensuring the highest possible mitigation efforts by all Parties' (FCCC/CP/2011/9/Add.1 2011: paras 2, 7). The aim is, therefore, to include all Parties, thus also developing countries, in the new agreement. In order effectively to engage all Parties in the mitigation efforts, there is a need for dynamism in the commitments, so that they take into account, and may be adjusted according to, changes in the relevant circumstances of each Party.

In any case, the developed world will not remain the sole contributor to the solutions to persistent global environmental problems. For instance, in regard to Principle 7 of the Rio Declaration, it has been argued that the second sentence of the Principle ('in view of the different contributions to global environmental degradation'), serving as the basic conceptual justification for differentiation, is unqualified and is, therefore, hypothetically unrelated to the North–South dichotomy (French, 2000: 50). Arguably, this leaves open the possibility that developing countries will be required to accept greater responsibility for environmental degradation as their contributions to the problems increase (*ibid.*). On the other hand, one may ask whether contributions to environmental degradation provide a solid basis for differentiation; as poor countries should perhaps be granted special treatment on the basis of their insufficient capacity to act, or because of the expected significant damage they might suffer from severe environmental degradation.

It could also be argued that the whole practice of using sustainable development, for example (and the principle of CBDR too, for that matter), as a framing device in international environmental negotiations replicates and sustains a twofold distinction between sets of countries (Williams, 2005: 66). In other words, by making distinctions among groups of countries and differentiating obligations, the dichotomy between the developed and developing worlds would only become wider. This argument probably holds some truth. However, it must be remembered that the distinction between developed and developing countries is intensified by numerous other factors besides the concepts of sustainable development or CBDR.

Different interests of states for differentiation

Full, or at least significant, realization of the principle of CBDR under multilateral environmental agreements may be badly hampered by the different interests and motives that states often have for the application of the principle. Industrial countries are frequently possessed by international competitiveness concerns, which make them demand meaningful participation from the developing world in global environmental efforts; developing countries, for their part, often seek compensation for past wrongs and recognition of their fewer resources necessary for the taking of environmental action. The reality is that the promotion of environmental protection is not always primarily in states' intentions when MEAs are negotiated. In fact, the developments in the application of the CBDR principle so far have been interpreted to indicate that differentiation has only been successfully implemented where the North has also found an interest in its application (Cullet, 2003: 182). It could be said that CBDR is often made possible or required by states' heterogeneous environmental valuations, or at least by their different emphases in the field of environment and development.

Nevertheless, developed countries often have self-interested reasons for applying the differential commitments towards developing countries. This has sometimes been described as 'greenmail'; where initially rather reluctant developing countries are induced, if not bribed, to participate in the cooperative arrangements. The situation comes down to the capacities and vulnerabilities of the industrial countries. Probably equally often, however, developed countries remain rather reluctant to grant developing countries differential treatment. The principal reason is the cost burden that results from additional financing and technology transfer. Concerns over competitiveness and even fairness have also been voiced in this regard. It is clear that states tend to emphasize different elements of the CBDR principle; and to make interpretations that are, more often than not, favourable to themselves.

Bargaining and negotiation power of states

Thanks to the improved relative bargaining strength of developing countries, they have increasingly been viewing provisions for differential treatment, especially financial and technical assistance, as prerequisites for their participation in international environmental treaties. The subsequent outcome depends to a large extent on the relative importance of the given environmental problem to the industrial countries.

Many less developed countries have little to lose in the bargaining and so they can sometimes adopt rather impudent strategies. At the same time, in negotiations on global environmental problems, the industrial states in particular cannot really consider the option of 'walking away' and accepting an outcome of no agreement rather than making more substantial concessions. That would result in both material and symbolic costs. In this sense, the developing countries are often in stronger negotiating positions in this regard.

This increased bargaining strength of developing countries has been made use of in actual treaty negotiations. For instance, within the negotiations toward the Montreal Protocol, the developing world made it clear that unless they received preferential treatment, developing countries would not become Parties to the Protocol. Developing countries insisted that in the absence of financial support they would be bound only by moral commitments (Borione and Ripert, 1994: 84). The threat of refusing cooperation was credible and hit its target, as the participation of a large number of developing countries was crucial to the environmental effectiveness of the Protocol.

The principle of common but differentiated responsibilities has also been a core bargaining issue in the international negotiations on climate change. To begin with, developing countries agreed to participate in the negotiation process on the condition that their development priorities were recognized and that they were guaranteed 'new and additional' financial and technological aid. The strategy appears to have been relatively successful as the developing world was not subject to binding emissions reduction obligations provided for in the Kyoto Protocol, and various assistance mechanisms have been created in the regime. It should be noted, however, that the bargaining power of the developing countries may not be as strong, at least in theory, as it appeared to be in the ozone case. That is partly because it is possible, or even likely, that in the end the South will suffer from the adverse effects of climate change more than will the developed world, which limits the South's room for manoeuvre.

Precedents from the past as lessons for the future?

International environmental agreements are not negotiated, and nor do they work, in isolation. They draw inferences from past experience, whether this is considered desirable by the participants or not. Consequently, states are increasingly inspired by, or worried about, the possibility that, once agreed upon, a treaty rule or mechanism might become a precedent; in other words, that it will subsequently be used, or at least claims will be made for its use, in other treaty arrangements, to the discontentment of some Parties.

It is not surprising that states that will incur costs, due to more favourable treatment being granted in an agreement to a group of Parties, are generally very wary when such mechanisms are formulated. Such states may oppose the idea that the principle of CBDR would become a virtually automatically applicable rule in international environmental affairs. They do not want to create expectations to that end to which they would have to respond in every new MEA negotiation process. In contradistinction, the receivers of assistance and of concessions would be only too pleased if the arrangements held the value of precedents and, thereby, forced differentiation to become a norm in international environmental negotiations. It stands to reason that developing countries generally hope that the differentiation rules on financial resources and on technology transfers will set precedents for North–South relations also in other fields and more generally.

The fear of creating precedents has a stagnating effect in international environmental treaty negotiations. This makes the negotiation process proceed more slowly, as states cautiously consider what they can commit themselves to in the long term; and, consequently, the emergence of ambitious rules and new innovations may be hindered. Ultimately, this fear also leads to vaguer language and less decisive commitments in agreed texts.

The issue of 'fear of precedent-setting' was not as visibly present at the early stages of the climate change negotiations as it had been several years earlier under the ozone regime where potential donor countries made it clear that they would not agree to an 'open cheque' for the receivers of the aid. There may have been various reasons for this. One is that the negotiations on climate change were focused on such a variety of issues, all at the same time, that financing questions did not receive so much attention; while the granting of preferential treatment for developing countries was, in general, already quite clear from the beginning. In addition, experience had perhaps shown that, despite the potential precedent created under the Montreal Protocol for developing country financing, the forms of differential treatment would still be negotiated on a case-by-case basis under

MEAs, leaving industrial countries with some power to influence the particular outcomes. Nevertheless, the climate change negotiation process has been reported as having given developing countries a fear of a precedent as to the formulation of their possible future commitments. The fact that the emissions reduction targets of developed countries were determined quite haphazardly (without, or with only little, *ex ante* or *ex post* equitable justification) has increased suspicions in developing countries that they will be forced to accept targets inappropriate to their social and economic capabilities, disproportionate to their historic contribution and their greater vulnerability to the adverse effects of climate change (Yamin, 1999: 270). These fears may be quite well-founded, although perhaps not entirely due to the past experience of how the process went with the developed countries. Moreover, both the developed and developing countries have shown awareness of the potential of climate change issues to influence the wider North–South agenda (see, for instance, Sebenius, 1995: 67).

The crucial role of information

State heterogeneity in bargaining makes the role of information-supply crucial in negotiations toward international environmental treaties. The risk of problems of imperfect information emerging is evident especially when states raise their special circumstances as a justification for differential treatment. Incentives often exist to exaggerate the expected costs of the treaty; and to understate expected benefits, available domestic resources, and interests for fulfilling the obligations. States are likely to behave strategically when it is evident that the burden imposed upon them will depend on their revealed willingness and capacity to pay for environmental quality (see also Eyckmans, 1997: 315). It is clear that vast differences genuinely exist in these aspects between the North and the South, and their real extent is generally unknown. Probably equally valid is the claim that developing countries usually face far more significant opportunity costs than do developed countries, with regard to participating in an environmental treaty.

It should be remembered that misrepresentations of information in international negotiations and in regime governance are not necessarily intentional. The science behind many global environmental problems is, alone, so complicated that acquisition of correct information, no matter how much resources are invested in the relevant research, is difficult. Furthermore, national environmental governance and international negotiation capacities might be under such heavy stress in some developing countries that correct, or up-to-date, information is simply not available.

Misstated or hidden information may be disastrous to the application of the CBDR principle in multilateral environmental agreements. Differentiation is made based on countries' often vastly differing circumstances, wealth, resources, wills, and vulnerabilities. If treaty-makers do not have correct information on these issues, the whole regime becomes flawed and probably inefficient. Consequently, some Parties will benefit undeservedly; while others will almost inevitably lose.

The unclear status of the CBDR principle

Perhaps the most troubling issue with regard to the principle of common but differentiated responsibilities is its status in international law and policy. CBDR has developed rather rapidly during the last 20–25 or so years, and there has arguably been at least somewhat consistent practice in its application in international environmental agreements since the 1987 Montreal Protocol. Being thus increasingly commonly adopted and applied, it could be asked whether the principle is not developing into a customary norm of international environmental law; and what implications such a transformation might have for international environmental law.

Common but differentiated responsibilities is now, arguably, an inseparable part of international environmental treaty negotiations. Nevertheless, the language used tends to remain somewhat vague; or commitments made to be more akin to 'soft law' (for example, declarations in treaty preambles). On the other hand, the practical applications of the CBDR principle have largely been adopted in a binding form; for instance, as differentiated emissions reduction targets and specific financial mechanisms. In those cases there is no question about the impact and force of the principle. Views about CBDR as a principle of customary law in the international environmental field are divided (see, as examples, Harris, 2000: 237; Rajamani, 2006: 124; Honkonen, 2009: 301–306; Nanda and Pring, 2013: 43). Moreover, negotiating parties may well have different views about the status of the CBDR principle, with such different views being subsequently reflected in the treaty itself. Developed countries often regard the principle as being based on *ad hoc* arrangements at the international level; whereas developing countries are more eager to give differentiation the status of customary international law. Overall, it is probably too early to classify CBDR as a principle of customary international environmental law.

The process of shaping and defining the status of the principle of CBDR is multi-faceted and ongoing. The principle of common but differentiated responsibilities is becoming an integral part of an increasing number of international legal instruments; but the actual content and scope of the differentiation are still too difficult to define accurately.

Categorization of countries for the purposes of differentiation

An interesting aspect in the practical realization of CBDR is the classification of countries into categories for differentiation. Negotiation toward international environmental treaties used to be concerned with two main negotiating blocs: the developed and the developing countries. However, nowadays there may be numerous different groups present, most of them also making demands for more individual treatment within the regime under negotiation.

Categorization of countries tends to be reductionist. Especially, the group of developing countries is by no means a unitary unit; indeed, such countries sometimes adopt markedly different policies, for instance the positions of the Organization of the Petroleum Exporting Countries (OPEC) and Alliance of

Small Island States (AOSIS) groups in the climate change negotiations (Rowland, 1995: 212). A crude North–South differentiation largely overlooks the diversity in national situations: countries' varying levels of development, available resources, preferences and so on. In addition, there is a need for dynamic definitions of the country positions. It is important that the criteria for forming categories of countries for differential treatment in MEAs also permit certain flexibility and dynamism. This would allow, or force, a certain country that has, for example, reached a specified level of development, to move to another group.

At present, international environmental treaty regimes usually draw from UN practice in their classification and treatment of countries, possibly supplementing this with specific guidance for the particular MEA in question. The Montreal Protocol, for instance, establishes in Article 5(1) that only those Parties which (i) are by a Meeting of the Parties classified, based on the UN scale of assessments, as 'developing countries', and (ii) have less than 0.3 kg annual per capita consumption of the controlled substances, may benefit from the positive incentives laid out in Article 5. In contrast, funding under the Protocol is available to all developing country Parties and countries with economies in transition, without similar qualifications. The Montreal Protocol does not provide a definition of a developing country as such, since the terms in Article 5 are too contextual to work as a definition. The calls for further and more specialized differentiation have been answered to a degree within the global climate change regime, where countries are placed into a variety of categories for the commitments.

Concluding remarks

The principle of common but differentiated responsibilities is of utmost importance for both the political and the environmental effectiveness of international environmental regimes. It is important to remember that CBDR consists of two sides: common responsibility denotes that we cannot afford to exclude countries from participating and taking action to ameliorate global environmental problems; differentiated responsibility means that not all Parties need to adopt an equal burden in the effort.

To determine the more specific ways of promoting equity and realizing an equitable burden-sharing within international environmental agreements, multiple criteria probably need to be used. Distributional effects of treaty commitments must, in any case, be accounted for in the arrangements; often a rather pragmatic approach to seeking solutions to international environmental problems is needed. The question to be asked is not *whether* developing countries should participate and act to ameliorate global environmental problems; but rather *how*, and *when*.

In general, differentiation in states' international obligations is quite a youthful phenomenon. One might wonder why exactly it is that differentiations emerged so late; and why they do not appear more frequently than they do (Stone, 2004: 282). Applications of the principle of CBDR can be found in virtually all 'modern' international environmental agreements. The influence of the principle, or approach, on multilateral environmental regimes is indisputable. It can be said that differentiation has developed from a limited practice of granting exceptions to a more or less general rule, or consistent practice, in international environmental treaty-making. The concrete application of CBDR is still highly context-based and happens from a variety of motivations; but that does not lessen the value of the principle. Inclusion of the principle of common but differentiated responsibilities has apparently become a permanent feature of international environmental law-making and diplomacy.

References

Agenda 21 (1992) 'UN Conference on Environment and Development', UN Doc. A/CONF.151/26/Rev.1.

Birnie, P. and Boyle, A. (2002) *International Law and the Environment* (2nd ed.), Oxford University Press, Oxford.

Borione, D. and Ripert, J. (1994) 'Exercising Common but Differentiated Responsibility' in Mintzer, I.M. and Leonard, J.A. *Negotiating Climate Change: The Inside Story of the Rio Convention*, Cambridge University Press, Cambridge, 77–96.

Brunnée, J. and Streck, C. (2013) 'The UNFCCC As a Negotiation Forum: Towards Common but More Differentiated Responsibilities', *Climate Policy*, 13: 589–607.

Chichilnisky, G. (2000) 'Equity and Efficiency in Global Emissions Markets', in Revesz, R.L., Sands, P. and Stewart. R.B. (eds) *Environmental Law, the Economy and Sustainable Development*, Cambridge University Press, 263–279.

Cordonier Segger, M., Khalfan, A., Gehring, M. and Toering, M. (2003) 'Prospects for Principles of International Sustainable Development Law after the WSSD: Common but Differentiated Responsibilities, Precaution and Participation', *Review of European Community and International Environmental Law*, 12: 54–68.

Cullet, P. (1999) 'Equity and Flexibility in the Climate Change Regime: Conceptual and Practical Issues', *Review of European Community and International Environmental Law*, 8: 168–179.

Cullet, P. (2003) *Differential Treatment in International Environmental Law*, Ashgate Publishing, Aldershot.

Draft Resolution on a Protocol Concerning Chlorofluorocarbons (proposal based on discussions in the informal working group) (1985), www.ozone.unep.org/Meeting_Documents/adhoc/other-meetings/adhoc-draft_resolution_on_protocol_on_cfcs.85-03-31.doc (accessed 24 May 2015).

Drumbl, M.A. (2002) 'Poverty, Wealth, and Obligation in International Environmental Law' *Tulane Law Review*, 76: 843–960.

'Establishment of an Ad Hoc Working Group on the Durban Platform for Enhanced Action', UNFCCC Dec. 1/CP.17 (2011), in Report of the Conference of the Parties on its seventeenth session, held in Durban from 28 November to 11 December 2011, UN Doc. FCCC/CP/2011/9/Add.1, Appendum, Part Two.

Eyckmans, J. (1997) 'Nash Implementation of a Proportional Solution to International Pollution Control Problems', *Journal of Environmental Economics and Management*, 33: 314–333.

French, D. (2000) 'Developing States and International Environmental Law: The Importance of Differentiated Responsibilities', *International and Comparative Law Quarterly*, 49: 35–60.

Harris, P.G. (2000) 'International Norms of Responsibility and U.S. Climate Change Policy' in Harris, P. G. (ed.) *Climate Change and American Foreign Policy*, Martin's Press, New York, 225–239.

Honkonen, T. (2009) *The Common but Differentiated Responsibility Principle in Multilateral Environmental Agreements. Regulatory and Policy Aspects*, Kluwer Law International, AH Alphen aan den Rijn.

Kolari, T. (2008) 'The Principle of Common But Differentiated Responsibilities as Contributing to Sustainable Development through Multilateral Environmental Agreements' in Bugge, H.C. and Voight, C. (eds) *Sustainable Development in National and International Law: What Did the Brundtland Report Do to Legal Thinking and Development*, Europa Law Publishing, Groningen, 251–267.

Metz, B. (2000) 'International Equity in Climate Change Policy', *Integrated Assessment*, 1: 111–126.

Nanda, V. and Pring, G. (2013) *International Environmental Law and Policy for the 21st Century*, Koninklijke Brill, Leiden.

Papasavva, S. and Moomaw, W.R. (1997) 'Adverse Implications of the Montreal Protocol Grace Period for Developing Countries', *International Environmental Affairs*, 9: 219–231.

Plan of Implementation of the World Summit on Sustainable Development (2002) UN Doc. A/CONF.199/20.

Rajamani, L. (2006) *Differential Treatment in International Environmental Law*, Oxford University Press, Oxford.

Report of the Sixteenth Meeting of the Parties to the Montreal Protocol on Substances that Deplete the Ozone Layer (2004) UN Doc. UNEP/OzL.Pro.16/17.

Rowland, I.H. (1995) 'Equity and Global Environmental Politics' in Rowland, I. H. *The Politics of Global Atmospheric Change*, Manchester University Press, New York.

Sands, P. (2003) *Principles of International Environmental Law* (2nd ed.), Cambridge University Press, Cambridge.

Sebenius, J.K. (1995) 'Overcoming Obstacles to a Successful Climate Convention' in Henry, L. (ed.), *Shaping National Responses to Climate Change: A Post-Rio Guide*, Island Press, Washington, DC, 41–79.

Statement on Behalf of the Group of G77 and China by the Delegation of the State of Qatar at the Closing of the 12th Session of the Commission on Sustainable Development, 30 April 2004, www.g77.org/Speeches/043004.htm (accessed 24 May 2015).

Stockholm Declaration, Report of the United Nations Conference on the Human Environment, UN Doc. A/CONF/48/14/Rev.1 (1972).

Stone, C.D. (2004) 'Common but Differentiated Responsibilities in International Law', *American Journal of International Law*, 98: 276–301.

Third World Network (2012) '"Common but differentiated responsibilities" under threat', TWN Update on Sustainable Development Conference 2012 (Jun12/06), available at www.twn.my/title2/sdc2012/sdc2012.120606.htm (accessed 24 July 2015).

UN Declaration on Environment and Development, UN Doc. A/CONF.151/5/Rev.1 (1992).

UNGA (1970) 'Declaration on Principles of International Law Concerning Friendly Relations and Co-operation Among States in Accordance with the Charter of the United Nations', UNGA Res. 2625, 24 October 1970.

UNGA (2012) 'The Future We Want' Outcome Document, UNGA Res. 66/288, 27 July 2012.

Williams, M. (2005) 'The Third World and Global Environmental Negotiations: Interests, Institutions and Ideas', *Global Environmental Politics*, 5: 48–69.

Yamin, F. (1999) 'Equity, Entitlements and Property Rights under the Kyoto Protocol: The Shape of 'Things' to Come', *Review of European Community and International Environmental Law*, 8: 265–274.

Young, O.R. (2001) 'Environmental Ethics in International Society' in Coicaud, J. and Warner, D. (eds) *Ethics and International Affairs: Extent and Limits*, United Nations University Press, Tokyo, 161–193.

12 The Cartagena Protocol on Biosafety

A personal memoir on its creation, content and implementation

Tewolde Berhan Gebre Egziabher

Introduction

Negotiations toward the Cartagena Protocol on Biosafety were finalized on 29 January 2000 in Montreal, Canada. The Protocol was signed by 103 states during the signature period, and came into force on 11 September 2003, 90 days after its 50th ratification. As at 2015, the Protocol had 170 Parties. The history presented here by an author who was one of the main negotiators of the Protocol largely reflects the author's personal notes and unpublished reports. Both because the author knows the issues intimately, and in the belief that developing countries carried a heavier load owing to their position of greater disadvantage, more attention will be given to negotiations involving developing countries. Their load is heavier both because of their obvious limitations in terms of well-trained and experienced human resources, and the greater complexity of their biological diversity – developing countries generally being richer in biodiversity than are developed countries.

It should be pointed out that complexity of biodiversity increases the risks of introgression, the introduction of species from one gene pool into another, and thus complicates biosafety considerations. It is also more than likely that history from the perspective of developed countries is going to be better preserved and presented by their better endowed professionals and institutions than will that of the developing countries involved.

The Biosafety Protocol is complex both because of the inherent nature of regulating genetic engineering, and because of the compromises that had to be reached to accommodate a wide range of beliefs (ideologies) on the sanctity of, and acceptability of human-made modifications to, life. This complex situation was exacerbated by the wide range of perceived positions of advantage and disadvantage within human societies.

Little more than a decade has passed since the Protocol came into force, which is a brief time in international law. Its implementation is really only just beginning. In any event, the implementation of the Protocol will remain difficult so long as the country which is the most active in genetic engineering, the United States of America, remains a non-Party. It must also be noted that, like all international environmental agreements, the Cartagena Protocol on Biosafety lacks an enforcement mechanism comparable with the clout of the Dispute Settlement Body of the World Trade Organization, let alone to the Security Council of the United Nations organization.

A brief history of the Cartagena Protocol on Biosafety

The Convention on Biological Diversity

The Cartagena Protocol on Biosafety is a protocol to the Convention on Biological Diversity, which was adopted on 22 May 1992. In its Article 19(3), the Convention requires the Parties to 'consider the need for and modalities of a protocol setting out appropriate procedures ...in the field of the safe transfer, handling and use of any living modified organism [LMOs] resulting from biotechnology'. The protocol is to concern such organisms where they 'may have adverse effect[s] on the conservation and sustainable use of biological diversity'; and procedures are to include, 'in particular, advance informed agreement'. The Conference that adopted the Convention also adopted a resolution asking the UNEP Governing Council to 'consider requesting the Executive Director of the Programme, i.e. of UNEP, to convene an Intergovernmental Committee on the Convention on Biological Diversity starting in 1993 to consider ... the need for and modalities of' a biosafety protocol (Resolution 2, Para. 2(c)). This was intended to start the implementation of Article 19(3) of the Convention before it came into force.

Report of Panel IV

In preparation for negotiating a biosafety protocol, the Executive Director of UNEP, Mostafa Tolba, established a group of experts to analyse the need for and modalities of a biosafety protocol. This group of experts was referred to as Panel IV. It was co-chaired by Veit Koester of Denmark; and by the present author. Twenty-nine experts from 12 countries (including the European Community) as well as five organizations participated in the three meetings of Panel IV, which submitted its report to UNEP on 28 April 1993 (Expert Panel, UNEP, 1993).

International technical guidelines for safety in biotechnology

The Ministries of Environment of the Netherlands and the United Kingdom convened a meeting of international experts in March 1994 and developed the first draft of technical guidelines on safety in biotechnology. The draft was discussed by invited experts from 17 countries in May 1994. These draft guidelines were revised further, then promoted by UNEP and subjected to further consultations in the various regions. A 'global consultation of government-designated experts on [the] international technical guidelines for safety in biotechnology' was then held in December 1995; and this meeting adopted 'the final text of the United Nations Environment Programme International Technical Guidelines for Safety in Biotechnology' (Report on Global Consultation, UNEP, 1995a: 9).

Although the meeting was considered global, only 59 countries and the European Commission took part in it. Based on this meeting, however, UNEP organized an international workshop in late 1996 to review the Guidelines' implementation (Report on International Workshop, UNEP, 1995b). This workshop was attended by experts from 55 countries. The last statement in the recommendation from this workshop was a call for UNEP to review the Guidelines periodically.

Negotiations on the Cartagena Protocol on Biosafety

Introduction

UNEP's Panel IV Report produced a majority view that called for negotiating a biosafety protocol, and a minority view that stated that there was no need for such a protocol. The minority view was that of the representative from the United States, supported by two representatives of the Organization for Economic Cooperation and Development.

By the time the Report of Panel IV was finalized, the Executive Director of UNEP who had established the Panel, Mostafa Tolba, had been replaced by Elizabeth Dowdeswell of Canada. Under Dowdeswell's leadership, UNEP tried to keep the Panel IV Report from the meetings of the Intergovernmental Committee on the Convention on Biological Diversity (ICCBD), which was the body that had been created to prepare the ground for the implementation of the CBD while it was awaiting entry into force.

The Interim Secretariat of the CBD in UNEP oversaw the functioning of the ICCBD, and deliberately failed to mention the Panel IV Report in the document prepared for the ICCBD's work on biosafety. The first meeting of the ICCBD in 1993 focused only on capacity-building and international cooperation in biosafety (ICCBD, 1993: 1). The reason can be seen by studying the document on biosafety presented to the 2nd session of the ICCBD in 1994 (UNEP, 1994: 5). In its 19th paragraph, this document suggested to the ICCBD that the term 'protocol' should be defined and added that it 'may then proceed to consider whether or not a protocol is needed; whether it is an immediate need or whether its development is envisaged for the future'. However, in its 18th paragraph it states that '[a]s familiarity with LMOs increases and experience accumulates … the patterns of regulation will likely evolve from initial stringency to less stringent requirements'. In its 20th paragraph, it states that '[i]f a protocol is not needed at all or if it is only needed in the future, the Committee [ICCBD] may wish to consider whether other instruments such as voluntary codes of conduct and guidelines could be considered'. To make this view palatable, the document's 14th and 21st paragraphs emphasize the need for capacity-building in developing countries.

Calls for both stopping and starting negotiations on biosafety were reflected in the First Conference of the Parties to the CBD, which took place in November–December 1994. From among the NGOs, the Third World Network, Greenpeace, Community Nutrition Institute and Friends of the Earth distributed a statement on 5 December 1994 calling for the negotiation of a biosafety protocol. On 6 December, they again distributed a similar statement, this time joined also by Accion Ecologica. Several countries were condemned for attempting to stall the negotiation of a protocol. There were also suspicions that UNEP was attempting to stifle such negotiation by promoting the UNEP International Technical Guidelines for Safety in Biotechnology.

A Panel of Experts on Biosafety, established by the Secretariat of the Convention to prepare for the meeting of the Open-ended Ad Hoc Group of Experts on Biosafety, met in May 1995. This Panel's report (Report of the Panel of Experts on Biosafety, 1995) made no mention of the report of its predecessor, Panel IV. The Panel stated that it strongly believed that capacity-building is essential (para. 83(c)) and that immediate action is needed to assess biosafety frameworks (para. 83(d)). Furthermore, it was stated that the adoption of an international framework, such as guidelines, regulations, codes of conduct or a protocol, would not in itself ensure safety (para. 35). The overall tone of the Panel Report was that of letting things be; in other words, that of not taking any immediate international action.

Negotiations in the Open-ended Ad Hoc Group of Experts on Biosafety

Following Decision I/9 of CoP I, an Open-ended Ad Hoc Group of Experts on Biosafety met in July 1995. Experts from 83 countries, 21 from Africa, and one regional organization (the European Community) participated in a decisive debate that shaped the future of biosafety. The meeting examined the report of the Panel of Experts. It soon became clear that this document was not acceptable to all delegates. In fact, of all the Parties to the CBD, only Australia and Canada were fully in favour of this document. They were fully supported by the United States which, though not a Party, was active at canvassing opinion.

As the meeting continued, the call for recommending to CoP II that it authorize the negotiations on a biosafety protocol grew. Because of the role the present author had played in Panel IV, as its Co-Chair, virtually all delegates from developing countries rallied behind my making this call.

Perhaps feeling the need to break this unity among delegates from developing countries, some delegates from the United States apparently campaigned negatively against the author outside of the meeting itself. They pointed out, rightly, that the call for negotiating a protocol was strongest from within Africa, and this was depicted as being an unjustified fear held in ignorance of avant-garde biotechnology.

This began to cause defections from the call for a protocol. Fortunately, at this point, Professor Elaine Ingham from Oregon State University in the United States explained her research results on the genetically engineered soil bacterium *Klabsiella planticola*. She pointed out how this normally useful bacterium had been rendered dangerous to plant life by genetic engineering that had been intended to make it more useful for producing ethanol from cellulose. After that, the developing country delegates rallied around the author again and the call for a protocol grew louder. Of the industrialized countries, New Zealand, Germany, Japan and South Korea sided with Australia and Canada. Finally, after much debate, however, they accepted allowing a decision that recommended to CoP II that a biosafety protocol be negotiated. The main issues to be covered by the protocol were also identified (Elaboration of Terms of Reference, 1996). However, the industrialized countries, on the whole, did not want socio-economic considerations and liability and redress to be included in the protocol.

Negotiations in the Open-ended Ad Hoc Working Group on Biosafety

The Open-ended Ad Hoc Working Group on Biosafety was established by CoP II through Decision II/5 (Report of First Meeting, 1996). The first meeting of the Working Group was in July 1996.

On the first day, the African Group elected the author as its spokesperson. The meeting reviewed and elaborated the items identified by the Madrid meeting of the Open-ended Ad Hoc Groups of Experts. The question of whether or not to include socio-economic issues and liability and redress divided the G77 and China. Brazil, South Korea, Costa Rica, and Argentina took the stand of the industrialized countries that these two items should not constitute a part of the protocol. At the suggestion of Amarjeet Ahuja of India and the author, the developing countries – except for these four – formally pushed these two issues as essential; and the G77 and China ceased functioning in any meaningful manner in the subsequent biosafety negotiations.

The African Group then asked the author to draft a biosafety protocol on behalf of Africa. Upon returning to Ethiopia, the author initiated the drafting of the protocol. Experts from four institutions developed the working draft. There were diverging positions within the African Group (with South Africa advocating a weaker protocol text than was desired by other countries). Even though these were difficult for the author to manage, it was important to avoid any African delegations separating from the Group because this would have resulted in reduced political impact. The African Group then met in October 1996 to revise and adopt the draft protocol; and did so adopt and then submit to the CBD Secretariat at CoP III in November 1996.

The second meeting of the Open-ended Ad Hoc Working Group on Biosafety took place in May 1997. The submissions of views by governments on the provisions of the protocol were discussed by the meeting. A compilation of the views had been prepared by the CBD Secretariat (Individual Government Submissions, 1997). However, the submissions were descriptive in nature, except for the submission of the African Group, which was in the form of legal text, and so the former were not of great use for beginning negotiations. The meeting was, therefore, basically for exchanging opinions in which respect the compiled views were useful for showing the diversity of thinking.

The meeting established a Contact Group to consider how the definitions of key terms should be formulated. At its suggestion, the Working Group directed the Secretariat to compile a list of such terms from country submissions in alphabetical order for being defined by the Contact Group starting at the third meeting. The third meeting of the Open-ended Ad Hoc Working Group took place in October 1997. More detailed submissions (Government Submissions, 1997) by governments were made the basis of the negotiations. South Africa submitted its own separate text; but did not formally declare that it disagreed with, and was splitting from, the African Group.

The meeting of the Working Group widened the scope of the work of the Contact Group to include negotiating on Annexes. It also divided into two sub-Working Groups and began negotiating the consolidated text of country submissions to produce an agreed text. Delegates were able to move in and out of the sub-Working Groups and the Contact Group as their interests dictated. The fourth meeting of the Open-ended Ad Hoc Working Group took place in February 1998 (Report of Fourth Meeting, 1998). The negotiations became highly polarized. The second Contact Group focused on financial and institutional issues. The delegation of the United States requested that countries attend consultations on sub-regional bases. Attempts by South Africa to organize the delegates from the Southern African Development Community for a consultation with the United States delegation on their own failed because the other delegates refused to speak to the United States delegation except as the African Group as a whole. However, consultations were held with the European Community and with other regions as an African Group.

The fifth meeting of the Ad Hoc Open-ended Working Group took place in August 1998. Many states submitted final portions of their proposed detailed wording for the provisions of the protocol (Report of the Fifth Meeting, 1998), as had already been done by the African Region. As a consequence, the first draft text of the protocol, albeit with many brackets, was compiled (Open-ended Ad Hoc Working Group, 1998); and the negotiation process became clearly defined, as did the divisions between states and groups of states. It became difficult to obtain comment from developed countries on the issues of liability and redress; and the delegates from developing countries began refusing to comment on any other issues. One day of near total silence, however, forced the industrialized countries to agree seriously to negotiate also on liability and redress; and the negotiations then continued. The question of whether products of living modified organisms (LMOs) should also be regulated by the protocol became divisive, however. The African Group and most developing countries wanted such products covered by the protocol. The issue remained unresolved to the end of the negotiations.

When the negotiations began in 1996, communications within Africa had been very difficult. However, many changes in electronic communication had occurred since then and taking a common position on the negotiating text during the subsequent negotiation session became easier.

Trying to hasten the negotiations, in October 1998, amidst division, the Chair of the Working Group called a meeting of the Bureau of the Working Group –

which included the elected representative from each UN Regional Group – and a selected number of other delegates. This was dubbed the 'Extended Bureau' and it discussed ways to hasten the negotiations. For the author, the most intriguing suggestion was one proposed by the European Union, which 'strongly urged states and regional integration organizations to operate as many of the provisions as possible of the protocol…'. It is intriguing because this draft decision, if passed, would arguably have had the effect of reducing the protocol from being an international treaty to becoming a suggested procedure. This draft decision was not tabled at the subsequent meeting of the Working Group and, in the final analysis, the meeting of the Extended Bureau did not advance matters significantly.

The sixth and final meeting of the Open-ended Ad Hoc Working Group on Biosafety took place in February 1999. The negotiations were scheduled to be finalized at this meeting. The negotiating text had a great many brackets and it seemed certain that no consensus text would be produced from it. Living modified organism commodities, products of LMOs, socio-economic issues, the precautionary principle and the scope of the protocol were issues that remained divisive. On 15 February, the Chair formed a 'Friends of the Chair' group from among the members of the Regional Groups. The Chair said that this group was intended to advise him and not to negotiate. In practice, however, these functions became virtually indistinguishable.

On 16 February formal negotiations, open to all delegates, continued. In the evening, the Chair, with the Friends of the Chair, reviewed progress, and labelled it minimal. The next day, the Chair, following a suggestion by one of the Bureau Members, informed the Bureau, which met at the beginning of every morning, that anything agreed in the sub-Working Groups and Contact Groups would not be re-opened in Plenary, which would merely endorse the agreement. The author contended that this would not be transparent, and would therefore be undemocratic, especially since most developing countries were represented by single delegates who could not be present in both sub-Working Groups and Contact Groups simultaneously; however, the Chair tried to implement it, contributing to the failure of the negotiations. In the evening, he announced that he would return with a Chair's text the next day. Most of 18 February passed with the delegates waiting for this text; which arrived in the afternoon. The rest of the afternoon and the night were taken up with delegations studying the new text.

This new text galvanized the groupings into even greater confrontation. Developing countries, except for Argentina, Chile, Mexico and Uruguay, created the Like-minded Group of Developing Countries; and elected the author as their chief negotiator. Argentina, Australia, Canada, Chile, the United States and Uruguay had already formed the Miami Group. These two groups were the furthest apart on most substantive issues. As a result of these groupings, the usual UN Regional Groups could no longer continue. Mexico joined with Japan, New Zealand, Norway and Switzerland to form the Compromise Group. The Central and Eastern European Group remained intact. These two groups remained quiet throughout the confrontation. The European Union continued unaffected and very active, with its positions on most of the divisive issues being between those of the Miami and Like-minded Groups.

On Saturday 20 February, the chief negotiators of the various Regional Groups, with their advisors, met twice over the new draft. The next day, the Chair produced a revised text. It did not change the confrontation. In the night, the chief negotiators of the Miami, European and Like-minded Groups met. The chief negotiator of the European Group offered what he called 'a package' to the Miami Group. The chief negotiator of the Miami Group also had a list of changes which he wanted included in the Chair's revised text of the draft protocol. The suggested changes from both Groups wanted the provision on the precautionary principle to be deleted. Different groups found different proposals unacceptable, and the negotiations therefore failed.

In spite of strong attempts by the Chair, his new draft protocol was resoundingly rejected on the early morning of 22 February, and the negotiations by the Open-ended Ad Hoc Working Group on Biosafety were formally abandoned. It was agreed, however, that the text would be presented to the Extraordinary Conference of Parties of the CBD. A formal Extraordinary Session of the Conference of the Parties had been planned to approve the text of the finalized protocol. Instead, this Extraordinary CoP had to restart the negotiations almost from scratch; although, of course, it took into consideration the draft protocol passed on to it by the Ad Hoc Working Group on Biosafety.

Negotiations in the extraordinary sessions of the Conference of the Parties to the Convention on Biological Diversity

The meeting of the Extraordinary CoP started only 5 minutes after the negotiations of the Open-ended Ad Hoc Working Group ended in the early morning of 22 February 1999. The meeting was brief. At the end of the meeting, the Chair of the Extraordinary CoP convened another negotiation session involving the chief negotiators of the Miami Group, the European Union and the Like-minded Group. The chief negotiator of the European Union again presented his previous package, which, among other things, accepted the deletion of the precautionary principle; as did the chief negotiator of the Miami Group with his set of proposed changes. The two continued discussing their respective proposals and it looked as though they were about to agree. At this stage, even the European Union's package contained provision for virtually unregulated import and export of LMO commodities; with the proviso that this would be reviewed at the first Meeting of the Parties after the Protocol had come into force. The author, therefore, rejected both sets of proposals; and told the two chief negotiators that the practice of ignoring developing countries had 'completely died with the colonial era'.

The Chair tried to break the deadlock by introducing an enabling clause similar to that proposed by the European Union which, he thought, might have made it possible for the author to accept the Miami Group's position on LMO commodities. The enabling clause stated that the issue of LMO commodities would be re-negotiated after the Protocol came into force. The Miami Group's chief negotiator, however, rejected it. The author was also going to reject it, but one rejection was good enough and so kept quiet.

On 23 February, the last day of negotiations, the chief negotiators of all the Regional Groups (i.e. not only those of the Miami, European Union and Like-minded Groups) met. It became clear that there would be no agreement. The manoeuvring by each Group then turned into trying to avoid appearing to be the party that had wrecked the negotiations. After much wrangling, the negotiations in Cartagena were ended; with the chief negotiator of the Miami Group refusing the provision that would have made it possible to re-negotiate LMO commodities after the protocol came into force. The author would also have rejected it – although for the opposite reason – but did not have to; thinking it more strategically fitting that the Miami Group be the one that appeared to have wrecked the negotiations. The Miami Group promised to return to the negotiations after one year with a new proposal that took into account the difficulties on LMO commodities expressed by the author on behalf of the Like-minded Group.

However, the Chair of the Extraordinary CoP did not wait for one year. Informal consultation continued by all parties. The author had suggested informally that if the Miami Group understood the nature of the agricultural systems in developing countries, where most crop gene pools are found, its delegations would appreciate the problems of developing countries more clearly. Delegates from the Miami Group visited Ethiopia in September 1999, touring farms, homesteads and grain markets. They left Ethiopia enthusiastic that this would help them to produce an acceptable proposal for the next negotiation session. In the meantime, the author analysed the Cartagena negotiations, and the text of the draft protocol at the end of those negations, arguing to the delegates of the Like-minded Group what should be fought for. This did, it seemed, help to consolidate the views of this Group.

In September 1999 the Chair of the Extraordinary CoP invited delegations to informal consultations in Vienna. These consultations helped to show more clearly the difficulties that the protagonist Regional Groups had with each other's positions. It also helped further to consolidate the somewhat amorphous Like-minded Group, which the author continued to lead.

In November and December 1999 the Miami Group, led by the United States, attempted to have a decision on trade in LMO commodities passed in the Seattle Ministerial Session of the World Trade Organization. The author went to Seattle and lobbied, primarily amongst African delegations, against allowing this to happen. Others from different parts of the world also lobbied the delegations that they could reach. The result was that the WTO did not accept the passing of any decision on trade in LMO commodities. In fact, the ministerial negotiations as a whole collapsed in the face of sustained protests by anti-globalization protestors in the streets of Seattle – the protests being dubbed the 'Battle for Seattle' – and the author remains convinced that the issue of LMO commodities contributed to that general collapse.

The Miami Group then decided to negotiate on LMO commodities seriously in the biosafety protocol. The final negotiations by the Extraordinary CoP were held in Montreal in January 2000, and the text of the Cartagena Protocol on Biosafety was agreed. This final negotiation session of the Extraordinary CoP was also difficult.

The negotiations on LMO commodities were primarily between the Miami Group and the Like-minded Group. The European Union negotiators, presumably confident that their internal laws were robust enough to protect them from unwanted LMO commodities, were, although supportive of the Like-minded Group, not going to fight hard on the issue. On the other hand, they wanted clear provisions in the protocol on labelling of LMOs and LMO products. The Miami Group continued to oppose labelling, the precautionary principle and the treatment of products of LMOs. Both the Miami Group and the European Union continued to oppose any meaningful negotiations on liability and redress. The Like-minded Group had been wishing to join forces with the European Union to push for more secure and transparent product labelling. The prevaricating attitude of the Brazilian delegation had prevented this so far. In this session, however, the Brazilian delegation also became supportive of labelling. Nevertheless, the author decided to hold back on the issue until sure that the European Union would support the Like-minded Group until the negotiations on LMO commodities were finalized; which they did. The result was the somewhat clumsy compromise struck with the Miami Group that is now in Article 11 of the Cartagena Protocol.

The Like-minded Group also wanted the scope of the Protocol (Art. 4) to include all LMOs and not explicitly to exclude any categories of LMOs. Although we realized, since the Miami and European Groups were united on the issue, that pharmaceuticals (Art. 5) and transit and contained use (Art. 6) would not be subject to the advance informed agreement procedure (Arts 7–10) fully under the Protocol, as we had wanted, we did not want these exceptions to be made at the level of the scope of the Protocol (Art. 4). We wanted to make it always possible for the Protocol to consider all LMOs. Therefore, because the Miami Group wanted a separate provision on LMO commodities and the European Union wanted labelling, we managed to bargain (obstinately!) with them both to accept an all-inclusive scope (*ibid.*).

The European Union negotiators had changed their position since the failed negotiations of Cartagena and, with the support of the Like-minded Group, they pushed for the inclusion of the precautionary principle (Arts 10(6) and 11(8)). The Miami Group was therefore under pressure to accept the precautionary principle. The author suspects that it was the unprecedented collapse of the WTO negotiations in Seattle, not merely the unity between the European Union and the Like-minded Group, which forced them to give up their wish that the Protocol not be subjected to the precautionary principle.

LMOs that are in transit through a country are not subject to the advance informed agreement procedure (Art. 6(1)). The Like-minded Group did not want this exception. The compromise that was forced upon us was that of being allowed to prohibit, through the Biosafety Clearing-House, those specific LMOs that a state considers particularly dangerous. This will require capacity to access information through the Biosafety Clearing-House; and also alertness to place objectionable LMOs in the Biosafety Clearing-House. Such capacity was often lacking in developing countries. The ability to access the Clearing-House has now been established in most developing countries. However, the capacity to evaluate the information downloaded from the Clearing-House is still deficient in the majority of developing countries.

Excluding contained use from the advance informed agreement procedure was unacceptable to the Like-minded Group. Norway proposed that agreement could be reached on the issue if the definition (of what legally constitutes 'contained use') were to be left to the country of import. This made it possible for Article 6(2) to be formulated in a way that we could accept.

Unlike the Miami and European Union Groups, we wanted LMO pharmaceuticals for human use also to be subjected to the advance informed agreement procedure. We were convinced that there were (and that there still are) no 'other relevant international agreements or organizations' that are responsible for LMOs that are pharmaceuticals for humans. Therefore, these LMOs must be governed by the Cartagena Protocol. It thus became possible for us to accept Article 5 of the Protocol as a compromise. This will, however, require alertness in the World Health Organization, and possibly also in other fora, so that rules on LMO pharmaceuticals for humans that violate the advance informed agreement procedure are not adopted anywhere. It should be noted that, because Article 5 of the Protocol is restricted to pharmaceuticals for humans, pharmaceuticals for animals have to be subjected to the advance informed agreement procedure (Arts 7–10) of the Protocol.

The Miami Group and some members of the European Union opposed the position of the Like-minded Group on products of LMOs; and we were forced to accept giving it up. However, the Risk Assessment Annex (Paragraph 5 of Annex III) enables the assessment of risks posed by LMO products. This, in combination with national laws on environment and health, can hopefully be used to fill the gap created.

The most significant deficiency of the Protocol as far as developing countries are concerned is in the absence of provisions to govern liability and redress. A promise was made to continue negotiations after the coming into force of the Protocol (Art. 27), and the Like-minded Group felt that this promise was all that the negotiations of the Protocol could yield and accepted the negotiations of the Protocol as finalized.

Another issue left pending by the Protocol in spite of the push by the European Union, supported towards the end of the negotiations by the Like-minded Group, was that of packaging and labelling (Art. 18, paragraphs 2(a) and 3). This was the last issue to be negotiated before the Cartagena Protocol on Biosafety was adopted by the Extraordinary CoP at about 06h00 on 29 January 2000 after an all-night session.

Negotiations on issues left pending by the Cartagena Protocol on Biosafety

The first issue left pending at the adoption of the Protocol has two components. The first (Art. 18(2)(a) of the Protocol) requires the Conference of the Parties to the Convention on Biological Diversity serving as the meeting of the Parties to the Cartagena Protocol (CoP/MoP) to take a decision on the detailed labelling of LMO commodities 'no later than two years after the date of entry into force of this Protocol'. The Protocol entered into force on 11 September 2003. A labelling scheme should, therefore, have been finalized at the second CoP/MoP, which took place in May–June 2005. However, Brazil and New Zealand had concerns that prevented a consensus from being reached on labelling requirements for LMO commodities. The issue was therefore taken up again in the third meeting, in March 2006.

Brazil had moved away from its previous position and was now asking for a labelling system that gave sufficient detail; as all of the other Parties, except for New Zealand, had been doing. It is possible that New Zealand was acting as a surrogate on behalf of the Miami Group. As a Party to the Protocol, New Zealand could block consensus but, since they were non-Parties, the Miami Group of countries could not. However, the position of New Zealand's delegation attracted criticism from organizations both at home and abroad. In the meeting in Curitiba, New Zealand thus refrained from opposing the call for labelling. Therefore, in spite of attempts by the Miami Group to prevent it, a decision was passed that requires detailed labelling of LMO commodities (Report of the Third Meeting, 2006: 60–2). The second component (Art. 18(3) of the Protocol) requires the Cartagena Protocol's CoP/MoP to evaluate the need for and modalities of developing standards for the packaging and transport of LMOs. The completion of this requirement is not time-bound. The process started in the third meeting in Curitiba, at which the CoP/MoP recognized that standards on packaging and transport already exist under various other international bodies, and that there is a need to create synergies and avoid duplication of efforts in this regard (Decision BS-III/9). Since CoP/MoP3, the process has continued to focus on identifying existing rules and standards, and assessing whether there are gaps in the existing framework that justify the development of new rules and standards. No new standards have yet been introduced under the Cartagena Protocol.

Article 27 of the Protocol stipulates that, at its first meeting, the CoP/MoP shall 'adopt a process with respect to the appropriate elaboration of international rules and procedures in the field of liability and redress for damage resulting from transboundary movement of' LMOs. Through its Decision BS-1/8 (CBD Secretariat, 2005, *Handbook*: 1333, 1408–11), the first CoP/MoP, which convened in February 2004, adopted the terms of reference of an Open-ended Ad Hoc Working Group of legal and technical experts to negotiate a liability and redress regime for the Protocol.

Article 27 of the Protocol requires that the Working Group endeavour to complete its negotiations within four years, i.e. before February 2008. This was not realized. Key points of division included the question of whether the regime should be legally binding and the legal approach to be taken by the instrument. Most developing countries called for a legally binding regime based on a civil liability approach (which would establish international requirements for addressing cases of damage through domestic procedures for civil liability); while most developed countries instead supported a domestic administrative approach (in terms of which damage, and threats thereof, would be monitored and addressed by competent national authorities) (Jungcurt and Schabus, 2010: 198–199, 201–202). In the face of such polarization, the fifth meeting of the Working Group, in March 2008, ended with no agreement on liability regarding LMOs. However, the process did not stop there, as the Working Group decided to convene a Friends of the Co-Chairs group (Group of the Friends of the Co-Chairs on Liability and Redress in the Context of the Cartagena Protocol on Biosafety) in May 2008, immediately before the Cartagena Protocol's fourth CoP/MoP. A contact group was established to continue negotiations on redress and liability throughout CoP/MoP4 and made an important step forward by agreeing to work towards a legally binding instrument, focusing on an administrative approach, which would include a provision on civil liability and be complemented by non-binding guidelines. It was further decided that the Group of the Friends of the Co-Chairs would be reconvened to continue the negotiation process (Decision BS-IV/12).

The Group held its first independent meeting in February 2009, where again minor progress on liability and redress under the Biosafety Protocol was made. After the second meeting of the group, in February 2010, it could be said that a treaty on liability for damage from LMOs was in sight. The treaty text was further negotiated by the Group in its third meeting, in June 2010. Finally, in its fourth meeting, in Nagoya in October 2010, the Group of the Friends of the Co-Chairs adopted the text of a draft protocol. The draft was then considered at the Cartagena Protocol's fifth CoP/MoP and, after intense discussions, the Nagoya–Kuala Lumpur Supplementary Protocol on Liability and Redress to the Cartagena Protocol on Biosafety was adopted by consensus on 15 October 2010 (Decision BS-V/11). The Supplementary Protocol received 51 signatures and, as of April 2015, had been ratified by 30 states and the European Union. It will enter into force on the ninetieth day following ratification by 40 Parties to the Cartagena Protocol (Art. 18(1)). Rather than establishing a binding civil liability regime, as some states had hoped it would, the Supplementary Protocol is based on an administrative approach. The author considers the Supplementary Protocol to be satisfactory. However, its effectiveness will obviously hinge on the willingness of both exporters and importers of LMOs to ratify and implement the instrument. Although a detailed discussion of the Supplementary Protocol's negotiation and text falls outside the scope of this chapter (see further Jungcurt and Schabus, 2010; Etty, 2011: 320–326), it is noteworthy that the negotiations witnessed a shift in the positions of several developing countries, which have begun to invest in biotechnology or become producers and exporters of agricultural LMOs (Jungcurt and Schabus, 2010: 203).

A brief evaluation of the appropriateness of the provisions of the Cartagena Protocol on Biosafety

In evaluating the provisions of the Cartagena Protocol on Biosafety, it is useful to state the assumptions from which this chapter has been written. These are, first, that since, once released into the environment, LMOs cannot be recalled, strict adherence to the precautionary principle is required for biosafety. Second, that since, on the whole, the number of living species increases towards the equator, unforeseen impacts of LMOs also increase towards the equator: furthermore, risk assessment becomes more complex towards the equator. Third, since the countries with the least scientific capacities are found towards the equator, mistakes in both risk assessment and risk management are likely to increase towards the equator. Fourth, since the poorest countries are found towards the equator, mistakes in managing LMOs are likely to be most devastating towards the equator. Finally, since, on the whole, the number of species increases towards the equator, the possibilities of solving perceived problems of development by choosing from among the diverse varieties of the species available, rather than trying to create transgenic organisms, increase towards the equator. This makes genetic engineering less relevant towards the equator.

General provisions

Article 2(4) begins by stating that any Party can take action more protective than provided for in the Protocol. However, it then weakens this possible action by qualifying it. It specifies that such action must be consistent with the objective and the provisions of the Protocol. The objective of the Protocol (Art. 1) is broad and would thus allow a lot of room. However, the provisions are of necessity much more detailed and they thus restrict the more protective action that can be taken. Article 2(4) also allows international law, for example on trade, to restrict the more protective action that can be taken.

The scope

The scope of the Protocol (Art. 4) appears good, but Article 5 weakens it when it comes to LMOs that are pharmaceuticals for humans. It does so by making it essential, especially for the countries with least wealth and scientific capacity, actively to watch the World Health Organization and other international institutions lest they institute procedures or laws that bypass the advance informed agreement procedure. Article 6 similarly weakens the scope with regards to LMOs in transit and LMOs for contained use.

LMO commodities

Although the provisions of Article 11 of the Protocol make advance informed agreement the basis of decision-taking in importing LMO commodities, the notification process takes place via the Biosafety Clearing-House (Arts 11(1) and 11(6)). This requires well-developed capacity even in a poor importing country. It would have helped poor importing countries if LMO commodities had been treated in the same way as LMOs intended for direct release into the environment (Arts 7–10).

Simplified procedure

Article 13 of the Protocol allows for simplification of the advance informed agreement procedure in dealings between Parties that wish to do so. This might expose poor developing countries to undue pressure from rich and powerful countries that produce LMO commodities to accept simplified procedures, and thus potentially weakens the applications of the precautionary principle.

Bilateral, regional and multilateral agreements and arrangements (Art. 14) and non-Parties (Art. 24)

Article 14 of the Protocol, especially in combination with Article 24, can also potentially be used to lower protection in weaker countries. For example, Mexico, although a Party to the Protocol, has had to opt out of the labelling requirements finalized in the third meeting of the CoP/MoP by insisting on including Paragraph 4(f) of the Decision BS/III/10. This occurred because Mexico is a member of the North American Free Trade Area (NAFTA) and thus has to import unlabelled LMO commodities from Canada and the United States. The potential exists for the United States to insist on similar concessions when it makes bilateral or multilateral agreements with other Parties to the Protocol.

Confidential information

Article 21 of the Protocol allows for an exporter of an LMO to ask for any of the items of information it supplies the importer to be kept confidential. Although this same Article 21 allows the importer to refuse keeping confidential information that is necessary for biosafety, it makes this refusal conditional upon giving reasons. Again, this may subject a poor importing country to complications that it has little capacity to deal with. The consequence is then likely to be that it will accept treating as confidential the information that is important for ensuring biosafety.

Socio-economic considerations

Article 26 of the Protocol allows importing Parties to 'take into account, consistent with their international obligations, socio-economic considerations arising from the impact of' LMOs when deciding to import or reject those LMOs. For a poor developing country, socio-economic considerations should have a very high weight in decision-making on whether to import a given LMO or not, especially when that LMO is a commodity. However, Article 26 diminishes this weight by invoking 'international obligations'.

Concluding remarks

The Cartagena Protocol on Biosafety is the first international environmental agreement negotiated to pre-empt possible problems with the entirely new issue of recombinant DNA technology. It is not surprising, therefore, that the Protocol is firmly based on the precautionary principle. Nor is it surprising that the process toward negotiating was extremely divisive, with polarized positions appearing not only between, but also *within*, traditional negotiating blocs. It is equally not surprising that it satisfied nobody completely. During the Cartagena Protocol's negotiation, developing countries made a significant concession by agreeing to defer a decision on liability and redress. With the adoption of the Nagoya–Kuala Lumpur Supplementary Protocol on Liability and Redress, this gap in the international biosafety regime has finally been filled. The positions of various states during the final stages of the Supplementary Protocol's negotiation also suggests that the divide between developed and developing countries has become less pronounced than it was during the negotiation of the Cartagena Protocol itself. However, several commentators have expressed concern regarding the legal weakness of the Supplementary Protocol's provisions (see Etty, 2011: 325–326), and only time will tell whether it is able to make a meaningful contribution to achieving the Cartagena Protocol's objectives.

References

CBD Secretariat (2005) *Handbook of the Convention on Biological Diversity* (3rd ed.), CBBD.

Compilation of views of Governments on the Contents of the Future Protocol, Montreal (1997) 12–16 May 1997, UN Doc. UNEP/CBD/BSWG/2/2.

Considerations of the Need for, and Modalities of, a Protocol on Biosafety (1994) UN Doc. UNEP/CBD/IC/2/12 (unpublished).

Elaboration of the Terms of Reference for the Open-ended Ad Hoc Working Group on Biosafety, Aarhus (1996) 22–26 July 1996, UN Doc. UNEP/CBD/BSWG/1/3 (unpublished).

Etty, T.F.M. (2011) 'Biotechnology', *Yearbook of International Environmental Law*, 22(1): 318–332.

Expert Panels Established to Follow-up on the Convention on Biological Diversity – Panel IV (1993) UN Doc. UNEP/Bio.Div./Panels/Inf.4 (unpublished).

Government Submissions (1997) 13–17 October 1997, UN Doc. UNEP/CBD/BSWG/3/5.

Individual Government Submissions on the Contents of the Future Protocol, Montreal (1997), 12–16 May 1997, UN Doc. UNEP/CBD/BSWG/2/Inf.2.

Interim Secretariat of the Convention on Biological Diversity, Informal Note no 2 – Summary of the Results of the ICCBD Meeting of October 11–15, 1993 (unpublished).

International Technical Guidelines for Safety in Biotechnology, 21 May 1994 Draft, Netherlands Ministry of Environment and UK Department of Environment (unpublished).

Jungcurt, S. and Schabus, N. (2010) 'Liability and Redress in the Context of the Cartagena Protocol on Biosafety', *Review of European and International Environmental Law*, 19(2): 197.

Open-ended Ad Hoc Working Group on Biosafety (1998) Extended Bureau Meeting, Agenda Item 12, Document No. 10, Proposal from the European Union on Voluntary Application of the Protocol (unpublished).

Report of the Fifth Meeting of the Open-ended Ad Hoc Working Group on Biosafety (1998) 17–28 August 1998, UN Doc. UNEP/CBD/BSWG/5/3.

Report of the First Meeting of the Open-ended Ad Hoc Working Group on Biosafety (1996) Aarhus, 22–26 July 1996, UN Doc, UNEP/CBD/BSWG/1/4.

Report of the Fourth Meeting of the Open-ended Ad Hoc Working Group on Biosafety (1998) 5–13 February 1998, UN Doc. UNEP/CBD/BSWG/4/4.

Report of the Panel of Experts on Biosafety (1995) CBD/Biosafety Expert Group/2, presented to the Open-ended Ad Hoc Group of Experts on Biosafety, Madrid, 24–28 July 1995 (unpublished).

Report of the Third Meeting of the Conference of the Parties to the Convention on Biological Diversity serving as the Meeting of the Parties to the Cartagena Protocol on Biosafety (2006) UN Doc. UNEP/CBD/BS/COP-MOP/3/15.

Report of the Third Meeting of the Conference of the Parties to the Convention on Biological Diversity (1995) UN Doc. UNEP/CBD/COP/3/38.

UNEP (1995a) 'Report of the Global Consultation of Government-designated Experts on International Guidelines for safety in Biotechnology', UNEP/Global Consultation/ Biosafety/4 (unpublished).

UNEP (1995b) 'Report of the International Workshop to Follow-up on UNEP's International Technical Guidelines for Safety in Biotechnology' (unpublished).

UNEP Sponsored Worldwide Consultations on Technical Guidelines for Safety in Biotechnology and Related Capacity-Building Requirements – Conclusions and Recommendations of Regional Consultations (1995) Biosafety Guidelines /Inf.1, UNEP (unpublished).

13 Future prospects for enhancing sustainable use of natural resources

The role of international environmental governance after Rio+20

Niko Urho and Ville Niinistö

Introduction

The world is confronted with the twin challenges of achieving a high level of human development, while at the same time not exceeding earth's finite natural resources. Today, the consumption of biological resources is one-and-a-half times higher than what the world can provide (Global Footprint Network, 2013: 6). Developed countries have achieved a satisfactory level of human development, but their ecological footprints exceed significantly the threshold for environmental sustainability. In contrast, most developing countries are not able to provide sufficient services and material well-being to their citizens although their ecological footprints remain comparatively low. In essence, to date, not a single country has achieved sustainable development that both satisfies human needs and respects nature (UNEP, 2011: 21).

Against this backdrop, the United Nations Conference on Sustainable Development (UNCSD), more commonly known as Rio+20, was organized in June 2012 in Rio de Janeiro, Brazil, where world leaders came together to tackle the twin challenges of eradicating poverty and achieving sustainable development. High expectations for the UNCSD attracted altogether 44,000 participants from 191 countries, making it the largest sustainability conference ever organized (Bulkeley *et al.*, 2013: 958). The meeting resulted in a 53-page Outcome Document entitled 'The Future We Want' that was, subsequently, adopted by the General Assembly in its 68th session (UNGA, 2012b, Res. 66/288).

After the meeting, many environmental non-governmental organizations (ENGOs) expressed disappointment with the results of the Conference; whereas government representatives, including the writers of this chapter, took a more positive stance and argue that Rio+20 represented a turning point for strengthened environmental governance structure, development of global sustainable development goals and growing interest in greening the economy. In addition, the birth of several new initiatives means that more time is needed to understand the Conference's long-term impacts.

Now, three years after Rio+20, it is relevant to take stock of the follow-up to the Conference. To this end, we shall discuss the main achievements of the Conference, particularly in the context of sustainable use and the conservation of natural resources. The chapter will show that Rio+20 initiated various significant processes that aim to spearhead a more balanced relationship between the three dimensions of sustainable development.

Key areas in the follow-up to Rio+20

This section covers three key areas in the follow-up to Rio+20 with regard to natural resources. These include strengthening the international environmental governance (IEG) system, developing a Post-2015 Agenda that satisfies human needs and respects nature, and enhancing sustainability of natural resources use by 'green economy-based policies'.

Enhancing international environmental governance and its coherence

Introduction

The current IEG system has been largely created during the last four decades. In 1972, global environmental concerns received widespread attention through the United Nations Conference on the Human Environment (UNCHE), which resulted in the creation of the United Nations Environment Programme (UNEP). UNEP was given a mandate to institutionalize environmental matters across existing UN agencies and to improve cooperation and communication amongst them (Ivanova, 2011: 1). The 1997 Nairobi Declaration further redefined and strengthened UNEP's mandate as the '…leading global environmental authority that sets the global environmental agenda, that promotes the coherent implementation of the environmental dimension of sustainable development within the UN system and that serves as an authoritative advocate for the global environment' (Nairobi Declaration, 1997, para. 11).

Upon its establishment, it was envisaged by its founders that UNEP would gradually grow and achieve a more stable financial basis, so that it could fulfil its relatively broad mandate (Ivanova, 2010: 33). However, UNEP's Environment Fund (EF) relies on voluntary contributions and its annual budget has, in contrast to expectations, remained miniscule in comparison to other UN counterparts (*ibid.*: 49). Despite its small annual budget, UNEP has been effective in catalysing action and creating new instruments – in particular, multilateral environmental agreements (MEAs). Today there exist 540 MEAs, 477 amendments and 220 protocols, bringing the total number above 1,200 (Mitchell, 2013). However, a significantly smaller number of MEAs are considered globally significant, for instance the UN's Joint Inspection Unit (JIU) lists eight thematic clusters that consist of 60 MEAs, including four on atmosphere, nine on biodiversity and five on chemicals and wastes (Inomata and Cazeau, 2014: 62–65).

The vast array of MEAs and other instruments and entities active in the international environmental arena shows that environmental problems have been widely acknowledged and a high degree of action has been taken to overcome them. However, as a result largely of fragmentation, the UN system struggles with a blurred division of labour and unclear mandates resulting in duplication of work and unhealthy competition for funds (Council of the European Union, 2010). In 2008, the JIU assessed that the cost for operating the current MEA-system is four times higher than in other sectors (Inomata, 2008: 11).

Against this backdrop, discussions on enhancing international environmental governance have focused on UNEP's reform and enhancing synergies among MEAs. Consensus on the IEG-reform has evolved in a step-by-step manner since 2002, when UNEP's Governing Council (GC) adopted the 'Cartagena Package' (UNEP GC Dec. SS.7/1, 2002). In 2005, the need for IEG reform was covered in paragraph 169 in the '2005 World Summit Outcome' Document (UNGA, 2005, Res. 60/1), which provided impetus to initiate an informal process in New York. This resulted, in 2007, in the 'Options Paper' (Co-chairs' Options Paper, 2007), which identifies seven building blocks to strengthen IEG. In late 2008, an attempt to reach an IEG-resolution in the General Assembly failed, due to highly polarized views.

Consequently, UNEP's GC launched a political process to continue the IEG-debate: two formal ministerial groups convened in subsequent years to identify forms and functions to meet both incremental and fundamental needs for the IEG-reform. In 2009, the first group (also known as the 'Belgrade process'; Set of options, 2009) identified a set of options to improve the IEG-system. These were further elaborated by the latter group, culminating in 2010 in the 'Nairobi–Helsinki Outcome' (Nairobi–Helsinki Outcome, 2010), which identifies six functions and system-wide responses and five institutional reforms to address the challenges in the current IEG-system. The Outcome was transmitted by the request of UNEP's GC to the preparatory process of Rio+20 (UNEP GC Dec. 26/1, 2011: para. 4).

Paragraph 88: reinforcing UNEP's three F's

Careful preparation and consensus-building leveraged Rio+20 to agree on UNEP's reform. In fact, paragraph 88 of 'The Future We Want' not only responds to every functional element identified in the Nairobi-Helsinki Outcome (Bernstein, 2013: 17), but also addresses form and funding. UNEP's reform has progressed through UNEP's GC decision on institutional arrangements (UNEP GC Dec. 27/2, 2013) and subsequent UNGA resolutions (UNGA, 2012a, Res. 67/213; UNGA, 2013a, Res. 67/251). These decisions significantly strengthen UNEP's 'three *F*s' – functions, funding and form – and, thereby, reinforce its leadership role in international environmental governance.

Addressing functions was always considered key in the IEG-discussions in order to strengthen UNEP's mandate to meet the needs of the twenty-first century. The reforms to UNEP's functions are stipulated in paragraph 88 of 'The Future We Want', which reinforces UNEP's mandate in several areas, allowing it, *inter alia*, more legitimately to create a strong science-policy interface, coordinate the formulation of UN system-wide strategies, disseminate and share evidence-based information, raise awareness on environmental issues, provide capacity-building to countries, facilitate access to technology, and promote transparency and the effective engagement of civil society. The reform of functions has progressed promisingly, although no formal assessment of progress has been made to date.

Rio+20 also strengthened UNEP's financial position, with paragraph 88 of 'The Future We Want' reaffirming the need to '...secure, stable, adequate and increased financial resources from the regular budget of the UN and voluntary contributions to fulfill its mandate'. In December 2013, the UNGA approved a US$ 21 million increase for UNEP over 2014–2015 from the UN regular budget, including 24 new posts (UNGA, 2013b, Res. 68/248). As a sign of confidence in UNEP's reform, several industrialized countries (such as Finland) have increased their contributions to UNEP's Environment Fund in the wake of Rio+20. Since voluntary donations to UNEP's trust fund today rely mainly on a small number of regularly contributing countries, it is important for non-traditional donors to step forward now and show financial as well as political commitment to UNEP (UNEP, 2014). Some donors have already shown such willingness. During Rio+20, Brazil and China pledged US$ 6 million each toward UNEP's Trust Fund.

The highlight of UNEP's reform was the decision taken at Rio+20 to expand UNEP's GC from 58 countries to universal membership. To this end, in February 2013, UNEP's GC decided to transform itself into the United Nations Environment Assembly (UNEA) (UNEP GC Dec. 27/2, 2013: para. 1), which concludes in a High-level Segment (HLS) with actual political decision-making power. The transformation was approved a month later by the UNGA (UNGA, 2013a, Res. 67/251). This makes UNEP the only UN subsidiary body with universal membership (Ivanova, 2013: 224). Since universal membership in UNEA will involve all UN member states in decision-making, the legitimacy of decisions should be greatly improved. Previously, the UNEP GC, with only 58 members, lacked legitimacy to coordinate MEAs that had a significantly higher number of Parties. Thus, the reform grants UNEP greater authority in relation to MEAs (*ibid.*) and, thereby, facilitates UNEP's role in enhancing synergies among MEAs.

The institutional reform of UNEP has provided it with some key attributes of a specialized agency: universality, more stable and predictable finances, and formal authority (*ibid.*). However, the lack of actual discussion at Rio+20 on the organizational form left many unsatisfied. Over 100 countries, including those in the European Union (EU), were in favour of upgrading UNEP into an independent specialized agency. The host country's refusal to discuss the organizational form was surprising, as many relied on this issue being discussed once the functions had been agreed, in accordance with the 'form follows function' principle, known as the underlying precept of IEG-reform. Presumably, the resistance originated from the fear of creating an imbalance in favour of the environmental dimensions of sustainable development (Biermann, 2013: 1102). Nevertheless, Rio+20 forms a significant milestone towards the UN's ultimate goal to transform UNEP into a specialized agency.

Paragraph 89: enhancing synergies among MEAs

Enhancing synergies among MEAs is at the core of the IEG-reform, since it aims to strengthen implementation by tackling fragmentation where it is greatest. Enhancing synergies among MEAs is not covered under paragraph 88 of 'The Future We Want', which deals with UNEP's reform. Instead, synergies are covered in paragraph 89, which makes no reference to UNEP, but encourages Parties to MEAs to '... consider further measures, in [the chemicals and waste cluster] and other clusters, as appropriate, to promote policy coherence at all relevant levels, improve efficiency, reduce unnecessary overlap and duplication, and enhance coordination and cooperation among MEAs...'. Since Rio+20, synergies have progressed in two MEA clusters: the chemicals and waste cluster and the biodiversity cluster.

Work done to enhance synergies among MEAs in the chemicals and waste cluster since 2006 has been exemplary. As a result, the Basel, Rotterdam and Stockholm Conventions share a joint secretariat, with a joint head and functions, operated through a matrix management system. Decision-making has been streamlined with the synchronization of the Conference of the Parties (CoP) cycles: simultaneous extraordinary meetings of the CoPs were organized in 2010 and 2013 and ordinary meetings of the CoPs were held back-to-back in 2015. Implementation has been facilitated through the adoption of a joint program of work for the biennium 2014–2015, with altogether 17 joint programmatic activities (Dec. BC-11/26, RC-6/16 and SC-6/30, 2013). The logical continuum for the synergies process is to expand the cluster to include the Minamata Convention, the new Convention on Mercury. In October 2013, in the Kumamoto signatory meeting, the Minamata Convention gave a positive signal for the possibility to co-locate its secretariat with the joint chemicals and waste secretariat ('Final Act of the Conference', UNEP(DTIE)/Hg/CONF/4, 2013: para. 9). Furthermore, the inclusion of SAICM (strategic approach to international chemicals management) in the cluster is natural, since it provides an umbrella framework to foster sound management of chemicals and addresses new and emerging chemicals challenges.

Recently, discussions have centred on enhancing synergies among six biodiversity-related MEAs: the Convention on Biological Diversity (CBD); the Convention on International Trade in Endangered Species of Wild Fauna and Flora (CITES); the Convention on Migratory Species (CMS); the International Treaty on Plant Genetic Resources for Food and Agriculture (ITPGRFA); the Ramsar Convention on Wetlands; and the World Heritage Convention (WHC). Consequently, two mutually supportive processes have emerged. Firstly, in 2013, as part of a project initiated by UNEP, a paper elaborating options for synergies among biodiversity-related MEAs has been developed through the organization of two multi-stakeholder experts meetings. The final output of UNEP's project is envisaged to provide a set of recommendations for the UNEP Executive Director to present to the second session of the UNEA in 2016. Second, in October 2014, the 12th CoP to the Convention on Biological Diversity established a Party-led process aimed at supporting Parties to the biodiversity-related conventions to enhance synergies and improve efficiency among the conventions, with a view to enhancing their implementation at all levels. As part of the process a workshop will be organized to prepare options for synergies, as well as to identify a possible roadmap to carry out a clustering process ('Cooperation with other conventions', CBD Dec. XII/6, 2014). The output from the UNEP project may be used to inform the CoP-driven process.

The Rio+20 outcomes and UNEP's role with respect to sustainable use of natural resources

The Outcome Document 'The Future We Want' also covers many thematic governance gaps, including oceans and biodiversity, aiming to strengthen the sustainable use of natural resources. It is relevant to ask how the upgraded and strengthened UNEP has dealt with issues arising from Rio+20, which relate to the sustainable use of natural resources. In June 2014, the first session of UNEA adopted decisions concerning international trade in endangered species and marine debris.

Generally, the international community is becoming more aware of the magnitude of transnational organized environmental crime, which includes illegal action concerning logging, fisheries and other wildlife trade, mining, and dumping of toxic waste (UNEP/EA.1/INF/19, 2014: 1). Consequently, Rio+20 led to renewed commitment to halt biodiversity loss, including a strong call for action to halt illegal wildlife trade (UNGA, 2012b, Res. 66/288: paras 197–204). The value of transnational organized environmental crime is estimated to be between US$ 70–213 billion annually (UNEP, 2014: 1). CITES is widely considered to be among the most effective global environmental regimes, but it operates with a yearly budget of only US$ 5 million, which does not correlate at all with the magnitude of the problem. To this end, the 1st session of UNEA decided to take decisive action against illegal trade in wildlife (UNEA, 2014, Res. 1/3).

Oceans were high on the agenda at the Rio+20 Conference, since governments recognized that oceans are under growing pressure: overexploitation, pollution, climate change and ocean acidification are severely damaging marine biodiversity and food production capacity (see, for instance, Couzens, 2011: 187–191). 'The Future We Want' addresses marine debris and includes a time-bound target to achieve significant reductions in this form of pollution by 2025 to prevent harm to the coastal and marine environment (UNGA, 2012b, Res. 66/288: para 163). In response, the 1st session of UNEA requested UNEP to carry out a study on marine plastic debris and marine microplastics in order to identify key sources of marine debris, effective measures to minimize debris and most urgent research needs (UNEA, 2014, Res. 1/6: para. 14). The study will be presented to the 2nd session of UNEA with recommendations for most urgent action.

Bringing together the agendas of poverty eradication and eradication of overconsumption of natural resources in the Post-2015 Agenda

Sustainable development goals

The Millennium Declaration and Millennium Development Goals (MDGs; UNGA, 2000, Res. 55/2) have steered development efforts in the twenty-first century focusing on poverty eradication. The MDGs have underscored the power of global vision that has catalysed action to meet the goals (Ivanova, 2013: 7). Since the adoption of the Millennium Declaration (UNGA, 2000, Res. 55/2), many developing countries have experienced significantly faster economic growth than have developed economies (Report of the Intergovernmental Committee, 2014: 8). However, the Millennium Declaration does not propose sustainable development as the overarching paradigm for achieving development and poverty eradication (Dodds *et al.*, 2014: chapter 1). Consequently, the MDGs cover only three environmental topics: water, biodiversity and urbanization – and do so in isolation from other goals.

Against this backdrop, one of the main achievements of Rio+20 is the strong call for integrating the three dimensions of sustainable development. At the Conference, countries agreed to establish a set of 'action-oriented, concise and easy to communicate' sustainable development goals (SDGs; UNGA, 2012, 'The Future We Want': para. 247). The goals are to be developed through an inclusive and transparent intergovernmental process that is open to all stakeholders. An Open-ended Working Group (OWG) was established in 2013 and finally in July 2014 the OWG put forward a proposal for SDGs (Open Working Group proposal for Sustainable Development Goals, 2014) comprising 17 goals and 169 targets to be achieved by 2030 at the latest. The sustainable development goals will build upon the Millennium Development Goals but are expected to be broader in geographical scope, since they apply to all countries, whereas the MDGs concern primarily developing countries.

In September 2014, the UNGA decided that the OWG's proposal on SDGs shall be the main basis for integrating sustainable development goals into the Post-2015 Development Agenda in the intergovernmental negotiation process (UNGA, 2014, Res. 68/309). In December 2014, the UN Secretary-General issued a synthesis report on the Post-2015 Agenda that calls for the creation of an integrated global sustainable development agenda that is people-centred and planet-sensitive ('The road to dignity by 2030', 2014, Synthesis Report of the Secretary-General: 5–6). The report recommends the United Nations Statistical Commission (UNSC) to take a leading role in the production and monitoring of data relevant to the new agenda (*ibid.*: 29). The next phase of the process will be the development of indicators for the goals and targets that can capture the integration of the three dimensions of sustainable development and their interlinkages.

The Post-2015 Agenda is to be adopted in the Post-2015 Summit organized in September 2015. Prior to this, intergovernmental negotiations had been scheduled for every month from January to July. The co-facilitators of the intergovernmental negotiations requested the UNSC to produce an initial proposal for an effective indicator framework. In response, an initial list with 338 indicators was provided to the intergovernmental meeting held in March 2015. In general, governments supported the preliminary list of indicators and hoped that their elaboration would continue as a technical exercise. To this end, the indicator framework will be refined by an Inter-agency Expert Group on SDGs (IAEG-SDG) that was established in March 2015 by the 46th session of the UNSC. The indicator framework will be advanced until the end of 2015 with a view to its adoption by the 47th session of the UNSC in March 2016 (United Nations Statistics Division, 2015). Consequently, the development of indicators for the Post-2015 Agenda will have to continue beyond September 2015.

Institutional implementation of sustainable development

It will be necessary to provide the most suitable institutional base to ensure follow-up on the implementation of the SDGs. At Rio+20, governments decided to abolish the Commission on Sustainable Development (CSD) and to replace it with the High-level Political Forum (HLPF; UNGA, 2012, 'The Future We Want': paras 84–85). The HLPF has huge potential as it has universal membership and will meet every four years under the UNGA at head-of-state level, and in other years under the United Nations Economic and Social Commission (ECOSOC) at the ministerial level. Since the HLPF has the mandate to coordinate sustainable development within the UN-system and has a high political profile, it should be tasked with reviewing the implementation of the SDGs. The Global Sustainable Development Report, a subsidiary scientific process operating under the HLPF, could be harnessed to compile and present data and visualize global trends, drawing from various sources.

Similarly, an efficient monitoring, accountability and review mechanism needs to be in place at the national level. Ideally, it should have sufficient political clout and strong connections to all sectors of society, and should ensure equal and inclusive participation of all stakeholders. In Finland, for instance, the National Commission on Sustainable Development (NCSD) was established in 1993 and, since then, has promoted sustainable development and monitored its implementation in the Finnish society.

Financing for development

The Post-2015 Agenda will need effective means of implementation, including sufficient funding, mobilization of resources and capacity support, to ensure that the new goals and targets will be met. To this end, at Rio+20 it was agreed to establish an expert group on financing that will propose a Sustainable Development Financing Strategy to facilitate the mobilization of resources (UNGA, 2012, 'The Future We Want': para. 255). An Intergovernmental Committee of Experts on Sustainable Development Financing (ICESDF), consisting of 30 regionally nominated experts, was established in June 2013 and was Co-Chaired by Finland and Nigeria. In August

2014, the Committee submitted its final report for the consideration of the UN Secretary-General (Report of the Intergovernmental Committee, 2014).

The Committee proposed more than 100 options, together with recommendations for a global partnership that encompasses key aspects of aid, trade, debt, taxation and financial market stability ('The road to dignity by 2030', 2014, Synthesis Report of the Secretary-General: 10). At present, many of the proposals of the ICESDF are being incorporated in the zero draft of the so-called Addis Ababa Action Agenda, adopted in the third International Conference on Financing for Development in July 2015 in Addis Ababa. The Addis Ababa Action Agenda is a global framework for financing sustainable development to further strengthen the means of implementation of the Post-2015 Agenda. Ideally, the Addis outcome will constitute the 'Means of Implementation' part of the Post-2015 Agenda so that these processes will end up in a single comprehensive agenda.

Naturally, the official development assistance (ODA) commitment of 0.7 per cent of gross national income (GNI) is still valid and needs to be honoured. (The figure refers to a commitment first made in an UNGA Resolution in 1970 [UNGA, 1970, Res. 25/2626], and repeated in many international agreements, in terms of which 'rich countries' would commit 0.7 per cent of their gross national income to Official Development Assistance.) However, it will not be sufficient to achieve the required transformative change to sustainability. Thus, at the same time, new and innovative financial sources need to be deployed, including mobilization of domestic resources. Tackling illicit financial flows and tax avoidance by promoting transparency and accountability would provide an important new financial source. In addition, environmentally harmful subsidies, including fossil fuel subsidies, should be identified and redirected to provide incentives for domestic action to achieve sustainable development.

Furthermore, mandatory corporate sustainability reporting would increase transparency and accountability of the private sector's contribution to promoting sustainable development (Dodds *et al.*, 2014: chapter 4). Today, sustainability reporting is generally voluntary and many large companies do not report on their activities in this regard. Sustainability reporting is highly topical given that the UN High-level Panel on the Post-2015 Development Agenda has proposed that it should be made mandatory for large companies by 2030 (UN, 2013: 17, 48). After Rio+20, a Group of Friends of Paragraph 47, consisting of nine countries (Austria, Brazil, Chile, Colombia, Denmark, France, Norway, South Africa and Switzerland) and supported by UNEP, was established to develop sustainability reporting.

Making the environment and natural resources a central part of economic decision-making by means of green economy

In the run up to Rio+20, it was recognized that existing economic models need to be restructured and that the full engagement of all sectors, including the private sector, is required to achieve sustainability and to increase human well-being.

At Rio+20, countries reaffirmed their commitment to phase out fossil fuel subsidies by removing market distortions, including restructuring taxation (UNGA, 2012, 'The Future We Want': para. 225). The International Energy Agency (IEA) estimates that fossil fuels are subsidized by US$ 544 billion annually (IEA, 2013b: 3); whereas renewables are subsidized only by US$ 101 billion annually. To this end, eliminating fossil fuel subsidies and channelling them to renewables and energy efficiency is key for greening the economy and meeting the target to limit the global temperature rise to 2 °C (IEA, 2013a: 2). The Friends of Fossil Fuel Subsidy Reform, a group of eight like-minded countries (these being Costa Rica, Denmark, Ethiopia, Finland, New Zealand, Norway, Sweden and Switzerland), is committed to taking the lead in reforming inefficient fossil fuel subsidies. The European Commission has committed to a concrete target to phase out all environmentally harmful subsidies, including fossil fuel subsidies, by 2020 (Communication from the European Commission, 2011: 10).

One of the highlights of Rio+20 was the adoption of the 10-Year Framework of Programmes on Sustainable Consumption and Production (10YFP on SCP). The 10YFP aims to increase resource efficiency and decouple economic growth from environmental degradation, creating jobs and economic opportunities, contributing to poverty eradication and shared prosperity. Sustainable consumption and production is an integral part of the OWG proposal on SDGs. Goal 12 on 'ensuring sustainable consumption and production patterns' features as a standalone goal for SCP. In addition, SCP-related targets are integrated in 13 out of the 17 proposed SDGs, thus making SCP a cross-cutting enabler for achieving sustainable development globally. The 10YFP provides an existing implementation platform and financial mechanism for the goals and targets on SCP.

'The Future We Want' recognizes the need to develop indicators to measure progress beyond GDP and assigns the UN Statistical Commission to develop the new measures for growth (UNGA, 2012, 'The Future We Want': para. 38). In response to Rio+20, the 45th session of the UN Statistical Commission adopted a work programme for developing broader measures of progress, emphasizing the need to link these to the Post-2015 Agenda. Many new accounting systems have already been developed, although none of them are yet fully mature. One of the most evolved models includes the System of Environmental-Economic Accounting (SEEA) that was approved in February 2012 by the UN Statistical Commission as an international statistical standard. The SEEA goes far beyond GDP, since it covers natural resources like minerals and timber, as well as accounting for environmental protection expenditures, taxes, and subsidies.

The importance of creating enabling frameworks that foster environmentally sound technology and of investing in technology development and innovation for achieving the green economy transition is emphasized in 'The Future We Want' (UNGA, 2012: para. 73). UNEP has estimated that the greening economies would require investing 2 per cent of the global GDP in the transition (UNEP, 2011: 6). For example, technologies exist to increase material-efficiency five-fold in several sectors, including the agriculture, transport, building and construction sectors, but these technologies are still largely underutilized (see, for example, von

Weizsäcker, 2009). UNEP's Partnership for Action on Green Economy (PAGE) emerged as a response to Rio+20 and aims to support 30 countries over seven years in building national green economy strategies (UNEP, 2015b). This is expected to generate new jobs and skills, promote clean technologies, and reduce environmental risks and poverty.

Conclusions

An overall picture of the state of the environment is emerging as information is being synthesized and it shows that the pressure on the earth's resources is already unbearable. Human activity has already crossed several planetary boundaries, including climate change and change in biosphere integrity, which may result in a cascade of irreversible and unpredictable biophysical changes of the planet (Steffen *et al.*, 2015). Population growth, urbanization and increasing per capita consumption rates are featured to put an additional pressure on the environment. The world cannot sustain this level of demand and development trend.

In a time of human history in which almost all of the planet's ecosystems bear the marks of our presence, the writers of this chapter are convinced that it is not too late to turn a new leaf. Our optimism derives from Rio+20, which in our view represents a turning point for integrating the environment into economic and social considerations, as well as for mobilizing greater action through means of green economy and the development of global sustainable development goals. In other words, Rio+20 represents a turning point – a rebirth of sustainable development that draws its essence from the two complementary approaches: a planet-centred approach and a people-centred approach (Dodds *et al.*, 2014: chapter 1).

Now, three years after Rio+20, headway has been made on several processes. Most importantly, in respect of the institutional reform of UNEP. The institutional reform of UNEP has provided the Programme with some key attributes of a specialized agency: universality, more stable and predictable finances, and formal authority (Ivanova, 2013: 224). In addition, Rio+20 provided a strong call for enhancing synergies within MEAs, thereby providing a political push to advance the clustering of MEAs beyond the chemicals and waste cluster to the biodiversity cluster. Undoubtedly, in the long run, this will enhance the sustainable management of biodiversity and natural resources, as cross-cutting issues will be addressed jointly both at the national and international levels. In response to Rio+20, the first session of the UNEA addressed illegal trade of wildlife and marine debris two large-scale problems that will definitely continue to receive political attention followed, hopefully, by some efforts to take corrective action.

The foundations for the Post-2015 Agenda have been set and include 17 SDGs and 169 time-bound targets. In contrast to the MDGs, the environmental dimension is spread across the entire sustainable development agenda, helping to match global action to the level of the threat facing the world's natural capital. The last step in establishing the Post-2015 Agenda is to develop SDG indicators, which can support the level of ambition, capture the three dimensions of sustainable development and retain the political balance of the current proposal (UNEP,

2015a). Efficient review and monitoring will be needed both at the national and international levels.

Lastly, at Rio+20, the green economy concept was accepted for the first time in a UN political document. The concept is still relatively new, but has already inspired action and development of new business models for green growth all around the globe. In addition, many government-driven green economy initiatives sprang up in Rio+20 that need to be urgently formalized into all walks of society. Introducing and implementing economic incentives that boost green growth and resource- and energy-efficiency is crucial. They not only improve the state of the global environment but contribute also to achieving climate and poverty eradication targets. Increases in productivity and resource-efficiency gained from the shift to more sustainable consumption and production patterns can eventually deliver increased environmental, social and economic returns to the investments and the whole society.

References

Addis Ababa Action Agenda, Outcome of the Third International Conference on Financing for Development, Addis Ababa, 13–16 July 2015, www.un.org/esa/ffd/wp-content/uploads/2015/08/AAAA_Outcome.pdf (accessed 21 August 2015).

Bernstein S. (2013) 'Rio+20: Sustainable Development in a Time of Multilateral Decline', *Global Environmental Politics*, 13: 12–21.

Biermann F. (2013) 'Curtain Down and Nothing Settled: Global Sustainability Governance after the 'Rio+20' Earth Summit', *Environment and Planning C. Government and Policy*, 31: 1099–1114.

Bulkeley, H. *et al.* (2013) 'Governing Sustainability: Rio+20 and The Road Beyond', *Environment and Planning C: Government and Policy*, 31: 958–970.

'Co-chairs' Options Paper of the Informal Consultative Process on the Institutional Framework for the United Nations' Environmental Activities' (2007), www.un.org/ga/president/61/follow-up/environment/EG-OptionsPaper.PDF (accessed 15 September 2014).

Communication from the European Commission to the European Parliament, the Council, the European Economic and Social Committee and the Committee of the Regions (2011) 'Roadmap to a Resource Efficient Europe', COM/2011/0571 final.

'Cooperation with Other Conventions, International Organizations and Initiatives' (2014) CBD Dec. XII/6.

Council of the European Union (2010), 'International Environmental Governance: Preparations for the 2nd meeting of the Consultative Group of Ministers: Information from the Finnish delegation', www.register.consilium.europa.eu/doc/srv?l=EN&f=ST%2014634%202010%20INIT (accessed 17 October 2014).

Couzens, E. (2011) 'International Law Relating to Climate Change and Marine Issues', in Couzens, E. and Honkonen, T. (eds) *International Environmental Law-making and Diplomacy Review 2010*, UEF-UNEP Course Series 10, University of Eastern Finland, Joensuu, 185–216 at 187–191.

Dodds F., Laguna-Celis J. and Thompson E. (2014) *From Rio+20 to a New Development Agenda. Building a Bridge to a Sustainable Future*, Routledge, New York.

'Final Act of the Conference of Plenipotentiaries on the Minamata Convention on Mercury, Res. on arrangements in the interim period' (2013) UN Doc. UNEP(DTIE)/Hg/CONF/4.

'Financing and budget for the biennium 2014 – 2015' (2013) Basel Convention Dec. BC-11/26.

'Financing and budget for the biennium 2014 – 2015' (2013) Rotterdam Convention Dec. RC-6/16.

'Financing and budget for the biennium 2014 – 2015' (2013) Stockholm Convention Dec. SC-6/30.

Global Footprint Network (2013) *The National Footprint Accounts*, Global Footprint Network, Oakland, www.footprintnetwork.org/images/article_uploads/National_Footprint_Accounts_2012_Edition_Report.pdf (accessed 24 May 2015).

IEA [International Energy Agency] (2013a) *Redrawing the Energy-Climate Map. World Energy Outlook Special Report. Executive Summary*, www.iea.org/media/freepublications/weo/WEO2013_Climate_Excerpt_ES_WEB.pdf (accessed 18 October 2014).

IEA [International Energy Agency] (2013b) *World Energy Outlook 2013. Executive Summary*, www.iea.org/publications/freepublications/publication/WEO2013_Executive_Summary_English.pdf (accessed 17 September 2014).

'Illegal Trade in Wildlife: The Environmental, Social and Economic Consequences for Sustainable Development' Information document to support discussions of the Ministerial Dialogue on Illegal Trade in Wildlife, UN Doc. UNEP/EA.1/INF/19.

'Implementation of paragraph 88 of the Outcome Document of the United Nations Conference on Sustainable Development' (2013) UNEP GC Dec. 27/2.

Inomata T. (2008) 'Management Review of Environmental Governance within the United Nations System', Joint Inspection Unit (JIU) Report 2008/3, www.unjiu.org/en/reports-notes/archive/JIU_REP_2008_3_English.pdf (accessed 15 August 2014).

Inomata T. and Cazeau J.W. (2014) 'Post Rio+20 Review of Environmental Governance within the United Nations System', Joint Inspection Unit (JIU) Report 2014/4, www.unjiu.org/en/reports-notes/JIU%20Products/JIU_REP_2014_4_English.pdf (accessed 19 August 2014).

'International Environmental Governance' (2002) UNEP GC Dec. SS.7/1.

'International Environmental Governance' (2011) UNEP GC Dec. 26/1.

Ivanova, M. (2010) 'UNEP in Global Environmental Governance: Design, Leadership, Location', *Global Environmental Politics*, 10: 30–59

Ivanova, M. (2011) 'Financing International Environmental Governance: Lessons from the United Nations Environment Programme', Center for Governance and Sustainability, University of Massachusetts, Boston.

Ivanova, M. (2013) 'Reforming the Institutional Framework for Environment and Sustainable Development: Rio+20's Subtle but Significant Impact', *International Journal of Technology Management & Sustainable Development*, 12: 211–231

'Marine plastic debris and microplastics' (2014) UNEA Res. 1/6.

Mitchell, R.B. (2013) *International Environmental Agreements Database Project 2002–2014* (version 2013.2), iea.uoregon.edu/ (accessed 19 April 2015).

Nairobi Declaration on the Role and Mandate of the United Nations Environment Programme (1997) UN Doc. UNEP/GC.19/1.

Nairobi–Helsinki Outcome from the Second Meeting of the Consultative Group of Ministers or High-level Representatives on International Environmental Governance, Espoo, Finland, 21–23 November 2010, www.unep.org/environmentalgovernance/Portals/8/documents/Events/NairobiHelsinkifinaloutcomeedited.pdf (accessed 15 August 2014).

Open Working Group proposal for Sustainable Development Goals (2014) http://sustainabledevelopment.un.org/content/documents/1579SDGs%20Proposal.pdf (accessed 19 April 2015).

Report of the Intergovernmental Committee of Experts on Sustainable Development Financing, final draft (2014) www.un.org/en/ga/president/68/pdf/letters/8142014 ICESDF%20Co-chairs_PGA_Final%20report%20-%2014%20August%202014.pdf (accessed 16 September 2014). (Report of the Intergovernmental Committee, 2014)

'Set of options for improving international environmental governance', Second meeting of the Consultative Group of Ministers or High-level Representatives on International Environmental Governance, Rome, 26–29 October 2009, www.unep.org/environmentalgovernance/Portals/8/documents/IEG-Draft-Report-Rome-final-edited.pdf (accessed 15 September 2014). (Set of options, 2009)

Steffen, W. *et al.* (2015) 'Planetary Boundaries: Guiding Human Development on a Changing Planet', *Science*, 347 (6223): 736–746.

'The Road to Dignity by 2030: Ending Poverty, Transforming all Lives and Protecting the Planet' (2014) Synthesis Report of the Secretary-General on the Post-2015 Agenda, www.un.org/en/development/desa/publications/files/2015/01/SynthesisReportENG.pdf (accessed 6 April 2015).

UN (2013) 'A New Global Partnership: Eradicate Poverty and Transform Economies through Sustainable Development', the report of the high-level panel of eminent persons on the Post-2015 Development Agenda (New York: UN), www.un.org/sg/management/pdf/HLP_P2015_Report.pdf (accessed 24 May 2015).

UNEA (2014) 'Illegal trade in wildlife', UNEA Res. 1/3.

UNEP (2011) *Towards a Green Economy – Pathways to Sustainable Development and Poverty Eradication* (UNEP), www.unep.org/greeneconomy/Portals/88/documents/ger/ger_final_dec_2011/Green%20EconomyReport_Final_Dec2011.pdf (accessed 24 May 2015).

UNEP (2014) 'The Environment Fund contribution statistics 1973–2012', www.unep.org/about/funding/portals/50199/documents/Environment%20Fund%20contribution%20statistics%201973-2012.xls (accessed 19 April 2015).

UNEP (2015a) A Common Approach for developing SDG integrated indicators (UNEP), http://unstats.un.org/unsd/post-2015/activities/egm-on-indicator-framework/docs/Common%20approach%20for%20developing%20SDG%20Integrated%20indicators.pdf (accessed 24 May 2015).

UNEP (2015b) *Green Economy. Partnership for Action on Green Economy*, www.unep.org/greeneconomy/PAGE (accessed 24 May 2015).

UNGA (1970) 'International Development Strategy for the Second United Nations Development Decade', UNGA Res. 25/2626, 24 October 1970.

UNGA (2000) 'United Nations Millennium Declaration', UNGA Res. 55/2, 18 September 2000.

UNGA (2005) '2005 World Summit Outcome', UNGA Res. 60/1, 15 September 2005.

UNGA (2012a) 'Report of the Governing Council of the United Nations Environment Programme on its Twelfth Special Session and on the Implementation of Section IV.C, entitled "Environmental Pillar in the Context of Sustainable Development", of the Outcome Document of the United Nations Conference on Sustainable Development', UNGA Res. 67/213, 21 December 2012.

UNGA (2012b) 'The Future We Want' Outcome Document, UNGA Res. 66/288, 27 July 2012.

UNGA (2013a) 'Change of the Designation of the Governing Council of the United Nations Environment Programme', UNGA Res. 67/251, 13 March 2013.

UNGA (2013b) 'Programme Budget for the Biennium 2014–2015', UNGA Res. 68/248, 27 December 2013.

UNGA (2014) 'Report of the Open Working Group on Sustainable Development Goals

Established Pursuant to General Assembly Resolution 66/288', UNGA Res. 68/309, 10 September 2014.

United Nations Statistics Division (2015) 'Multi-Stage Process for Developing an Indicator Framework and Establishment of an Inter-Agency and Expert Group on SDGs', www.unstats.un.org/unsd/post-2015/activities/egm-on-indicator-framework/docs/Establishment%20of%20IAEG-SDG.pdf (visited 7 April 2015).

von Weizsäcker, E.U. *et al.* (2009) *Factor Five: Transforming the Global Economy through 80% Improvements in Resource Productivity*, Earthscan, London.

Index

For Product Safety Concerns and Information please contact our EU
representative GPSR@taylorandfrancis.com
Taylor & Francis Verlag GmbH, Kaufingerstraße 24, 80331 München, Germany

www.ingramcontent.com/pod-product-compliance
Ingram Content Group UK Ltd.
Pitfield, Milton Keynes, MK11 3LW, UK
UKHW021722240926
475702UK00029BA/1784
* 9 7 8 0 8 1 5 3 9 5 4 2 3 *